Scottish Highlanders in Colonial Georgia

Scottish Highlanders in Colonial Georgia

THE RECRUITMENT, EMIGRATION, AND SETTLEMENT AT DARIEN, 1735–1748

Anthony W. Parker

THE UNIVERSITY OF GEORGIA PRESS

ATHENS AND LONDON

Paperback edition, 2002
© 1997 by the University of Georgia Press
Athens, Georgia 30602
All rights reserved
Designed by Erin Kirk New
Set in 10 on 13 New Caledonia
by G&S Typesetters
Printed and bound by Sheridan Books
The paper in this book meets the guidelines for
permanence and durability of the Committee on
Production Guidelines for Book Longevity of the
Council on Library Resources.

Printed in the United States of America
06 05 04 03 02 P 5 4 3 2 1

The Library of Congress cataloged the hardcover edition of this book as follows:
Library of Congress Cataloging-in-Publication Data
Parker, Anthony W.
Scottish highlanders in colonial Georgia : the recruitment, emigration,
and settlement at Darien, 1735–1748 / Anthony W. Parker.
xiv, 182 p. ; 24 cm.
Includes bibliographical references (p. [167]–178) and index.
ISBN 0-8203-1915-5 (alk. paper)
1. Scottish Americans—Georgia—Darien—History—18th century.
2. Great Britain. Army—Scottish regiments—History—18th century.
3. Scotland—Emigration and immigration—History—18th century.
4. Georgia—Emigration and immigration—History—18th century.
5. Darien (Ga.)—History.   I. Title
F294.D26 P37 1997
975.8′737—dc21   97-015730

ISBN 0-8203-2456-6 (pbk. : alk. paper)

British Library Cataloging-in-Publication Data available

To the memory of my parents,
Mr. Frank S. Parker and Mrs. Vonnie H. Parker,
and to my teacher, mentor, and friend,
Professor B. Phinizy Spalding,
all of whom were lost to us
during the preparation of this work.

CONTENTS

PREFACE

WHEN I FIRST BEGAN collecting the material for this project, it soon became apparent that the subject offered too much substance and too many questions for adequate treatment within a single volume without being too burdensome. Decisions had to be made about the parameters and the approach to this fascinating topic of Highland Scots in colonial Georgia. The most logical method was to find some division of chronology and activities and to work exclusively within those boundaries. In Georgia's unique colonial experience, the division was easily defined. During Georgia's prerevolutionary history, the colony had two distinct phases—one as a trusteeship and one as a royal province.

During the trusteeship, Highland Scots were recruited as a group and immigrated as a community. Georgia's laws under the authority of the trustees in London were restrictive. Slavery was prohibited, so the Scottish community labored together. Land grants were limited, thereby keeping the people of Darien in close proximity to one another; and the reason for their recruitment—that is, military security—kept the Highlanders together in a regiment stationed in and around the settlement of Darien. The town of Darien was the center of political, social, and economic activity, and the affairs that would affect the individual would affect the entire society of the Scottish settlement.

This situation changed, however, when the colony reverted to Crown control. During the transition from trustee rule to royal government, the Highland regiment was disbanded (1749), slavery was permitted (1750), and limitations on land grants were removed (1752). This meant that Darien society changed with the times. With the regiment gone, the young men were free to move from the frontier settlement and seek their fortunes in other ways, such as the Indian trade. Many Darien Scots took up additional land grants from the Crown, bought slaves, and moved into the countryside. The emphasis shifted from corporate contributions to the colony by the Highland community during the trustee era to individual initiatives working within the now expanding community of Scots during the royal period. While this transition was taking place, the town of Darien suffered, but the individuals of Darien prospered under the changes.

Although the progress of these pioneers from the Highlands of Scotland to the frontier settlement in Georgia and ultimately to becoming many of the leading citizens in the closing days of the colonial period is fascinating, it is also encyclopedic. Therefore, to give adequate treatment to the pioneering efforts of the first settlers, I chose to concentrate my work on the trustee era and the initial struggles of these new immigrants on the southern frontier, and to leave the further growth of the community of Darien to a later effort.

Having made the decision to research the conditions in Scotland, the recruiting efforts of the colony, and the settlement of the Highland Scots in Georgia, I now faced a new set of challenges. As any student of Highland history will attest, a people with an oral tradition leave few records, and the majority of emigrants from Scotland to Georgia were from the ranks of cadets and tenants in the clans. After scouring the family records and muniments housed in the Scottish Record Office and the National Library of Scotland, I found considerable material on life in the Highlands but little correspondence between the emigrants to Georgia and their families in Scotland.

To study the Darien settlement I had to rely primarily on journals, diaries, and the colonial records of Georgia. That in itself was not a problem since the leading contemporary authorities of Georgia—John Percival, the first Earl of Egmont, and William Stephens, the secretary and first president of the colony—kept meticulous journals and diaries, which have been published, and the Trustees for Establishing the Colony of Georgia in America kept letterbooks of all correspondence to and from the colony.[1] Due to time limitations and financial considerations, I had to choose whether to spend more effort in London at the Public Record Office or in Georgia among the collections of the Earl of Egmont Papers at the University of Georgia Library, the collections found in Savannah at the Georgia Historical Society, the Georgia Department of Archives and History in Atlanta, and personal records in the town of Darien. I chose Georgia.

In that decision I was fortunate. The records kept in the above-mentioned collections are a treasure trove of colonial information. Many of the letters to and from James Oglethorpe found in the Egmont Papers of the Phillips Collection at the University of Georgia have been published.[2] The colonial records found in the Georgia Department of Archives and History are

copies of the letters, reports, and other documents on deposit in the Public
Record Office in London. This is in part because of the varied history of
Georgia's colonial records. Her custom records were destroyed in 1776
when the vessel upon which they had been stored was burned during the
"Battle of the Rice Boats" at Savannah. During the Revolutionary War many
of the records were sent north for protection; most never returned. Other
losses have taken their toll over the years. The State of Georgia had the
records restored by having them copied from the London offices.

Between 1904 and 1910, twenty-five volumes of these transcripts were
compiled and faithfully published along with their PRO reference numbers
as the *Colonial Records of the State of Georgia.* In 1977 seven additional volumes were published by the University of Georgia Press, and there remain
seven further typescript volumes in the Georgia Department of Archives
and History in Atlanta. By having access to the collections and the advantage
of published original records, I was able to forage through almost all available primary source materials for evidence about the lives and struggles of
the Highland Scots who settled in Darien between the years 1735 and 1748.
It has been an exhausting effort and is by no means complete, but it is a good
start on a lifetime of study.

ACKNOWLEDGMENTS

AS WITH ANY PROJECT that extends over five years in preparation, no one works alone. I owe sincere appreciation to several institutions and many individuals. To the helpful staffs of the University of Georgia Library, State of Georgia Department of Archives and History, University of Florida Library, Georgia Historical Society in Savannah, National Library of Scotland, Scottish Public Record Office in Edinburgh, Public Record Office at Kew, and especially to R. N. Smart and Christine Gascoigne at the University of St. Andrews Library, Scotland, I wish to extend my deepest gratitude.

My sincere thanks go to the fine people of Darien, Georgia, who welcomed me into their midst and shared their knowledge and friendship, especially Maurice and Martha Mixson, who opened their home and hospitality to my wife and me on our visits. The Mixsons' home, "The Thickets," has become our second home in Georgia. To Bill Haynes of Ashantilly Place, Doris Rab and staff at the Fort King George State Historical Site, Mattie Gladstone at "The Ridge," Isabel Mealing, Geneva E. Stebbins, and the helpful people at the *Darien News,* I thank you for your help.

Of course no book could be accomplished without proper support and guidance, and I could not have been more pleased with the efforts of T. C. Smout, Historiographer Royal of Scotland and head of the Centre for Advanced Historical Studies at the University of St. Andrews, in bearing with me and offering timely direction and comment on my research and writing. Thank you. I also wish to express my appreciation to David Stevenson of the Scottish History Department at the University of St. Andrews for his valuable assistance in the formation of this work.

On a more personal note, I cannot express my thanks enough for the patience of my friends, flatmates, and family for enduring these past five years. To my sons Jason, Ray, and Joshua, thanks for understanding my absence from Georgia and allowing me the time away from you to finish this endeavor. To Ken and Sarah Laird I owe a debt of gratitude for their unwavering support while I took their daughter, my wife, from Georgia to Scotland.

Finally, I want to express to my wife, Lisa, my love and deep appreciation for her patience, continued interest and encouragement, and the occasional kick in the seat to keep me on track. For her assistance in proofreading and correcting obvious errors in my judgment over the years, I also give my thanks.

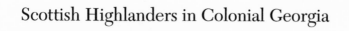
Scottish Highlanders in Colonial Georgia

INTRODUCTION

IN THE MONTH OF JANUARY 1736, the first group of Scottish High-landers arrived in the fledgling British colony of Georgia. They settled on the banks of the Altamaha River along the southernmost border of the province in a town they first called New Inverness, later to become Darien. These immigrants had been recruited, screened, and selected by represen-tatives of the Trustees for Establishing the Colony of Georgia in America.[1] According to William MacKenzie, a professor of history at the University of Edinburgh in the 1840s, these Scots were carefully "picked men" because of their "military qualities."[2] It was the design of the Trustees and of James Oglethorpe to people the borders of the colony with settlers who were ac-customed to hardship, militant in nature, and willing to become frontier farmer-soldiers. In this endeavor, the Trustees were successful.

The founding of Georgia in 1733 is most often seen as being a philan-thropic undertaking to find a home for the poor of England, and as such Georgia is considered a "debtor's" colony. While the concept for the colony did include the ideal of giving the poor of England a chance to improve their station in life, this was only one of several goals in the minds of the Trustees for establishing Georgia.

The Trustees also envisioned economic prosperity, not only for the colony but also for the mother country. The idea was to produce, in a similar cli-mate, those goods that were being imported at great expense to England. By employing the poor and destitute of England to supply the raw materials for the market at home, Georgia could be a valuable asset for Great Britain. These grandiose ideas, however, were overly optimistic and not very prac-tical. It would be hard to create a yeoman's utopia in the pine barrens of Georgia.

There was a third consideration in the designs of the Trustees. Colonial expansion and, in turn, colonial defense were of paramount importance to the governments of Spain, France, and Great Britain in the seventeenth and eighteenth centuries. It was for this reason—British imperial defense—that Georgia's real worth was recognized.

In Benjamin Martyn's account of the progress of the colony of Georgia, he wrote that it was thought necessary for the Trustees to send over "poor [English] people and foreign Protestants" willing to live in Georgia, "not only to cultivate the lands, but at the same time to *strengthen His Majesty's Colonies* [emphasis mine]. For which purposes they considered each inhabitant, both as a planter and as a soldier."[3] To the dismay of the Trustees, the first English immigrants to Georgia were neither farmers nor soldiers and most were unwilling to change.[4] This caused the Trustees to look elsewhere for suitable settlers, and the Highlanders seemed the perfect solution.

Recruiting and settling the Scottish Highlanders as the first line of defense on the southern frontier in Georgia was an important decision on the part of the Trustees and crucial for the survival of the colony; however, this portion of Georgia's history has been sadly neglected. While much has been written on the exploits of James Edward Oglethorpe, the town of Savannah, and the settlement of the German Salzburgers in Georgia, little of scholarly merit has been accomplished on the importance of the Scottish Highlanders during this critical period of the colony's history. Although vital to the survival of the infant colony, the Scots have received at most a passing mention in most general histories of Georgia and they are totally ignored in others.

When the subject of the Highlanders has been addressed, it is usually in broad romantic episodes of claymores flashing, kilts flying, and bagpipes skirling in the heat of the Battle of Bloody Marsh and does not take into account the sacrifices and hardships of frontier life that the Scots in Darien faced. J. P. MacLean leads as a glaring example of the romantics in a chapter devoted to the Scots' Georgia settlement in *An Historical Account of the Settlements of Scotch Highlanders in America.* The subject received some attention in the *Georgia Historical Quarterly* when it printed a special issue in 1936 celebrating the two-hundredth anniversary of the coming of the Scots Highlanders.[5] The aforementioned works were published relatively early in this century, and since that time there has been little serious research in this area.

The initial importance of the Highlanders to Georgia is mentioned in passing, but not developed, in Harvey H. Jackson's *Lachlan McIntosh and the Politics of Revolutionary Georgia,* as a backdrop to his study of Lachlan Mackintosh, one of the Scottish immigrants in 1736. A meaningful scholarly work dealing seriously with the contributions of the Highlanders is Edward Cashin's *Lachlan McGillivray, Indian Trader,* which appeared in 1992. However, Cashin too relegates the importance of the Scottish community to the background and concentrates upon Indian affairs and the inland trade.[6]

The most recent endeavor addressing Scottish emigration before the clearances to the colonies is the 1994 publication *Scottish Emigration to Colonial America, 1607–1785* by David Dobson. Dobson's work is the first published book that has dealt with the Georgia settlement by Scots in any detail. Until now, there has been only one treatise focusing on Scottish immigration to Georgia in the first half of the eighteenth century, and it aspires to include all immigrants of Scottish extraction in the colony, whether from the Lowlands, Highlands, or from other colonies. That work, although informative, remains unpublished.[7] The efforts and contributions of the Highland Scots in stabilizing Georgia as a permanent colony have largely been overlooked in past scholarship and are only now beginning to receive the attention they deserve.

Current interest in migration and cultural history of the colonial settlers has brought the importance and uniqueness of the Highlanders into focus. Perhaps the leader in the field of migration history is Bernard Bailyn, whose work *Voyagers to the West* deals exclusively with English and Scottish migration on the eve of the American Revolution.[8] Although Bailyn's research into the motives for migration by the Highlanders of Scotland begins during the period immediately following the end of the Seven Years' War in 1763, the same forces were already at work in the Highlands as early as 1735. However, in 1735 the Highlanders had to be actively recruited and persuaded to emigrate, while in 1763 the Scots were anxious and willing to migrate. The first Scots recruited by the Georgia Trustees were the pioneers who opened the way for those who followed.

From the cultural standpoint, David Hackett Fischer has broken new ground in regional and ethnic research in his *Albion's Seed: Four British Folkways in America.*[9] In this significant work Fischer details the values, mores, and cultural distinctions transferred from the varying regions of Great Britain to the American colonies. He argues that the people from Great Britain did not forswear their heritage in migrating to America but rather maintained their familiar lifestyle and transported their cultural values with them. Grady McWhiney takes Fischer's premise further in his controversial book *Cracker Culture: Celtic Ways in the Old South.*[10] McWhiney details the cultural differences and animosities between the American Antebellum North and South as being determined by settlement patterns of primarily East Anglian English in New England and the Celtic settlement of Scots, Irish, Ulster Scots, and Welsh in the South. Fischer's and to a lesser extent McWhiney's arguments find strong support in this study of the Highland Scots who came to Georgia and settled at Darien in the first half of the eighteenth century.

In this present study, I aim to put the Highlanders of Scotland at Darien in Georgia into perspective, concentrating on three specific groups recruited in Scotland and transported by the Trustees for settlement from 1735 to 1742. I do not deal with the Lowland Scots from Glasgow and Edinburgh who were to become known as the "Malcontents" nor with those Scots who were already in Georgia, having migrated from South Carolina or taken earlier passage from Scotland individually.

An examination of the immigration of Scottish Highlanders into Georgia should throw new light on the subject of southern colonial history. In addition to being farmers and soldiers as the Trustees had hoped, these Highlanders also proved to be effective Indian traders and merchants, who provided the colony of Georgia with the necessary vitality to sustain itself during its infancy. Their particular presence in Georgia not only produced a colorful change—with their plaids and pipes—from the dreariness of frontier life but also gave the colony strength and stability that held it together in times of crisis.

Additionally, the organized recruitment for Georgia in 1735 would be the first successful large-scale attempt in the Highlands since the Union in 1707. Groups from Clan Campbell migrated three years later in 1738 to the colony of New York, and the settlement of Highland Scots in Cape Fear, North Carolina, would follow in 1739.[11] The Highland Scots who ventured to Georgia would be the forerunners to the massive exodus from the Highlands that would ensue during the following decades. This study is an attempt to establish the importance of the Scottish Highlanders at Darien to the history of the southern colonies, especially Georgia.

CHAPTER 1

Discovery, Exploration, and First Contests in the Debatable Land Called Georgia

Has Heaven reserved, in pity to the poor,
No pathless waste, or undiscovered shore?
No secret island in the boundless main?
No Peaceful desert, yet unclaimed by Spain?
Quick, let us rise, the happy seats explore,
And bear oppresion's insolence no more!
—Samuel Johnson, *London; A Poem*

THE TRACT OF LAND in the New World known at various times as the land of Ayllón, Gualé, La Florida, Carolina, and ultimately Georgia became the scene of the first attempts at settlement and colonization within the present boundaries of the United States and the theater for many of the international conflicts that arose in the years following its discovery. Herbert Bolton and Mary Ross labeled the territory along the southern frontier of the British colonies in America, between the Savannah and St. John's rivers, as the "Debatable Land" because of the 250-year-long contest among the Spanish, French, English, and Native Americans for control of this land.[1] It would be in this context of continuous conflict that Scottish Highlanders would ultimately be used to settle the matter.

An expedition led by Juan Ponce de León for Spain in 1513 is the first recorded European contact with the mainland of North America.[2] Some historians suggest that he might have traveled as far north as the Georgia coast.[3] Having received royal permission to discover and settle the "Islands of Bening [Bemini]" to the north of Cuba in 1512, Ponce de León set about making the arrangements for an expedition the following year.[4] In March

1513, he sailed with three ships from his base in San Juan, Puerto Rico, in search of the Fountain of Youth and the fortune he thought could be found on Bemini. The Spanish ships reached land on the eastern coast of the Florida peninsula in April and named it La Florida because they had arrived during the time of the "Feast of Flowers" (Pasqua Florida).[5] Several modern experts claim that Ponce de León's landing was south of Cape Canaveral instead of the traditionally accepted site of Saint Augustine, further north.[6] His attempts at settlement failed before they had a chance to begin due to Indian resistance; however, the mainland would not long be free from Spanish incursions. The coastline of Georgia would be the next entry point for colonization.

Lucas Vásquez de Ayllón, a wealthy lawyer and legal official in Hispaniola, inspired by the same desire for wealth and power as was Ponce de León, went to Spain in 1523 to discuss a proposed exploration and conquest of a new land north of Ponce de León's grant. He received from Spain's Charles V a royal charter to the lands known as Chicora. The charter had certain specifications that reflected the change in attitude by the Spanish government over the previous few years. It directed Ayllón to deal with the natives in the same peaceful manner in which Spain dealt with other sovereign nations. This was in response to pressure by the Dominican friars, who were staunch defenders of Indian rights in the New World. The objective was to incorporate the Indians into Spanish society by peaceful rather than violent means, which had been the tactic used by previous *conquistadores*.[7]

During his audience with the king, Ayllón raised an issue that would reappear many times in future schemes for the development of a colony in the debatable land—that being the possibility of a silk industry in the New World. Ayllón averred that Chicora had a mild climate where mulberry trees abounded and was perfectly situated for the production of the finest silk.[8] Charles V was persuaded and ordered the Spanish explorer to take silkworms with him on his colonizing effort.[9] He was also to explore up to eight hundred leagues (about 2,560 nautical miles) of coastline before making settlement.

In 1525 Ayllón sent two caravels under the direction of Pedro de Quejo on a reconnaissance mission up the coast to survey the land he intended to settle. The voyage covered some 250 leagues (650 miles) of shoreline from the tip of Florida to an area just south of the Cape Fear region of North Carolina. It was on this preliminary voyage that the Spanish are believed to have landed at the mouth of the Savannah River, identified as the Río de la Cruz on the Juan Vespucci map of 1526. The expedition then proceeded north to the site of a former Indian contact. After brief contact with the natives there, the Spaniards continued their travels, first to the Cape Fear area, then south to a point around Amelia Island on the Florida-Georgia coast. At both stops along the Georgian coast, the travelers met the inhabitants of the land.[10] Having found large Indian settlements and cultivable land, Ayllón felt the way was clear for an attempt to establish a colony in the new land of North America.

The fleet of six ships that left Puerto Plata, Hispaniola, in July 1526 carried some five hundred men and women, who included soldiers, two priests and one lay brother of the Order of Dominic, and the first known black slaves to reach American shores.[11] According to Jane Landers, the African slaves among the colonists were not *bozales* or unacculturated agricultural laborers but rather *ladinos*—skilled artisans and domestics—from Spain.[12] The expedition sailed directly to a site where Indian slaves had been captured in 1521.

A portent of things to come greeted Ayllón's fleet upon arrival at the mouth of the Jordan River, which had been found on Quejo's previous exploratory voyage. Ayllón's flagship ran aground and was lost, along with most of the supplies it carried. Insult was added to injury when scouting parties vainly searched the area for the Indian villages that had been located during Quejo's previous trip. The Indians had apparently fled, leaving no avenue for food supplies, opportunities for trade, or guides for exploration. To make matters worse yet, Francisco de Chicora, an Indian guide who had traveled back from Puerto Plata with the colonists, promptly shed his civilized trappings and fled to his native forests, leaving the Spanish settlers on their own in a foreign land.[13] Ayllón could neither stay on the site nor carry out his contract with the Spanish king. He chose to move his colony further south to a point where large Indian populations had been located the year before—the land of the Guale (pronounced "wallie") Indians on the Georgia coast.[14]

Exploring parties, using a vessel made from the remnants of the wrecked flagship, found a fairly dense native population right on the coast living in the Saint Catherines–Sapelo Sound area. The location was some forty to forty-five leagues south of the Jordan (Santee) River. The movement to Guale began during the first days of September 1526, when Ayllón put the women and the sick along with a detachment of able-bodied men on board the ships and sent them south. Ayllón and the remaining company headed inland and south on horseback.

When his forces reassembled on the banks of the tidal river in Sapelo Sound with the remainder of the colonists who had come by ship, Ayllón had his settlers build a town, which he named San Miguel de Gualdape.[15] This would be the first known European settlement within the boundaries of the United States since the Vikings some five hundred years before. Most of the houses built would likely have been made of wattle and daub, a mixture of sand, mud, and seashells. Perhaps there would have been a few buildings of timber and all would have had thatched roofs.[16] Although no exact details of the buildings exist, there is enough evidence to suggest that these were not temporary dwellings but solid houses. Shallow wells would have been dug for fresh water and possible irrigation ditches excavated for crops (see note 14 for possible explanation of earthworks).

The autumn storms brought sickness and troubles for the infant colony. The search for food became an all-consuming passion and disease became rampant within the settlement. A few of the Spanish newcomers, desperate for food, abused the surrounding Indian villages. Retaliation followed, making it unsafe for the settlers to leave town. Bodies began to fill the church cemetery. Ayllón himself was not immune to the events; his body was added to the list of the dead on 18 October 1526, during the Feast of St. Luke.[17]

At the time of his death, Ayllón had been making preparations to send a ship back to Hispaniola for food and provisions. Many of the remaining colonists, disenchanted and demoralized, took the opportunity to mutiny. During the ensuing struggle between the settlers, the African slaves staged their own mutiny. Houses were burned and men murdered. Ayllón's lieutenant, Francisco Gomez, was able to overpower the Spanish and African mutineers and reestablish control. At least one mutineer was executed. Nothing is known as to what happened to the African slaves; however, many ethnohistorians maintain that the Africans took up residence among the Guale Indians and became *cimarrones,* as their counterparts had done in Hispaniola, Puerto Rico, Jamaica, Cuba, and Mexico.[18]

The decision was made to abandon San Miguel de Gualdape and return to Hispaniola. Of the six ships and some five hundred persons who had made the trip to the new land, only one vessel, *La Santa Catalina,* and 150 survivors are known to have arrived in the Antilles.[19] It is not known whether disease, internal rebellion, or Indian attack was the most devastating to the short-lived colony; however, the legacy of the attempt would bring others from Europe to Georgia's shores. In a small Spanish settlement on the shores of a river feeding Sapelo Sound in a remote area of the Georgia coastline, the contest for the debatable land had begun.

Other Spanish expeditions followed, by Panfilo de Narváez in 1528 and Hernando de Soto in 1539, and the French made their presence known in

1562 by Jean Ribault's small fortified settlement at Port Royal Sound on the coast of Carolina. St. Augustine, the oldest permanently inhabited European establishment in the United States, was founded by the Spanish on the coast of Florida in 1565 by Pedro Menéndez de Avilés in response to the French incursions.[20] After removing the French, the Spanish remained in control of the Georgia-Florida coast for the next hundred years.

The Spanish utilized two basic institutions in their colonization efforts: the presidio and the mission. The presidio was a small frontier fort defended by a contingent of Spanish troops and Indian allies. The mission was the spiritual training center for Indian converts under the supervision of a friar (initially Jesuit, later Franciscan). Unlike the English approach, in which the natives were removed or eliminated, the Spanish built their system around the Native Americans. By using this method, the Spanish were able to secure a line of presidios and missions along the entire coast of Guale.[21] There were Indian revolts and attacks by the English and French pirates against the Spanish; however, no serious threat to Spanish domination would appear until the later half of the seventeenth century.

In April 1670, a small fleet of English ships sailing from Barbados with some 150 colonists arrived at the mouth of the Ashley River to settle on the site of the former Spanish town of Santa Elena, known to the English as Port Royal. The proposed settlement was in response to a charter by Charles II of England in 1663, granting Sir John Colleton and seven other Lords Proprietors of Carolina all those lands lying between the thirty-sixth and thirty-first degrees north latitude, from the Atlantic Ocean to the Pacific.[22] It apparently did not matter to the English king that he was giving away lands claimed and occupied by both the French and the Spanish. In 1665, Charles II extended the boundaries of the grant to thirty-six degrees and thirty minutes north and along the twenty-ninth parallel to the south. This new grant included St. Augustine and a line of Spanish missions and presidios stretching 150 miles up the Georgia coast.[23]

Although initially intending to settle at Port Royal, the new colonists soon moved because of the Spanish presence. Fifty miles upriver at Kiawah, out of harm's way, they founded Charles-Town (present day Charleston). The fear in Charles-Town was real. One of the settlers complained that they found themselves "in the very chaps of the Spaniards."[24] To the Spanish, Charles-Town was regarded as a flagrant intrusion to be driven from Spanish soil.[25] The conflict was not only over territory but, more important, it was over the allegiance of and trade with the Indians.

The Englishman Dr. Henry Woodward had been in Indian country for several years as a trader before the founding of Charles-Town. He had taken the time to learn the native language and customs; now, he had begun to lure the Native Americans away from the Spanish by offering them cheap goods and by purchasing prisoners of war taken during their raids into Spanish Guale—raids instigated at times by the Englishman. The Spanish responded by sending a punitive expedition against their wavering allies. This move, in effect, forced many of the Indians into the waiting arms of the English.

Early in 1680, Santa Catalina, Spain's northernmost mission in Guale, was attacked by three hundred Indians led by Englishmen. They were repulsed by the Spanish garrison, but the attack raised the alarm in Saint Augustine.[26] One terrifying feature of these early raids into Guale was the growth of traffic in Indian slaves. Many native prisoners were taken back to Carolina and either sold to local planters or shipped to various points in the West Indies.[27] These actions, along with encroachments upon Indian lands and unfair treatment in trade, provoked reprisals both by the Indians and the Spanish.

Into this tense atmosphere a group of 148 Scottish Presbyterian Covenanters led by Henry Erskine, third Lord Cardross, and William Dunlop, who later became principal of Glasgow University, arrived at Port Royal to build a small settlement on the Spanish Point in 1684.[28] The Covenanters had come seeking in Carolina a colony of refuge from the persecution and repressive legislation they suffered in England and Scotland.[29] They were attracted by the provisions of the Carolina charters, which granted freedom of conscience to colonists, and by the influence of Anthony Ashley Cooper, Earl of Shaftesbury, a strong supporter of the Covenanters in Parliament and one of the original Lords Proprietors of Carolina.[30] Sir John Cochran of Ochiltree and Sir George Campbell of Cessmock negotiated the agreement with the Carolina proprietors for the Scots' settlement at Port Royal harbor.[31]

In the early planning stages of the new colony, there were high hopes and grandiose ideas. The scheme called for a thousand settlers and a thousand cows to be transported to the American colony the first year.[32] However, political intrigues in London cast a dark shadow over the bright hopes of a Presbyterian sanctuary in Carolina. Many of the covenanting Scots who were prominent in the Carolina project were charged with using the scheme as a cover for plotting an insurrection with the Whigs in England against the government.[33] Although some Scots were actually involved, others, such as Lord Cardross and William Dunlop, were not. The plan continued but the former zeal for the project had gone. With much reduced numbers, the Scots came to Carolina.

The settlement, which Lord Cardross named Stuart's Town, became the first barrier of defense in the colony of Carolina against the Spanish from Florida; a defense strategy the English would use again in Georgia in 1735. The Lords Proprietors of Carolina desired the Scots and the English to be settled apart, with open and unsettled lands between them.[34] This decision was made at the request of Lord Cardross to avoid possible conflict between the Scots colonists and the English at Charles-Town. Cardross wanted autonomy apart from the jurisdiction of the authorities in Charles-Town. He was given permission, provided that the Scots established their settlement "far enough inland to render it safe from surprise by ships . . . [and] to settle together as may be best for their defense and safety."[35]

Bitter controversy immediately arose between Stuart's Town and Charles-Town over the lucrative Indian trade.[36] In March 1685, Charles-Town Indian traders John Edenburgh and Dr. Henry Woodward were arrested and brought before Lord Cardross for trading with the Indians within his borders. Cardross warned "that noe Englishman should trade from Santa Helena to the Westoe River [Savannah River] for all the Indians were his and that noe Englishman should trade between the Westoe River and St. Katerina for that hee had taken up one County and had liberty to take up another County."[37] When the traders complained to the authorities in Charles-Town, an arrest warrant was issued for Lord Cardross; he ignored the summons.[38] In May, Cardross again arrested Woodward and several companions despite their having Grand Council of Carolina credentials for trading with the Indians.[39] A second warrant for Cardross's arrest was issued, which again was refused and returned with an excuse claiming illness. Cardross complained to the Lords Proprietors, who in turn ordered the governor and council in Charles-Town to drop all proceedings against the Scot.[40]

The arrest of the Charles-Town traders and the refusal of Cardross to accept authority from the English in Carolina were not the only sources of contention between the two settlements. The Scots had already begun to send raiding expeditions into Guale for both trade and slaves. In February 1685, a large band of Yamassee Indians from Guale arrived under the leadership of Chief Altamaha to settle under the protection of the Scots. At first, the Scots feared that the Indians were part of a Spanish plot; however, after an alliance was formed, the Scots supplied the Indians with arms for a raid against the Spanish missions in Guale.[41] The Scots-armed Indians invaded Guale in the spring of 1685 and attacked the Spanish mission of Santa Catalina (Saint Catherine), which "had a Chapel and a Spanish Friar," bringing back "twenty prisoners as slaves and a manuscript of prayers produced" to the Scots at Stuart's Town.[42]

This and other actions of the Carolina traders provoked a determined response from the Spanish at St. Augustine. Open hostilities began in September 1686 when three ships carrying a raiding party of Spanish soldiers, Indians, and mulattos descended on the Carolina coast with instructions to destroy the Scottish settlement at Port Royal and then the English one at Charles-Town. The defenders of Stuart's Town were ill-prepared to ward off the invaders due to sickness; only twenty-five Scots were able to bear arms. The settlement was completely destroyed and Stuart's Town was burned. Cardross, Dunlop, and the remaining survivors took refuge in Charles-Town.[43] Some of the survivors settled in Charles-Town, while others may have moved north or returned to Europe; however, little is known of their further impact on Carolina.[44] The Spanish went on to sack the plantation of the governor of Carolina and then moved north toward Charles-Town.[45] They wanted to complete the destruction of the English in Carolina, but a hurricane intervened and the mission was aborted.[46] The Spanish retreated with their booty back to the safety of St. Augustine.

The English prepared a retaliatory strike but were stopped by the newly appointed governor, James Colleton. He was supported in his decision by the Lords Proprietors, who felt that the attack by the Spaniards was in revenge of the plundering of Spanish settlements by Indians "set on by the inhabitants of Port Royal"—that is, the Scots.[47] They further declared that "such action was unjustifiable by the Scots" and that they would offer no protection for the guilty parties.[48]

The increased influence of the Scots and English traders over the Guale Indians and the frequent savage attacks of English and French pirates forced the Spanish to retreat from Guale to the protection of the fort at St. Augustine. By the end of 1686, the remaining missionaries and neophytes were ordered south of the St. Mary's River, and the era of Spanish missions and presidios in Georgia was at an end.[49] The struggle for the debatable land was not over; however, an old adversary was making new inroads in the backcountry.

By 1700, the French, led by Pierre Iberville, had taken possession of the lower Mississippi and the surrounding Gulf coast.[50] In response, the Spanish moved quickly to settle the area around Pensacola to protect their territory.[51] This race by England, Spain, and France for control of the northern coast of the Gulf increased the interest of each in the Carolina backcountry, which included the Georgia territory. The rivalry was not for possession of the land but rather over the lucrative Indian trade. At the turn of the eighteenth century, South Carolinians were more worried about the French

menace from the Mississippi than they were about the Spanish at St. Augustine.[52] Fear over the loss of the Indian trade and uneasiness over possible
French and Spanish attacks caused many South Carolinians to push for settlement south of the Savannah River (formerly known to the English as the
Westoe).

The English in South Carolina had good reason to fear the designs of the
French and the Spanish. Iberville had drawn up for Louisiana and the Mississippi region a comprehensive frontier policy that included dealing with
the English in Carolina.[53] Not only did he want a strong defense for the
Louisiana settlements, but he also sought French expansion into the Georgia
territory. He planned to pacify and unite the Native Americans under
French authority and to cooperate with the Spanish to destroy Carolina. In
1702, Mobile was established as a point of support for the Indians allied with
the French and Spanish against the English.[54] For the French, the conquest
of Carolina would pave the way for an Indian alliance that would be strong
enough to make possible a grand encircling movement, from Canada down
the Mississippi River to the Gulf coast, against all of the English seaboard
colonies.

The English at Charles-Town were not passive during Iberville's planning
stages. Queen Anne of England had turned openly aggressive with a declaration of war against Spain and France in 1702. The English took the of-
fensive and from 1704 to 1706 waged a successful campaign against the
Apalache Indians, who were being used by the French and Spanish against
English-allied Indians.[55] The success of the mission thwarted Iberville's plan
to develop a strong Indian alliance against the English. It did not, however,
stop the determination of the French and the Spanish to eject the English
from Carolina.

During the international struggle on the Georgian frontier, England was
facing another threat at home. The question of succession to the throne
of both England and Scotland was being raised in the parliaments of both
countries. The English had come to terms with the idea that a new line of
succession would be needed. In 1701 they declared the Act of Settlement,
which provided the Electress of Hanover, a Protestant and granddaughter
of James VI of Scotland (James I of England), and her descendants the throne
of England if Anne died without heirs. The Scottish Parliament responded
by passing the Act of Security in 1703, which stated that Scotland would
choose its own sovereign after the queen's death unless it had the same trading privileges as England.[56] This act caused an uproar in England for fear
that Scotland would choose the next person in direct line to the throne, who

was Catholic and living in exile. After much negotiation and questionable conduct, and despite strong opposition, the Treaty of Union between the two countries was passed and made law in January 1707, thereby creating Great Britain.

The political maneuvering in Great Britain was not without its significance to the colony of Carolina in the New World. New visions of Scottish colonization for the protection of the Carolina border were being trumpeted in London. Former Governor John Archdale declared,

> If it please God that the Union succeed with Scotland, the principle place in Carolina, call'd Port Royal may be setl'd with English and Scots in a considerable body, because 't is a bold port, and also a Frontier upon the Spaniards at Saint Augustine which is but a weak settlement about 200 miles to the South West of it. The Scots did, about twenty years since, begin a settlement with about 10 families, but were disposs'd by the Spaniards. O might the Scots, that go now as Switzers to serve Foreign Nations, how might they, I say, strengthen our American colonies and increase the trade of Great Britain and enrich themselves both at home and abroad.[57]

Archdale seemed to be pleading for soldiers on the colonial southern frontier. He would not have to wait long for a new influx of Scottish soldiers to make the journey to Carolina.

After the Treaty of Utrecht ended Queen Anne's War in 1713, an uneasy peace followed. None of the provisions in the treaty dealt with the boundaries along the southern frontier—the Spanish were still in Florida, the French were in the Alabama basin, and the English were in the Carolinas. The fight for the Indian trade and the allegiance of the various tribes continued unabated, but the Native Americans themselves caused the next round of trouble for the Carolinians. The abuses and mistreatment of the natives by the Charles-Town traders finally led to a revolt.

In 1715, the Yamassee Indians formed an alliance with several other tribes and launched hostilities by murdering a party sent to them by South Carolina's Governor Charles Craven to settle their grievances.[58] Violence spread; the colony reeled at the devastation and death resulting from the Indian raids. The reaction was swift and the revolt was put down by the Carolinians; however, the Yamassee War of 1715–16 exemplified the need for control of the land south of the Savannah River. South Carolina realized that there could be no real security until this region was settled by people loyal to the British crown, capable of fighting and defeating any English enemies.[59] They found such men among the Scottish prisoners of the failed Jacobite uprising of 1715. Out of a total of 608 Jacobite prisoners exiled to the colonies, 150 were sent to the colony of South Carolina.[60] A large number of those prisoners banished to South Carolina were from the Highland Clan Chattan in the shire of Inverness and would later play a major role in the life of the colonies of South Carolina and Georgia as soldiers and Indian traders.[61]

While the new Scottish immigrants were settling on the frontier in Carolina, the French were moving quietly into the Carolina backcountry (Georgia). The Indian traders notified the Charles-Town authorities, and a report was sent by Richard Beresford to London expressing strong fears of renewed French encirclement, especially in the Carolinas.[62] Beresford's letter received immediate attention from the Council of Trade and Plantations. Letters were sent out to all of the governors in the colonies asking for defense strengths and plans of action.[63] In January 1720, Governor Robert Johnson of South Carolina made a long, detailed report to the council on the defense of the colony, and he also expressed fears of the French along the Mississippi.[64] The Grand Council in South Carolina followed Johnson's letter with a document of their own, describing the movement of the French in Indian country, and declared that Carolina was a "place of no real security."[65] This document was transmitted to the Board of Trade and became the basis for later action in both England and Carolina.

In order to guard against further French and Spanish encroachments on South Carolina and to preserve peaceful trade with the Indians, the British government instructed the governor of South Carolina to build a fort on the Altamaha River in Guale at the precise location that the French were desiring.[66] The area would later become the Highland Scots' Darien settlement. The result was Fort King George, located on the river's north bank. The Board of Trade suggested that a town should be laid out contiguous to the fort, with adjoining farm lots granted on military tenure to settlers who would become citizen-soldiers.[67] Clearly the board thought it was time to secure the debatable land for Great Britain.[68] But the fort did not prosper. The site was unhealthy, the Spaniards were incensed,[69] troops stationed there were quarrelsome, and the cost of upkeep proved exorbitant. Much to the delight of both the French and the Spanish governments, the fort was abandoned in 1727.[70] At roughly the same time in England, forces were being consolidated that would result in the formation of the British colony of Georgia, the last in a series of projected schemes aimed at providing adequate defense for Britain's southernmost continental colonies.

The English Privy Council had long recognized the need to protect the southern boundaries of Carolina. London was alive with various schemes that would meet Privy Council demands. As early as 1708, Thomas Nairn, a Scot and a South Carolina Indian agent, advocated a British settlement in the Mississippi River area to halt the advancement of the French into the lucrative Indian trade in the backcountry.[71] He proposed that a line of forts be built across the frontier in the same manner as the French had done in Canada. The effort never got past the planning stages before he was killed by being burned at the stake by the Yamassee Indians.[72] In 1713, a Welsh gentleman by the name of Hughes Pryce, traveling with the Carolina traders, suggested a new English colony near the mouth of the Mississippi, to be settled by the poor from Wales, but nothing was done before he, too, was killed by the Indians in 1715.[73]

Thomas Coram put forth an idea in 1717 for a new settlement that fore-shadowed the Georgia colony. Coram, who would later serve as one of the Georgia Trustees, envisioned a colony to be called "Georgeia."[74] Although it was to be located on the northern frontier, the design was similar to the plan adopted later by the Georgia Trustees. He advocated settling "waste lands" and islands between Nova Scotia and Maine under royal grant to "Thirty or more men in trust, with full power for settling it."[75] The people of New England rejected the idea and it was dropped. However, the foundation for Georgia's plan had been expressed: public trustees were to have charge of settlement, families were to be established on farms, foreign Protestants were to be accepted on equal terms with British subjects, Indians were to be protected against the evil influence of liquor, and a frontier was to be secured against hostile natives and enemies of the British Empire.[76]

The first scheme to be considered for the situation on the southern border was a proposal by Sir Robert Mountgomery, a Scottish baronet. In 1717, he published *A Discourse Concerning the Design'd Establishment of a New Colony to the South of Carolina, in the Most Delightful Country of the Universe*,[77] in which he explained that his design "arises not from any sudden motive, but a strong bent of genius" that he inherited from his ancestors.[78] Mountgomery was the son of Sir Robert Mountgomery of Skelmorlie, Ayrshire, an associate of Lord Cardross in the Stuart's Town venture and descended from on of "those Knights of Nova Scotia purposely created near a hundred years ago, for settling a *Scots colony* in America."[79] The young Sir Robert proposed to the Carolina Lords Proprietors that he be allowed to settle a colony between the Savannah and the Altamaha rivers. Coming as it did on the heels of the Yamassee War, the plan was readily accepted by the people of South Carolina. The Carolina proprietors recommended the scheme to the Privy Council, who strongly favored the idea of a barrier province.[80]

According to Mountgomery, the colony, called the "Margravate of Azilia,"[81] would prevent Spanish and Indian invasions of Carolina and would produce silk, wine, olives, raisins, almonds, and currants—products imported into England from the Mediterranean area.[82] Sir Robert's settlers were to be citizen-soldiers who would produce these items while at the same time, through his symmetrical design of land allotments as "one continued fortress,"[83] defending the area from the Spaniards in Florida, the French on the Mississippi, and the Indians in the backwoods.[84] Mountgomery's plan was accepted. On 9 June 1717 the Lords Proprietors of Carolina granted Mountgomery all the land between the Savannah and Altamaha rivers for the express purpose of erecting his province. The contract was to be operative only if settlement had commenced within three years. Unfortunately, Mountgomery was unable to establish the colony within the time allocated and the land reverted to the Lords Proprietors. "Paradise with all her Virgin Beauties" had slipped through the hands of the baronet due to lack of investment and the collapse in 1720 of the South Sea Company, which brought financial panic and skepticism about all overseas schemes.[85]

The importance of Azilia and Sir Robert's ideas lies in the suggestions that were incorporated into the Georgia plan. He advocated the concept of a buffer colony between the Savannah and Altamaha rivers. As Georgia would be, Azilia was to have been settled in a compact township plan with the settlers living in a town surrounded by contiguous farm lots. The colonists were to have been citizen-soldiers who would fight when needed and cultivate the land for their support. In Kenneth Coleman's words, "the approval of this settlement in London made it clear that by 1720 the British government was ready to contest the Spaniards for the area south of the Savannah River."[86] With the failure of Mountgomery to execute his colonial plan, the Privy Council approved the building of Fort King George on the banks of the Altamaha with his ideas for settlement in mind.

Mountgomery's idea and plans were not forgotten elsewhere and were reintroduced by Jean-Pierre Purry of Switzerland in 1724. He petitioned the Crown to be allowed to settle six hundred Swiss on the Carolina frontier and to form a regiment of soldier-workers with himself serving as colonel and judge. In his *Memorial* about Carolina written in 1724, Purry idealized the potential for producing such items as fruits, oil, wax, cotton, tobacco, indigo, cocoa, leather, furs, wood for building and other purposes, resin, tar, hemp, wool, silk, brandy, wines, wheat, rice, and other products useful as medicines and dyestuffs.[87] He also encouraged the settlement as a means of stopping the French from expanding into Carolina country and as a buffer to the Spanish in Florida.[88] Again, as with Mountgomery, the Carolina Lords Proprietors agreed to the idea and were anxious to see the plan put into effect; but it, too, initially failed because they could not finance the settlement. When Carolina became a royal colony, Purry at last received his grant and, in 1732, settled Purrysburg on the north bank of the Savannah River in Carolina. His original plans were overly ambitious, but they emphasized two vital points of interest to the British government: mercantilism and imperial defense.

The settlement schemes of Coram, Mountgomery, and Purry were further enhanced by Joshua Gee in 1729 when he published *The Trade and Navigation of Great Britain Considered: Shewing the Surest Way for a Nation to Increase Its Riches, Is to Prevent the Importation of Such Foreign Commodities as May be Rais'd at Home.*[89] Gee had been one of the promoters, along with Thomas Coram, of the project for settling soldiers in Nova Scotia. By 1729, however, his interest had shifted to the southern colonies. Gee expressed the fear that the southern frontier might be overrun by the French, Spaniards, and Indians, "for want of sufficient protection."[90] He ardently proposed that the English build a line of forts along the Appalachian Mountains, as the French had done along the Saint Lawrence, the Mississippi, and the Gulf of Mexico.[91] Verner Crane, a noted historian of the southern frontier, suggested that James Oglethorpe must have read Gee's pamphlet before meeting with the Earl of Egmont in February 1730, because Oglethorpe verbally reproduced Gee's proposals on the colony plan.[92] It was the incorporation of the ideas and schemes of Nairn, Coram, Mountgomery, Purry, and Gee that provided James Oglethorpe and the other promoters of the colony of Georgia with a basis for a new colonial venture, one that would succeed this time.

While the ideas about South Carolina's defense and imperial growth were circulating in the colonies and in London, other forces were at work to bring about the genesis of Georgia. In the summer of 1728, Robert Castell, a noted architect, was confined to Fleet Street prison in London for debt.[93] While imprisoned, he died of smallpox. Castell had pleaded with his jailers not to place him where the pox was raging, but his pleas had fallen on deaf ears.[94] During his confinement at Fleet Street, he was visited by his friend James Edward Oglethorpe, Member of Parliament representing the British borough of Haslemere. Oglethorpe, deeply moved by the young man's untimely death, asked for a parliamentary investigation into the state of English jails. In February 1729, he was appointed chairman of the committee that led the investigation.[95] The prison inquiry put an end to many abuses in the jail system in England; but, as Oglethorpe told the Earl of Egmont later, no provisions had been made by the Act of 1729 for "the miserable wretches . . . let out of gaol" and people were "starving about the town for want of employment."[96] Oglethorpe shared with Egmont his ideas for a settlement in America.

The petition for the charter for a charity colony was considered by the Privy Council on 17 September 1730. It was referred to the Board of Trade, which considered it in December 1730 and again in January 1731. Oglethorpe and others reported to the council on their aims for the new colony. The Committee of the Privy Council approved the charter in form and submitted it to the king for his approval.[97] On 9 June 1732, a charter was granted by George II to "The Trustees for Establishing the Colony of Georgia in America."[98]

There were three main motives behind the founding of Georgia: philanthropy, mercantilism, and imperial defense. In the first case, the colony was expected to give insolvent and unemployed persons in Britain, and persecuted Protestants from the continent of Europe, a chance to repair their fortunes and practice their religious beliefs (Papists excepted).[99] It was anticipated that Georgia would contribute to the mercantile prosperity of the British Empire by providing raw materials to the mother country while also acting as a market for finished products. As for the military security of the colonies, Georgia's presence was to protect South Carolina against encroachments by the French and the Spanish.

On Friday, 17 November 1732, the ship *Anne*, captained by John Thomas, left Gravesend heading for the birth of the new colony. Aboard were James Oglethorpe and approximately 120 settlers. The *Caledonian Mercury* and the *Gentleman's Quarterly* reported the departure on a grand scale, describing the emigrants as "25 families, consisting of carpenters, brick-layers, plummers, farmers &c. who take with them all proper utensils according to their respective occupations for building and manuring the lands there."[100] They further stated that the colonists were being trained for the military needs of the colony by "learning discipline from the guards" and they were to have muskets, bayonets, and swords "in case they should be attacked by the Indians or meet with any other resistance."[101] It is interesting to note that the ship was also stocked with "10 tuns of the very best and strongest beer brewed by Alderman Parsons . . . for the service of this colony."[102]

The immigrants arrived in Charles-Town in January 1733 and were welcomed with open arms; in these settlers the South Carolinians saw their defenders on the southern frontier. The Carolinians helped supply the colonists with farm animals, tools, rice, troops (primarily Scottish Highlanders patrolling the frontier), money, and boats. English colonization of the "debatable land" had begun.[103]

It did not take long for the principal reason for establishment of the colony to be underscored. On 9 April 1734, Governor Johnson of South Carolina and his Assembly sent a letter to the king stating the danger in which their province stood. Johnson feared the French particularly, and gratefully informed the king of the protection the Georgia settlement gave Carolina.[104] The Earl of Egmont, one of the most active of the Georgia Trustees, declared: "we [Georgia] are a guard to Carolina." He noted in his diary that he informed Prince Frederick that "our design was no less than to be a barrier to the Southern Colonies of America, which are in poor condition to defend themselves."[105]

Shortly after Johnson's letter was received, Parliament granted £26,000 "for the further settling and securing the Colony of Georgia."[106] The money was for the erection of forts: two of eighty men each and eighteen of forty men each to defend against the French and Spaniards by land.[107] Benjamin Martyn, secretary to the Trustees, recorded that "the Trustees thought it prudent to strengthen the Southern part of the Province, by making a Settlement on the Altamaha River." He continued: "Upon which inducements the Trustees resolved to make Embarkations for strengthening the Southern Part of Georgia; . . . they determined that these Embarkations should consist chiefly of Persons from the Highlands of Scotland, and persecuted German Protestants."[108]

The subject of sending Highland Scots to Georgia came up among the Trustees during an informal dinner at the Cider House in London on 25 June 1735. Egmont notes in his diary that he, Oglethorpe, and other Trustees discussed "sending over 100 Scotsmen under the leading of an experienced Lieutenant, for the defense and settlement of our new fort and town designed at the mouth of the Altamaha River."[109] Once the Trustees decided on enlisting the Highlanders as settlers, they commissioned Lieutenant Hugh Mackay and Captain George Dunbar, son of the Inverness merchant James Dunbar,[110] to go to Scotland and carry out the job of recruitment. By 9 July, the Committee of Embarkation had drawn up several orders to buy shoes and swords and to print advertisements; instructions were prepared for

Mackay and Dunbar to furnish the committee with a hundred Highlanders to go to Georgia.[111]

These instructions received the formal stamp of approval by the Common Council of the Trustees for Establishing the Colony of Georgia in America on 16 July 1735. Mackay was authorized to "agree with and bring together One Hundred and Ten Freemen and Servants, to which Fifty Women and Children are Allowed" for transport to Georgia.[112] These people were to be interviewed and carefully screened before being accepted for settlement in Georgia.

The question arises: Why would the Trustees look to the Highlands for immigrants into their new colony when they had hundreds of applicants applying daily for entrance from London and the surrounding English countryside? Obviously, the Trustees were looking for something more than settlers; they already had more petitioners than they could accommodate. The Scots the Trustees were looking to recruit were neither debtors nor persecuted foreign Protestants needing refuge. What was it about these people that made them more desirable than the English to the south?

Part of the answer can be found in Benjamin Martyn's *Account of the Progress of the Colony of Georgia*. He writes:

> In pursuance of his Majesty's charter, and in order to fulfil the good intents and purposes therein expressed, it was thought necessary for the Trustees to send over such poor people, and foreign Protestants, as were willing to live in Georgia, not only to cultivate the lands, but at the same time to *strengthen His Majesty's Colonies* [emphasis mine]. For which purposes they considered each inhabitant, both as a planter and as a soldier; they were therefore to be provided with arms for defense, as well as tools for their cultivation, and to be taught the exercise of both. . . . Each lot of land was to be considered as a *Military fief* [emphasis mine]. Provision was made to prevent the accumulation of several lots into one hand. Lest the garrison should be lessened.[113]

The problem, as Martyn and the Trustees had found out, was that many of the poor who had been useless in England were inclined to be just as useless in Georgia.[114] The settlers already in Georgia were neither farmers nor soldiers; nor were they likely to change. Logically, the Trustees looked elsewhere for suitable colonists, and the Highlanders of Scotland seemed to them to be the perfect solution—they were both farmers and soldiers by training and tradition. This effort in the Highlands would be more than a military recruiting exercise; the Trustees wanted families.

Another consideration for the choice of the Highlanders is alluded to in the provision of Martyn's account that each lot of land was to be considered as a "military fief." *Fief* is a feudal term signifying an estate held by a tenant on condition of services being rendered to an overlord, in this case the Trustees. In England during the 1700s, this practice no longer existed as a system; however, in the Highlands of Scotland, the clans were structured along strict feudal lines. A clan chief might allow extended family members to reside as tenants on his lands; he, in essence, was their liege lord. He would provide the land and necessities, and in return the tenants would render service and allegiance.[115]

In the Highlands before the failed Jacobite Rebellion of 1745, the tenants' allegiance and duty to their chiefs meant military service as much as any other responsibility. Any of the Trustees, including Oglethorpe, who had military experience, and especially those with knowledge of the pro-Stuart rising of 1715, would be familiar with the Highlanders and the clan system. If the Scots could be persuaded to leave the Highlands in family groups as opposed to the familiar military recruitment of individuals, then perhaps they could be induced to accept similar living conditions on the southern frontier in America. If the recruitment of families worked, the Trustees would have loyal soldiers as well as hardworking farmers in Georgia. A letter received by the Trustees from a Highlander named Daniel McLachlan in May 1735 indicated that the necessary volunteers might be found.[116] Two months later, with instruction in hand and a sum of money not to exceed one hundred pounds sterling credit "for the charge of raising, marching, and maintaining one hundred men till put on board the ship that is to carry them to Georgia,"[117] Lieutenant Hugh Mackay and Captain George Dunbar began their travels in the Highlands. Their aim: to recruit hardy frontier settlers for the colony of Georgia.

CHAPTER 2

Changing Conditions
in the Highlands of Scotland

Farewell to the land of the mountain and the wood,
Farewell to the home of the brave and the good,
My bark is afloat on the blue-rolling main,
And I ne'er shall behold thee, dear Scotland, again!
—Peter Crerar

THE HIGHLANDS OF SCOTLAND in the first half of the eighteenth century were in a state of flux. By 1735, when Captain George Dunbar and Lieutenant Hugh Mackay arrived in Scotland to recruit settlers for the new
colony of Georgia in America, the changing circumstances in the Highlands
were enough to encourage many to emigrate. Scotland, particularly the Highlands, had traditionally proven to be fertile ground for military recruitment
for service in Europe.[1] The Georgia recruiters, however, were not there just
for soldiers; they wanted families. This was not the first time that the Scots
were enlisted to man an English frontier and combine the sword with the
ploughshare.[2] There had been a proposal in the first quarter of the 1600s to
settle the land in Monaghan, Ireland, with a "wall of Scots" as a barrier between English farmers and the wild Irish.[3] The Trustees in Georgia were
hoping to recreate a similar situation for Highland Scots on the southern
frontier in Georgia to buffer the English in Savannah and South Carolina
against the wild Indians in the backcountry, the Spanish in Florida, and the
French in the Alabama basin.

The region of Scotland known as the Highlands is usually conceived of as
lying north of the Highland Boundary Fault, which bisects the country from
the mouth of the Clyde on the west coast at Campbeltown along the mountain line northeastward through Perthshire and Angus, and so around the

east side of Scotland to the North Sea. It includes the Western Islands (the Inner and Outer Hebrides) as well as the Eastern Slopes of the Grampians to within forty miles of Aberdeen.[4] In physical character, the Highlands varies immensely.

The island districts are dominated by the sea, with almost constant wind and cloud cover. As a result, most of the islands were and are not well suited for extensive farming, with the possible exceptions of Mull and Tiree. The northern Highlands, subject to subarctic conditions, also have severe limitations for arable agriculture, except in pockets along the western coastline. The Grampian or Central Highlands are alpine country with mountainous and rocky terrain, which made conditions for travel, communication, and agriculture difficult but not insurmountable for the inhabitants. This sector did, however, provide good grazing for the Highlanders' livestock.[5] It also produced rich woodlands that could be exploited and fertile strips of ground along the straths (Highland River valleys) for the few crops that were cultivated. Prior to the mid–seventeenth century, the people of the Lowlands to the south and to the east of the Highland boundary could obtain the profits of agriculture, industry, and commerce; north and west of the line, nature offered the Highlanders little but hunting, herding, subsistence farming, and the trade of war.[6] That would begin to change dramatically by the turn of the eighteenth century.

The social, political, and economic makeup of Highland society was largely the consequence of the region's diverse geography. Unlike the rolling hills and gentle countryside of the Lowlands and of England, in the Highlands the extensive moorland, high mountains, and invading arms of the sea along the firths (estuaries) divided the population into small, relatively isolated, tight-knit communities. Most communication came by way of the sea with trading merchants such as Bailie John Steuart of Inverness.[7] People lived mostly in groups of eight or ten houses in the glens and straths, along the banks of inland lochs (lakes), or on the cultivable land near the seashore. Although a few villages and towns existed, the largest being Inverness, there were no concentrations of population in the Highlands where large numbers of people lived within easy reach of one another.[8] Because of the seclusion of the various communities, the "clan" emerged.

The origins of the clan are obscure, but its functioning in the Highlands for generations before 1750 is clear. It has traditionally been suggested that all the emphasis of the clan was on ties of blood, linking members in an indissoluble relationship that, of itself, had nothing to do with land. While there is a strong element of truth in this concept, recent research indicates that this notion is overdrawn.[9] The Gaelic term *clann* meant nothing more than family or kin, but ultimately it evolved into a society incorporating feudal characteristics tied to land distribution. Because of the difficulty in traversing the mountainous country of the Highlands, unified military control, thence unified government, could not be established. Captain Edmund Burt,[10] an English agent for the forfeited estates of the Earl of Seaforth and later the manager of the lead mines at Suinart,[11] wrote in his letters from Scotland that no traveler could venture among the hills without a guide. He likened it to "making a sea voyage without sun, moon, stars, or compass."[12]

Clan society developed as small communities of related families organized themselves under the leadership of a chief and conducted their own affairs from a much stronger position of force.[13] The Clan Chattan, living in and around the region of Inverness with influences stretching into Sutherland,[14] was a case in point. The Chattan community was founded initially on kinship, but as time progressed it came to be based more on a cooperative effort for subsistence and defense. In 1268, Gillivray, the chief of the small clan McGillivray, took for himself and his clan the protection of Farquhar Mackintosh, chief of the larger clan Mackintosh. Other families began to affiliate themselves with the Mackintoshes, so that Strathnairn and the surrounding valleys were soon populated with Mackintoshes, McGillivrays, Farquharsons, McBeans, Macphails, Macphersons, McQueens, Frasers, Shaws, Clarks, and Davidsons, who together made up the powerful Clan Chattan.[15] Most of the names are found among the Highland Scots settled in Georgia in 1736.[16]

A chief, or supreme head, was linked by blood ties to the chieftains of the septs, or main branches of the clan. The dependents of the chieftains, down to the humblest herdsman on the mountain, believed themselves to be blood relations of one other and of the chief, or for the sake of convenience and protection they claimed to be.[17] The chief had the authority of the clan to settle all disputes and he regulated matters at his discretion; against his judgment there was no appeal. At the height of a clan's existence, the power of the chief might be almost unlimited. When Captain Burt commented on the offenses of one chief's clansmen, the chief offered to send "two or three of their heads" in apology. Burt laughed as though it were a joke, but the chief's expression intensified as he replied forcefully that "he was a man of his word."[18]

Generally, a clan chief lived among his clansmen, but not always. After the union of the Crowns in 1603 between Scotland and England and the union of parliaments in 1707, there was an increasing tendency among many chiefs to live in Edinburgh or in London.[19] This absenteeism and the high cost of living at court led to increased indebtedness that would strain the loyalties between chief and clan and help bring about the decline in the clan in the eighteenth century.[20] However, traditionally, the chief's castle was the court where rewards were distributed and distinctions conferred. A chief's home was the center of life for the clan, a number of whom constantly attended him both at home and away from home. Every chief surrounded himself with as large a retinue of followers as possible. His importance was measured not only by his annual income, of which there was sometimes very little, but also by the number and fidelity of his vassals and tenants. To his clan, the chief was both father and landlord.

Clan members, in turn, regarded themselves both as the chief's tenants and in some senses as his children, and they expected him to protect and maintain them.[21] Initially, the chief provided his clan with their "window to the world" and it was his assessment of external needs and threats, accepted by the clansmen without question, that determined collective action. In return for the chief's leadership and protection, clan members followed his standard in war, attended him in the chase, supplied his table, and harvested his fields.[22] As the eighteenth century approached and the intrusion of new economic and social forces began to take effect, the symbiotic relationship of clan chief and clansman changed.

The lands belonged to the chief and, without question, control over land was the key variable in the success of clan society. It enabled a clan chief to establish a network of loyal kinsmen and followers, which assured him of self-defense and sustenance in times of shortage. Traditionally, the best tracts of land were awarded at a modest rent to the chief's more important relations—not necessarily the best farmers. These men, in turn, parceled out the land to their friends and relations. In addition to being farmers, these principal tacksmen, or leaseholders, were the cadets or gentlemen of the family and acted as both military officers and administrators of the land. They lived a privileged and relatively comfortable life, by comparison with the standards of the common Highlander. Burt complained of the "inelegant and ostentatious plenty" with which the gentlemen of the clan feasted.[23] John Mohr Mackintosh, a nephew of William Mackintosh of Borlum and the leader of Georgia's Highland settlers, was of this class and was called in later times a Highland "gentleman farmer,"[24] although his family's lands were forfeited after the failed Jacobite Rising of 1715. By subletting and subdividing their holdings, these tacksmen were able to collect more rent than they paid, thus providing themselves with additional means of support "free from the drudgery of agriculture."[25]

Men and women who leased their land from the tacksmen were known simply as tenants and the men were the principal clan warriors when the need arose.[26] Unlike in England, women in the Highlands of Scotland commonly rented land and held property in their own right. In the tenants' rent-roll of the estate of Clunie in 1747 there are four women listed: Katerine Mackintosh, Lady Clunie, Katherine Macpherson, and Janet Rattray.[27] A lease by Mackintosh of Mackintosh, dated 14 March 1753, was granted to Ann McIntosh, relict of Duncan Smith, tacksman of Dalriach, of the lands of Dalriach, Parish of Moy, for fourteen years.[28] Each of these women had the same responsibilities for the land and paid rent at the same rate as men. This fact of women's equality in property rights and land tenure in the Highlands would have a major impact on the future of the colony in Georgia and the effectiveness of the Trustees' recruiting efforts in Scotland.[29]

Highland tenants lived mainly as pastoral farmers, keeping goats and sheep for household subsistence and black cattle primarily to pay rent.[30] Their lands were divided into rigs, or ridges, according to the ancient open-field or "runrig" system, to plant grains.[31] It was not until the 1730s and the introduction of the potato that anything other than oats or barley was grown on the small, inadequate patches of arable ground in the Highlands.[32] Tenants dared not improve their lands for fear that their rents might be raised, and as a result most tenant farmers barely produced enough for their families and livestock to exist.[33]

Below the tenants were the subtenants, called in different regions of the Highlands cottars, mailers, or crofters. A crofter held no more than a small strip of ground and the right to graze a cow or, perhaps, one or two goats in the pastures. The crofter paid the tenant rent by working without wages on the tenant's land for a certain time each week and the rest of the time tried to eke out enough produce from a tiny plot of land to survive.[34] Life for both tenants and subtenants was primitive, grim, and precarious. The physical circumstances of the Highlands left people vulnerable to crop failures and depletion of livestock by disease and climate.

Food—whether grain, livestock, or cheese—and whiskey played a vital part in sustaining clan bonds. Most of the produce from what little fertile ground existed was consumed by the clansmen themselves, with a large portion going to the chiefs or lairds to support their displays of hospitality and feasting.[35] Although the grain crops grown were critically important, they

were generally inadequate and had to be supplemented with grain purchased from the Lowland districts through sale of cattle or by importation
through merchants in Inverness.[36] This growing dependence on and integra-
tion into a trading economy, along with other changing conditions, would
cause many chiefs to explore new avenues of land management and to re-
evaluate their relationship with their clansmen.[37]

Livestock, particularly cattle and horses, proved to be the mainstay of
Highland economy and society. Cattle, as a form of accumulated wealth,
played an important part in local exchange schemes. Rent was paid to tacksmen and chiefs in cattle. Cattle droving was considered an honorable profession, and many drovers, who appeared to spectators to be gentlemen,
dressed in their finest plaids to drive cattle to the Crieff tryst, a great market
for Lowland buyers.[38] John Macky, traveling through the Highlands in the
1720s, described the Highland gentlemen assembled at Crieff in 1723 as
"mighty civil, dressed in their slashed short waistcoats, a trousing with a
plaid for a cloak, and blue bonnet." He noted further that "they have a pon-
yard knife and fork in one sheath hanging at one side of their belt, their pistol at the other, and their snuff-mill before; with a great broad-sword by their
side."[39] Obviously, to Macky they were an impressive sight. This sight would
change after 1725, however, when an order was sent throughout the Highlands by General George Wade on behalf of the Hanoverian government to
disarm the clans.[40]

Agriculture may have been the principal occupation for survival, but the
sale of cattle was a major force in supplying meal and other necessities in
times of great need. Cattle were the commercial currency of the Highlands
and their value to the health of the clan community could not be overesti-
mated in the first half of the eighteenth century. The only real obstacles in
exploiting the cattle export business were the acts of blackmail and "cattle-
lifting" in the Highlands. Because of the militaristic structure of the clan and
competition between clans by way of feuding, it was not advisable to graze
large herds of cattle for fear of being raided by opposing clans.

"Cattle-lifting" was the euphemism for stealing cows. In the Highlands, it
was an accepted occurrence in clan life. Both Edmund Burt in 1726 and
Martin Martin, a Highlander himself, in 1699 described cattle-lifting in their
writings.[41] Burt explained that, in the Highlands, "the gathering-in of rents
was called *uplifting* them, and that the stealing of cows they called *lifting*, a
softening word for theft; as if it were only collecting their dues."[42] He went
on to say that when a plan was formed for the purpose of lifting cattle, the
cattle thieves went out in parties of ten to thirty men and covered large

tracts of mountains until they arrived at the appointed place. Burt commented that these men chose to be "as distant as they can from their own dwellings."[43] The ideal time, according to Burt, was the Michaelmas moon, when the cattle were in "fit condition for the markets, held on the borders of the Lowlands."[44] If the thieves were caught, they were seldom prosecuted by the owners for fear of retaliation by the culprits' clan.[45]

In 1699, Martin Martin explained cattle-lifting in nostalgic terms of bygone days, less sinister and more heroic:

> EVERY heir, or young chieftain of a Tribe, was oblig'd in honor to give a publick Specimen of his Valor, before he was own'd and declar'd Governor or Leader of his people. . . . THIS Chieftain was usually attended with a Retinue of young Men of Quality, who had not beforehand given any Proof of their Valor, and were ambitious of such an Opportunity to signalize themselves. IT was usual for the Captain to lead them, to make a desperate incursion upon some neighbor or other that they were in Feud with; and they were oblig'd to bring by open force the Cattel they found in the Lands they attack'd, or to die in the Attempt. AFTER the Performance of the Atchievement, the young Chieftain was ever reputed valiant and worthy of Government.[46]

In this account of cattle-lifting, it would seem that it was little more than a right of passage, a ritual, condoned as a fact of life. This might explain Burt's reaction to the nonchalance of the typical Highlander in response to charges of theft. Neither description denies the fact that cattle stealing was endemic in eighteenth-century Highland clan society. These two accounts also demonstrate the differences in attitudes between those Highland clansmen who were trying to hold on to a time-honored style of life and the "improving" clan chiefs of all political persuasions who believed that the time had come to modernize the Highlands.

After the parliamentary union of 1707, the fabric of traditional Highland culture and society was being stretched from all sides by economic, social, and political influences. During the first half of the eighteenth century, Highland life was undergoing immense changes that would be the catalyst for migration to the British colonies of North America. Many historians, such as Ian Charles Cargill Graham, claim that the major changes in the Highlands did not occur until after the collapse of the Jacobite Rebellion of 1745, when the British government enacted repressive measures against the clans and the Highland lairds saw the value of modernizing the agricultural system by English technology.[47]

However, the evidence suggests that by the end of the second decade of the 1700s, "improving" land management and commercialization were already making a larger impact in the Highlands than ever before and that the bonds that tied the people to land and clan were loosening, from the perspectives of both clan chief and clansmen. By the 1730s, Highland improvers such as the Duke of Argyll and Duncan Forbes of Culloden advocated and instituted changes in their land policy by diminishing the powers of the tacksmen which would create a more favorable commercial opportunity for the lairds, while at the same time undermining the traditional relationship between chief and clan.[48]

Staunch Jacobites were not immune from the improving ideas toward their lands. Cameron of Lochiel and Brigadier-General William Mackintosh of Borlum were strong advocates of improved land usage. In 1729, Mackintosh, while imprisoned in Edinburgh, wrote *An Essay on Ways and Means for Inclosing, Fallowing, Planting, &c. Scotland; and That in Sixteen Years at the Farthest.*[49] T. M. Devine correctly states that "while the gentry were undergoing a profound metamorphosis, the clansmen still maintained traditionalist expectations."[50] It was this ideal—that traditional life was changing for the clansmen—that would prompt them to leave the Highlands in search of a place where their familiar lifestyle could continue.

As mentioned, the cattle trade between the Highlands of Scotland and English and Lowland buyers increased considerably after the union.[51] The influence of commercialization found its way into the straths and glens as town markets or fairs spread throughout the Highlands.[52] This influx of products and foreign influences opened the eyes of the Highlanders to a world outside their own. No longer were they isolated from the rest of the world. By 1729 William Mackintosh of Borlum, enjoying the commercial benefits but complaining of the changing culture, wrote, "When I came to a friend's house of a morning, I used to be asked if I had my morning draught yet? I am now asked if I have had my tea? And in lieu of the big Quaigh with strong ale and toast, and after a dram of good wholesome Scots spirits, there is now a tea-kettle put to the fire, the tea-table and silver and china equipage brought in, and marmalade and cream."[53] These changes signaled a rising cost of living and were not to the liking of everyone. Burt wrote in 1727 of four or five fairs a year when the Highlanders brought their commodities to market. One man would bring a roll of linen under his arm, another would bring a small piece of coarse cloth, while yet another carried two or three cheeses, a kid, or a little butter.[54] Although the offerings were meager, they were further signs of increasing commerce.

As trade increased, the Highlanders imported meal as a food, and by selling animals and dairy products for grain they could obtain far more calories for the same price, and thus either support a larger family or pay a higher rent to their landlord. It has been suggested that as a result, the population grew and the small Highland farms soon became overcrowded.[55] Another significant by-product of the emergence of trade and commerce in the Highlands was an increasing shift from an agricultural barter system to a cash society, which lessened the importance of ties to the land itself. By the 1740s, over three-quarters of the rents on the MacLeod estates in Harris and Skye were money rents, not rents paid in kind.[56] People would begin to look elsewhere for their survival. In 1727, Burt noted that it had recently become possible to get Highlanders to work as hired labor even when the landowners did not wish them to do so simply by offering higher wages.[57] In Inverness, at the beginning of the eighteenth century, there were a score or more merchants in good standing, most of them Highlanders.[58]

Industry arrived along with trade and commerce. Cattle, cod, herring, salmon, and oysters brought money into the Highlands;[59] so also did the exploitation of Highland forests. Burt related that the English Navy looked to Scotland instead of Sweden or Norway as a supplier of wood for masts and other naval uses.[60] Many of the Highland chiefs aimed to make money from their woodlands. In 1732 Mackintosh of Mackintosh floated timber from Glenfeshie down to Feshie for export.[61] Around 1725 the Earl of Cromarty got £1,600 for his fir trees at Achinall. York Buildings Company in 1728 purchased 60,000 fir trees at Abernethy on the estate of Grant of Grant for £7,000.[62] Later the same year, the company sent William Stephens, a former MP for Newport and destined to become a prominent figure in the affairs of the Colony of Georgia, to be superintendent and comptroller for their timber interests in the Highlands.[63] In 1730 Roderick Chisolm of Comer and Alexander Chisolm of Muckerach sold "all and every his wood and woods of whatever kind lying standing and growing within and on all and singular his lands and estate in the parishes of Kilmorack and Kiltarlity" to the York Buildings Company for £2,000.[64] The company was enthusiastic as it poured money into the Highlands. Numerous workmen were employed and houses erected; sawmills and machinery were set up. The Highlands of Scotland were experiencing pressures to which they were not accustomed, pressures that would severely test the Highlanders' loyalty to land and clan.

Highland timber was utilized to build houses and ships, but it was also used to smelt iron ore with charcoal. According to Burt, the York Buildings

Company set up ironworks for the sake of using the timber they had purchased in the Highlands and because "iron cannot be made from the ore with sea or pit coal to be malleable and fit for ordinary use."[65] The ore could be brought from Lancashire in England by sea to Loch Maree and, between 1727 and 1736, to the York Buildings Company's furnaces at Invergarry; or it might be mined locally, as between 1736 and 1739, at the Lecht outcrop workings near Tomintoul.[66] Those enterprises failed because the expense of transport made their products more costly than those in England, but the Highlands benefited, at least temporarily, from their outlay of wages, animals, and materials.[67]

Industry in the Highlands was not limited to timber and ironworks. Mining, although known for some time in Scotland, took on a new initiative due to the York Buildings Company's endeavors in the Highlands. News in *Caledonian Mercury* of 27 August 1728 reported that "his Excellency General Wade has been viewing the lead Mine belonging to Alexander Murray, Esq. of Stanhope, in which he is an Adventurer and whereof they give the following Account: That among the several Edge Veins already discovered, there is one lately found, that in appearance exceeds any Thing that hitherto has been seen in Great Britain."[68] A year later, the consortium that included Alexander Murray, General Wade, Sir Archibald Grant of Monymusk, and two Glasgow merchants received a royal charter for working the mines and subsequently leased the mines to the York Buildings Company.[69] By 1730 others were looking for opportunities in the mining industry. On 3 July 1730, Lachlan Mackintosh of Mackintosh received a letter from a certain John Smith, advising him of the likely existence of lead veins in Glenroy; however, it is doubtful that The Mackintosh was able to pursue the matter much further.[70]

Additional stress came to bear on the clans through the work of the Society in Scotland for the Propagation of Christian Knowledge (SSPCK). This work had begun in the first decade of the eighteenth century through the enthusiasm of a group of gentry in the Lowlands, "men of knowledge, solid piety, and estates,"[71] who had been moved by the perceived illiteracy, ignorance, and superstition of the Highlanders. These Protestant gentlemen of the South were concerned with the abiding Jacobitism of the Highlanders and with the current success of Catholic missionaries in winning converts in the north of Scotland.[72] To address these concerns, in 1709 they formed the SSPCK, and its work in educating and evangelizing the North was a major vehicle of social change in the eighteenth century.

The purpose of the society was to found schools "where religion and virtue might be taught to young and old" in the shape of reading, writing, arith-
metic, and religious instruction. Since Gaelic was believed to be the root of
the superstition and barbarity in the Highlands, the SSPCK would teach
only in English. Many Highlanders realized the advantage their children
would have in the external world if they could speak and read English. Lachlan McGillivray, one of Georgia's Highland settlers, learned to read and
write English through one of the society's schools in the Highlands.[73] The
SSPCK would also be the source of the first minister to the Scottish settlers
in Georgia.

However, not everyone was ready to discard Celtic ways and Gaelic culture. Some of the staunchest defenders of traditional Highland life were the
chiefs of Mackay and the Mackay clan. A full third of the Scottish emigrants
to Georgia in 1735 were from this clan, taking their heritage and culture
with them for preservation. It was not until the nineteenth century that the
house of Sutherland succeeded in implementing the policy for the Mackays
laid down earlier by Sir Robert Gordon to "purge the country piece by piece
of the Irish [Gaelic] barbarity."[74]

For the Highlanders, other conditions that were unique to the first half of
the eighteenth century were the result of the Jacobite Rising of 1715, the
failed effort to restore the Stuarts to the throne of Great Britain. In 1714
Queen Anne died; the heir apparent, Sophia, Electress of Hanover, had died
a short time before, and Sophia's son George became king under the title of
George I. His accession to the throne was a great disappointment to the
friends and followers of the exiled King James, whose supporters were
known as Jacobites. They had hoped that on Anne's death, James's son—in
their estimation the rightful heir to the throne—would be restored. In the
Highlands people began to arm themselves and to plot for the restoration of
the Pretender, or claimant to the throne. On 6 September 1715, the standard was raised at Castleton, in Braemar, for King James VIII under the
leadership of the Earl of Mar. Led by the Duke of Argyll, the British forces
defeated the Jacobites. The doomed rebellion lasted only five months and
was over by February 1716.[75]

The Rising of 1715 caused misery in both England and Scotland. George I's
government took immediate action to prevent another such outbreak. On
24 February 1716, two leaders of the rising, the English Earl of Dentwater
and the Scottish Lord Kenmure, were executed. In Scotland hundreds of
Highlanders were taken prisoner and tried. None were put to death, but

many were transported to the American colonies for treason. As noted, a number of Clan Chattan members were among the Stuart followers taken prisoner.[76] Sixteen of the Sept McGillivray were arrested and thirteen were exiled to the colony of South Carolina.[77] The men would be forerunners of the Clan Chattan settlers in Georgia.[78]

The British government feared a resurgence of Jacobite sentiment in Scotland and decided other measures must be taken to secure the peace. These measures would affect the clans and would provide the impetus for many to leave the Highlands. The Act of 1716, for "the more effectual securing the Peace of the Highlands in Scotland," ordered the commutation of a long list of feudal services for cash rents. These included personal attendance, hosting, hunting, watching, and warding, whether due by charter, contract, custom, or agreement. This section of the act, in effect, removed the military ties of the clansman to his chief.[79] The real purpose of the act was precisely to weaken the personal ties between chief and clansmen.

It is important to note that the basic organization of the clan was placed in jeopardy by the change in the method of landholding. Farms could now be let to the tacksmen or to the former subtenants, giving the latter the advantage of holding their land by lease or at fixed rent and bypassing the traditional tacksman as middleman. Also, instead of being tenants-at-will, the subtenants would not be subject to services unlimited and undefined. In many areas of the Highlands the traditional standing of the tacksmen was being threatened by changing attitudes of the landowners about their usefulness. As early as 1717 Bailie John Stuart, acting as factor to the Earl of Moray for the Petty estates, protested against his instructions to turn out tenants to make room for William McGillivray, a cadet of the Clan Chattan. He complained that he was "already sick of too many gentlemen tennents in Pettie."[80]

Duncan Forbes of Culloden, after surveying the Argyll estates in 1737, argued that the tacksman had outlived his usefulness and that subtenants could offer higher rents.[81] Forbes had seen the poverty and dire distress among those populating the Duke of Argyll's lands and strongly denounced the tacksmen as the culprits responsible. He reported that "had the tacksmen been suffered to continue their extortions a few years longer the islands would have been depeopled."[82] It is more likely that the pressures of emerging commercialism and a changing society were the real reasons. "The inhabitants," as E. R. Creegan points out, "living neither wholly under their traditional clan system nor wholly under a free individualistic, commercial system, were exposed to conflicting demands."[83]

Either under a tacksman or under direct leases from modern landlords, the tenants were faced with ever increasing rents. They were caught between two conflicting ideologies of traditional culture with familiar expectations and modern commercialism with unknown pressures. Throughout the Highlands, farms had been subdivided to such an extent because of the increase in population that most of the landholdings were far too small to be economically viable.[84] Already Highlanders were making the move to Lowland cities due to the increasing commercial pressures—in such numbers that, in 1727, the Glasgow Highland Society was founded by Glasgow citizens of Highland descent for the purposes of apprenticing poor Highland boys to trades.[85] People in the Highlands were becoming more mobile and were finding the idea of emigration a viable alternative.

In a letter dated 9 May 1735 to the Trustees for Establishing the Colony of Georgia, Daniel McLachlan expressed the desire of many to leave the Highlands.[86] He explained that their reason for wanting to emigrate was that rents were being raised of late, not, as he said, because of the avarice of the landlords but because of the vast "increase of people." McLachlan also complained that the price of cattle, "which is the only support and proper produce of this country," had fallen.[87] Between 1730 and 1740 the price of cattle remained consistently low.[88] As a result of cattle prices dropping and several years of bad harvests, the bulk of the people in the Highlands were "in a poor, starving condition."[89]

The Act of 1716 did more than release tenants from feudal manservice; it also declared unlawful the carrying of arms by any person or persons within the shires of Dumbartin, Stirling, Perth, Kincardine, Aberdeen, Inverness, Nairn, Cromarty, Argyle, Forfar, Banff, Sutherland, Caithness, Elgin, and Ross.[90] This provision of the act was ineffective because of the remoteness and inaccessibility of the Highlands. In 1725, another act was passed commanding that all arms should be taken from the Highland clans known to be friends or followers of the Stuarts.[91] To enforce this law, General George Wade was sent to the Highlands with a body of British troops. The great difficulty he faced, reported Wade, was that "the Highlands of Scotland are still more impracticable, from the want of Roads [and] Bridges . . . [and] very difficultly supported by the Regular Troops."[92]

General Wade was ordered to construct great roads, crossing the Highlands and connecting the garrisons at Fort George, Fort Augustus, and Fort William. He was also to build roads connecting Crieff to Inverness "for encouraging their Trade and Commerce with the Low Country; And to endeavor by mild and moderate Usage to convince them of the happiness they may enjoy by peaceably Submitting to Your Maty's [King George] Governmt."[93] The work on roads began in 1726 and took eleven years to complete. In the process Wade employed five hundred soldiers and constructed more than forty stone bridges.

The British troops did not work without help from the locals. In a letter from Edmund Burt to Mackintosh of Mackintosh in April 1728, Burt asks The Mackintosh to order his clansmen to furnish Wade's workmen with provisions and "Necessary's."[94] Obviously, this added additional strain to an already meager food supply in the Highlands. It was Wade's intention in building these roads to police the Highlands of Scotland better, both for criminal protection and to lessen the likelihood of a Jacobite resurgence. However, these roads would do more than provide an avenue for troop transport. They became a gateway for commerce and travelers into the Highlands—and an exit for emigrants from the region.

The residual effects of the "Fifteen Rising" and the invasion of commercialism, along with education, overpopulation, and poverty in the Highlands, created an underlying current for migration. All of these elements contributed significantly to the decline of the clan as an institution long before the Jacobite Rebellion of 1745. After the failed uprisings of 1715 and 1719, many of the clan chiefs forfeited their estates. The key position the chief held in the clan meant that prolonged absence, whether voluntary exile or of necessity (transport), was bound to affect his status adversely. Further, many of the forfeited estates had absentee owners and were overseen by unknown factors who were determined to run the estates as commercial enterprises.

In addition, the motive for commercial gain, introduced through the expansion of trade in cattle and timber and of industrial pursuits, was inconsistent with the patriarchal and military loyalty on which clanship was based. The advance of military roads built by General Wade through the Highlands contributed to the availability of commercial enterprise as well as supporting military strategy. Roads provided mobility and easier access to the various markets at Inverness and Crieff, besides serving the commercial needs of the garrisoned forts.

Considering all the various social, political, economic, and educational upheavals in process in the Highlands, the summer of 1735 was an opportune time for Captain George Dunbar and Lieutenant Hugh Mackay to come to Scotland to recruit families for the new colony of Georgia. All of the forces for emigration were at work among the Clan Chattan in the shires of Inverness and Nairn and among the Clan Mackay in Sutherland, Ross, and Cromarty. Relatives were already in the area of the Georgia colony, some having been sent to South Carolina as Jacobite prisoners and others already in the service of James Oglethorpe, the founder of the colony. General Wade's military roads passed along Chattan land, thereby easing trade and commerce in the area.[95] The changing conditions in the Highlands were such that many of the clans were eager for some sense of comfort in the familiarity of a traditional lifestyle, and emigration might provide the means for preserving a culture that was fast being lost in Scotland.

The Highlands were ready for the Georgia recruiters.

CHAPTER 3

Highland Recruitment:
Fertile Fields for Georgia Settlers

They carry with them their language, their opinions,
Their popular songs and hereditary merriment:
They change nothing but the place of their abode;
And of that change they perceive the benefit.
—Samuel Johnson, *Journey to the Western Isles of Scotland*

THE SUMMER OF 1735 was a busy time in the Highlands of Scotland for the recruiters from the colony of Georgia. News of the colony had already spread throughout the country via frequent reports in the *Caledonian Mercury* and *Edinburgh Eccho*, giving accounts of the progress and success of the settlements in America.[1] One especially encouraging article appeared in the 27 June 1734 edition of the *Caledonian Mercury*, reporting that "the people settled there [Georgia] is about 500, who have already cleared from 2 to 4 acres of land each, and planted them with corn, potatoes, pease, beans, yams, cabbages, &c. . . . They have plenty of horses, cattle, hogs, fish, poultry, and wild turkeys from 20 to 30 pounds weight each." The description goes on to say that "the climate and soil is equal in Goodness to the best part of [Italy]."[2] With stories such as this appearing in the press against the backdrop of the hardships in the Highlands, the lure of Georgia would have been considerable for prospective emigrants.

Lieutenant Hugh Mackay, already in Scotland in search of indentured servants for Georgia, was notified in a letter from Harman Verelst, the accountant for the Trustees for Establishing the Colony of Georgia in America, that Captain George Dunbar was to secure "forty men of the one hundred and ten [Highlanders] with the Proportions [of women and children] to that Number."[3] Mackay was then directed to obtain the remaining seventy with the like proportions. Enclosed with the letter were detailed instructions from Benjamin Martyn regarding the conditions for transport and settlement of the Highland emigrants. Mackay was told to bring them down to Cromarty, a town on the Moray Firth north of Inverness, where a ship would be prepared to take them on board for Georgia. The settlers were to be provisioned during the passage by allowing "four beef days, one pork day, and two Burgou [thick oatmeal porridge] days" per week. The instructions went on to "allow . . . seven pounds of Bread . . . by the week . . . three pints of beer and two Quarts of water . . . by the day for the space of a month, and a Gallon of water . . . each head by the day after, during their being on their passage."[4]

This meticulous planning by the Trustees exemplifies the care and control they used in dealing with all aspects of Georgia. From his instructions, Mackay could promise the prospective emigrant from Scotland "12 bushels of Indian corn at 56 pounds for each bushel, 100 pounds of meat, 30 pounds of butter, $\frac{1}{4}$ Cwt. of cheese and a bushel of salt" as maintenance for a year after his arrival in Georgia. He could also offer a cow, a calf, and a sow for "each five heads." This amount of foodstuffs offered to a starving Highlander and his family must have sounded like a dream. Moreover, the provisions did not stop there: "Each Freeman will have for his use in Georgia a Firelock, a broad Sword and an axe. And for the use of every five men there, a brass Kettle, a Shovel and Pick Axe will be provided. The better sort of Freeman will be provided with Targets [small shields]."[5] It was stipulated that the recruits be of "Gentlemen's familys" and of "good reputations," and Mackay was to determine if they were "Industrious, Laborious, and Brave." It is interesting to note that these gentlemen were also to speak "the Highland Language [Gaelic]."[6]

If these stipulations were met, then each Freeman would be granted fifty acres of land in "Tail Male," and that land would descend to the "Heirs Male of his Body for ever."[7] The Trustees' reasoning for tail male was "in order to keep up the Number of Men equal to the Number of Lots, for the better Defense and Support of the Colony."[8] This provision, as mentioned in chapter 2, caused trouble in the recruitment efforts of Mackay and Dunbar in Scotland and for the Trustees in the colony. By 1741, when the Trustees were determined to obtain more Highlanders from Scotland, they amended the Tail Male clause in favor of "Tail General," thus allowing daughters and wives to inherit the land grants.[9] However, for Mackay in 1735, the Tail Male clause proved to be a controversial stipulation from the start.

Not all of the Highlanders recruited were gentlemen and freemen; most were tenants too poor to travel any other way and who were indentured as servants for Georgia to work for the Trust or for individuals willing to pay their passage. The offer to these men was that "to each man servant and the Heirs Male of his Body for ever, after the Expiration of his Service; upon Certificate from his Master of his having served well, will be Granted Twenty Acres of Land."[10] The form of indenture for servants used by the Trustees of Georgia stated that everyone nineteen years of age and older would be indentured for five years; those under nineteen were bound until they reached twenty-four.[11] The advantage of indenture for the emigrant wanting to go abroad, but who had neither the means nor the knowledge, was that the passage and arrangements were paid either by the Trust or by someone in the colony needing a servant. After five years, the servant would become a landholder and a freeman.

The inheritance question was not to be Mackay's only problem in recruiting in the Highlands. After he left Inverness, he made his way through areas of Ross and Cromarty, visiting Lord Cromarty; Captain Monro, Sir Robert Monro's brother; and some gentlemen from the shire of Ross.[12] These men seemed supportive of Mackay's endeavors and, from the Earl of Egmont's list of settlers in Georgia,[13] Mackay apparently found recruits among the Monroes in the parishes of Alness and Kiltearn.[14] While he received encouragement from some of the gentlemen in the shires, he encountered strong opposition from other lairds reluctant to lose their tenants. Mackay wrote to the Trustees from Dornoch on 24 July 1735 complaining of waiting for two days in the shire of Sutherland for "my Lord Sutherland and Some other Gentlemen who Seem not so very favorable for fear of losing Those poor creatures, who they look on to be their property as Much as their Catle [sic]."[15] To some Highland chiefs, these tenants meant rent and a source of income, however meager. Loss of men in a clan also meant weakening the military strength of the chiefs.

Other chiefs feared that continued emigration would depopulate the Highlands. Of course, not every laird felt so protective of his clansmen before the '45 Rebellion. Duane Meyer, in *The Highland Scots of North Carolina, 1732–1776*, cites the example in 1739 of a betrayal of clansmen by their chiefs. MacLeod of Harris and MacDonald of Sleat in that year hired a press-gang and a ship to transport to America 110 clansmen whom they no longer desired as dependents. When the ship stopped in north Ireland, the betrayed clansmen escaped.[16] Granted, this was an unusual case, but the episode underscores the extent to which clan relationships were in flux.

Mackay had another demon to lay to rest. He claimed that a "Damnable Practice had prevailed and been carry'd on for Some time past, . . . to bind Servants by their Indentures for Georgia and Ship them off for Jamaica . . . which I am credibly informed is carry'd on in most of the Seaports of Scotland." This, he reported, "frightens many from coming near any person who would carry them to a better place."[17] Judging by his letters, by 24 July 1735, Mackay seemed discouraged and professed that he was "very indifferent whether any go or not," although he did admit that he had not yet "got among my own tribe."[18]

Verelst was sympathetic and encouraged Mackay, saying that he hoped "Dunbar would complete the Number."[19] However, on the same day that Mackay wrote his letter of complaint, the Trustees had granted him five hundred acres of land in Georgia.[20] On 26 July 1735, Verelst sent a letter to Dornoch to inform Mackay of the land grant and that he had paid on Mackay's account £1.1. consideration money and "Ten Shillings & Six Pence" for registering a memorial of it with the auditor of the plantations.[21] The news of the land grant and his journey into his own country apparently changed Mackay's attitude.

Mackay left Lord Sutherland in Dornoch and headed north into Mackay territory, finding success in the parishes of Dornoch, Rogart, Lairg, Eddrachillis, Durness, Tongue, and Farr.[22] Writing in September from the seacoast village of Kirktomie, about ten miles east of the Kyle of Tongue in Sutherland, he said he had recently been in the "most inaccessible parts of my Lord Reay's estate" and was on his way to Lord Sutherland's house.[23] His efforts had been successful in the land of his clan: a prime example of the kinship network in emigration at work. Mackay wrote to Oglethorpe and the Trustees that he now had "the pleasure to tell you that not withstanding of the Strongest opposition, and that carry'd on in the Vilest Manner, that is by under hand Agents instilling terrible apprehensions in the people's minds; I have at Last opened the people's eyes so far that severals have a good oppion [sic] of the project, and were it not for want of specie [ready cash] in the Country Many would embrace this opportunity."[24] He went so far as to boast that by this time, "if any convoy safely arrived [in Georgia] and accounts [are] transmitted here of their being happily settled, the Trust may annually have what numbers they please from the Northern Highlands."[25] This statement made in 1735 was prophetic of the mass emigrations of the next century.

The clergy played an important part in turning the minds of the people around, particularly one churchman, whom Mackay does not name:

"Shocked to see his fellow creatures in the utmost slavery and endeavour'd to be contenued so by their Masters by false aspersions against the scheme for the settling the Colony," said Mackay, this unnamed clergyman "did his utmost to open their eyes."[26] Mackay also had help from his family. One of his brothers, Robert Mackay, Tutor of Farr, and two of his nephews enlisted to emigrate,[27] along with a number of Trust servants from the area of Farr.[28] Lieutenant Mackay was able to take his family on the Trust's account in part due to the private instructions given him and Captain Dunbar on 16 July 1735, which stipulated:

> Out of the 110 Men there is to be 10 Servants to be distributed for Encourage-
> ments for raising the Men if Occasion shall so require 4 of which 10 are to be
> for the use of Lieut. Hugh Mackay and to be provided for at the Charge of the
> Trust as the others are, and the other 6 are to be allotted to Persons according
> to the Recommendations of the Said Lieut. Hugh Mackay and Mr. George
> Dunbar in proportion to the Numbers that each shall get.[29]

By the beginning of September, Mackay could declare "37 [recruits] on the public account and 34 on private account, including Mr. Baillie, Mr. Mackay in Georgia,[30] and Mr. Mackay of Strathy." He would write three weeks later that "if the colony subsists but three years there will be more Mackays in America than in the Highlands."[31] He was confident that if Captain Dunbar had acquired his forty men, then the Trustees could "safely venture to order the ship about."[32]

While Lieutenant Mackay was busy recruiting in the Highlands, the Trustees were beginning to make preparations for the new immigrants' arrival in Georgia. On 30 July 1735 they sent a petition to the "Queens most Excellent Majesty, Guardian of the Kingdom of Great Britain, and His Majesty's Lieutenant within the same," requesting armaments for a new settlement in Georgia "which will stand in great need of Defense."[33] There is no doubt that this ordnance was for the Scots. The Trustees asked for "24 pieces of Cannon from Six pounds to Eighteen pounds with Iron'd Carriages & Shott & Iron for 24 spare Carriages. 4 Small long Field Pieces with Carriages. 8 Cohorns & Granadoes.[34] 500 small arms & Shott Cartouch boxes & Moulds & Flints. 2 Flaggs & 2 Pendants. 50 Barrels of Powder, Spunges, Ladles, Rammers, Crows, &C. To be delivered to Your Petitioners as soon as possible."[35] The Trustees for Georgia knew that the Spanish in Florida would resent a new settlement on the Altamaha River and would likely respond quickly to any encroachment on the land they considered their own.

The Trustees wanted the ordnance in Georgia ready for the Scottish immigrants upon their arrival.

Fear of the Spanish was not the only concern of the Trustees for the new Scots in Georgia. Harman Verelst, in his instructions of 22 August 1735 to Thomas Causton in Georgia, wrote that the "Scotch must be supported. . . . You must strive to obtain the Indians consent for the Scotch settling at Barnwell's Bluff [Darien] & for that purpose you are to make them such Presents as shall be necessary and to get some of them to Go and hunt for them [the Scots immigrants] & show them the Country & be sure to satisfy the Indians upon this Occasion."[36] He was explicit in saying that "If any Persons should busy themselves in spreading any scandalous Reports & Rumours to hinder the settling the Highlanders You are to Commit them . . . and Prosecute them to the utmost severity of the Law & thereby prevent them from having Access to the new People and from doing any further Mischief."[37] The Scottish Highlanders were to be essential to the survival of the colony and the Trustees wanted to ensure their remaining in Georgia once they arrived.

The same day that Verelst wrote to Causton in Georgia, he also wrote to John Hossack in Inverness, asking him to go aboard the ship bound for Georgia before it sailed and count the passengers for accounting purposes.[38] John Hossack was Provost of Inverness from 1735 to 1738 and again in 1741–44. He had a daughter, Barbara, whose second husband was Phenias Mackintosh of Drummond, and likely assisted Captain Dunbar in his efforts among the Mackintosh Clan.[39] The Trustees would use Hossack's merchant business to supply most of the plaids and shoes for the Scots' use in Georgia.

Verelst stayed busy in his correspondence on behalf of the Highland recruits. On the following day, 23 August, he dispatched three letters concerning events in Scotland; the first was to Nicholas Spencer, secretary to the Society in Scotland for Promoting Christian Knowledge, asking him to recommend a minister to go to Georgia.[40] Verelst acknowledged receipt on 11 August of the society's letter of support for the proposal of sending a minister to Georgia for the Highlanders.[41] He expressed to the society the concern the Trustees felt for the welfare of their colonists. Furthermore, the Trustees thought it would be "a deplorable Condition for such a Number of poor people to be without Spiritual Help, they not speaking the English Language."[42] Verelst explained that the Trustees knew little of the lives, character, and conversations "of any Ministers who speak the Irish Language," and would appreciate it if the society "Would recommend a Godly Minister of the Gospel of an exemplary life."[43] To add to the missionary zeal of the society, the Trustees offered the thought that the minister's example might be useful to the "Heathern." They also promised to grant the minister sponsored by the society three hundred acres of land in their colony.[44]

The SSPCK responded by sending offers throughout the Highlands seeking a minister who was willing to go to Georgia on its behalf. Mackay refers to one such recipient, a Reverend Mr. Anderson in Sutherland, who, "Not knowing the terms, did not, by his answer engage to go."[45] Mackay, apparently after persuading Anderson to reconsider, asked the Trust that "if the place is not already supplied he [Anderson] may be the man."[46] However, the society was more fortunate with the Reverend John MacLeod from Skye, claimed by Captain Dunbar to be of "exceeding good character."[47]

The Reverend John MacLeod was not an ordinary Skianach, for he was related to the MacLeods of Dunvegan and a strong personality.[48] In his application to the SSPCK, MacLeod sent along letters of recommendation from brother ministers and other gentlemen in the Highlands giving their support of his character and abilities. These letters were read before the society in Edinburgh and his application was approved on 18 September 1735.[49] The Committee of Directors for the Society also appropriated £25 sterling per year as salary "during the continuance of his commission from the Said Society" and an additional £25 to defray his moving expenses.[50] The committee recommended to the "Praeses and Principal Smith to meet with the moderator of the Presbytery of Edinburgh . . . for taking Mr. MacLeod upon trials of ordination, and appoint a letter to be written to the Trustees of Georgia recommending him to them."[51]

At the 15 October 1735 meeting of the society MacLeod, having passed his trials the previous Wednesday, was ordained to be a "minister of the Gospel in order to his being sent to Georgia." In his commission and ordination instructions he was charged by the society to

> be one of the Society's Missionaries in the Colony of Georgia in America not only to officiate as Minister of the Gospel to the Highland families going thither from this country and others there who may incline to join with you in public worship but also to use your utmost endeavor for propagating Christian Knowledge among the Indian Natives in that Colony and in order thereunto you, as soon as you shall come to understand the language of the said natives are not only to preach to and catechize them but also to keep a school for teaching them and others under your care in the said colony—to read the Holy Scriptures of the Old and New Testaments and other pious and godly books—to understand and read the English Language and to direct them how to pray and to live as becometh the gospel and when you judge them fit to receive the seal of

the covenant of grace you are to administer the same to them and use your best endeavors to confirm such in the truth of our holy religion and engage them to persevere therein.[52]

With these instructions, MacLeod prepared to join the other emigrants bound for the frontier settlement in Georgia. On 29 October 1735, the Board of Trustees for Georgia signed a license for "Mr. MacCleod, a Scots minister, to perform Divine Service in Georgia; he going with Dunbar and Mackay's people."[53]

The second letter that Verelst sent on 23 August was addressed to Lieutenant Mackay and was to be left at the "Post House in Inverness." In it Verelst informed Mackay that his land grant and sealed instructions had been sent earlier to Dornoch and that Captain Dunbar "sails for Scotland this day."[54] Though the Trust had taken measures for Dunbar to make up the number of recruits since Mackay's last letter to Oglethorpe, they wanted Mackay to "continue Your Diligence in Your Parts of the Country" and to meet with Dunbar upon his arrival to "concert further Measures."[55] Mackay was then instructed to buy "Targetts, Mills & Charges on the Trust Accot. in Scotland."[56]

Captain Dunbar received Verelst's last correspondence of 23 August. Enclosed in the letter were lengthy instructions for his voyage to Scotland and the return trip to Georgia.[57] As with Mackay's first directions from the Trust, Dunbar's directives were meticulous and explicit. He was to "take in at Tilbury Fort[58] four cases of Arms marked G X C S No. 21 to 24 containing one hundred, all in List Cases."[59] Afterward, he was to proceed to "Leith Road [the port of Edinburgh] to give notice to the Proper People at Edinburgh of Your Arrival and desire their Assistance, and then proceed with the utmost Diligence to Crommarty or Inverness."[60] At Cromarty or Inverness, Dunbar was to "take in One hundred and thirty heads of Passengers . . . as soon as you can get them."[61] After meeting with Mackay and combining their efforts, Dunbar was to make up the "above-mentioned Number in such manner as You are directed by your other instructions"[62] The Trust, mindful of the sailing season and the onset of winter weather in the north of Scotland, advised Dunbar to set sail with whatever number of recruits they had "before the Season of the Year makes the Scotch Seas dangerous."[63]

Following up on Verelst's letter to John Hossack, Dunbar was to contact Hossack personally and ask him to come on board the ship and "in the Cabbin to have each single Man or Family brought before him" entering on a list each person with the ages and numbers of each family. Additionally, Hossack

was to list each man's profession and where he was born. Hossack was then
to verify and sign the list, testify that each was aboard, and send the list to
the Trustees by post, keeping a copy for himself.[64]

Dunbar was to inform the Trust of the day "all of the Passengers come on
board at Cromarty or Inverness at which time the extraordinary Charge for
the Ship ceases." He was further advised that "the Bedding Canvas and
Blanketting on board is to be delivered only to those who have no Bedding
of their own, and the residue You must be Accomptable for in Georgia to
Mr. Causton in Mr. Oglethorpe's Absence." The Trustees were not forgetful
of the purpose of recruiting Highlanders for the frontier of Georgia; they instructed Dunbar to make use of the gunpowder on board for the passengers
"not exceeding 25 pounds as also 50 pounds of Bullets for shooting at
Marks."[65] They were also mindful of the Scots' health during transport:
"Every Day that the Weather permits You are to Order the Passengers up
upon the Deck and Cause them to clean their Cabbins for the Preservation
of their health and for that purpose the Vinegar on board is for sprinkling
between Decks. And the Box of Medicines and 2 Stone Bottles of Theracle[66]
are for Use in the Voyage."[67] While in Scotland, in addition to his other duties, Dunbar was to purchase 200 yards of "bright colored Plads . . . from
12d. to 20d. a Yard, for the use of James Oglethorpe, Esqr."[68] It is not
recorded which pattern Oglethorpe wore but, as will be seen in the next
chapter, he did wear the garb of the Highlanders in their presence in Georgia. Dunbar was also to "take the Minister [MacLeod] on board accordingly
and to treat him with the utmost Civility during the Voyage, and to accommodate him in the best manner as the nature of the Sea Voyage will allow,
and assist him in making the People during the Voyage to behave in a sober
and Religious manner."[69]

If, upon his arrival in Georgia, Dunbar was to meet Captain James Gascoigne "in His Majesty's man-of-War the *Hawk*," which was to cruise off the
coast of Georgia to intercept Dunbar, then he was to obey such orders as
Captain Gascoigne would give him. If Dunbar happened to miss Gascoigne,
he was to enter the Savannah River and send word of his arrival to Mr. Causton, who would "assist in getting Pettiauguas[70] and other craft" to transport
some of the men to Barnwell's Bluff on the banks of the Altamaha. Half of
this advance party of Highlanders was to be made up of Mackay's recruits;
the other half was to consist of men raised by Mr. John Cuthbert, one of the
gentlemen from Draikes, near Inverness.[71] Lieutenant Hugh Mackay was to
stay with this group and make preparations for the "Reception of the Remainder of the Familys."[72] Dunbar was then to attempt to sail his ship, the

Prince of Wales, into the Altamaha for the more "commodious Landing of the Remainder of the Passengers and Goods." He was also to deliver to Mackay four pieces of cannon for the new settlement, taking his "Certificate of the Delivery thereof."[73]

Captain Dunbar attempted to follow the directions as ordered; however, bad weather forced him to bypass Edinburgh and sail directly to Inverness, where he arrived on 16 September 1735.[74] Dunbar's reception at Inverness was outstanding. Writing to Oglethorpe, he expressed his optimism for success:

> I put directly up to this place [Inverness] where I arrived the 16th and I hope will succeed to my wishes on bringing with me a parcel of the pertest fellows who ever left Scotland in one ship and I am convinced that I could get twenty for every one I can carry over. This day I have an appointment with them to seize and pitch upon the people. There are petitions from many parts of the Highlands in the name of considerable numbers and I intend to meet with some of the leading people to see what may be done another year of which I shall acquaint you. Most of my people will be to the southward of this place and I have appointed a meeting with them Friday and Saturday next when I'll be able to acquaint you of their number particularly. . . . I saw a letter from Lieutenant Mackay wherein he wrote that the people of that country have taken another turn and expects sixty. On my arrival here I sent him an express and expect to see him here this day or tomorrow when we'll be capable to give full satisfaction in every affair. I'll get Highland Plaids, nets, &c., and obey all my instructions to the utmost of my power nor will anything or consideration move me from the general sweep of our undertaking.
>
> P.S. The Magistrates of this place have such an esteem for you that they told me to put the only mark of distinction on you in their power & what they confer on every person of distinction that comes to this place. I mean a ticket of Freedom to the Town.[75]

Obviously, there was considerable interest in Inverness and the surrounding country for the proposal of emigration to Georgia. The magistrates did, as Dunbar mentioned, honor the work of Oglethorpe by making him a burgess and a guild brother on 22 September 1735.[76] Dunbar's method of recruitment was "to bring the enterprise into vogue with the chief Gentlemen" in order to gain favor with the cadets of the clans.[77] As a result, he was effective in his efforts, as evidenced by his above-mentioned letter of meetings with the gentlemen of the areas around Inverness, in particular, the gentlemen of Clan Chattan.[78]

Apparently word spread throughout the Highlands of the potential success

of the Georgia venture. Mackay's agents had been effective, the clergy had
helped, other agents of the Trust were at work (Mr. Cuthbert of Draikes and
Mr. Baillie), and newspaper advertisements had been used as well.[79] Whatever the reason, Dunbar reported that "there are petitions from many parts
of the Highlands in the name of considerable numbers."[80] By 22 October,
Dunbar was writing to tell the Trustees that he had a "young Gentleman, a
Son of McLean of Argours who takes passage for Self and Servant to See our
colony and his report will bring manie of his class there."[81] He further stated
that "the other Gentlemen are from different parts of this countrie, most of
them lades and I hope will answer to the benefit of Georgia Since I assure
you they are all of the best familys in this countrie and fit for any service."[82]
According to Dunbar, these young men did not expect the easy life and were
fully aware of the many hardships they would meet. He added that they
were willing to work with their own hands and, in the spirit of adventure,
would be "Disappointed on the Safe Side."[83]

The young men Dunbar mentioned might have come in response to an
item in the Edinburgh newspapers, to which Mackay referred in his letter
dated 1 September 1735. Mackay described an "advertisement . . . put in by
some Honest person telling that So many people are going from the Highlands to be setled in a new part of Georgia to be a barrier against the French
and Spaniards."[84] The piece, both concise and accurate, was a news article in
the 18 August edition of the *Caledonian Mercury:*

> We learn from London that the Trustees for the colony of Georgia have pro-
> jected a settlement of Highlanders from this country, and have actually sent
> round for Inverness and Cromerty, a ship commanded by Capt. Dunbar to take
> in 160 men, women and children, who are to be settled on the far boundary of
> the River Altamaha who will be a gallant barrier in case of war with France or
> Spain. And Mr. Oglethorpe with the other Trustees, are applying to the Society
> in Scotland for Propagating Christian Knowledge, to send a minister along with
> them who speaks Irish, with the proper encouragement. And we are assured
> the Society here [are] so well satisfied with the project that they have amply in-
> structed their committee of directors to close in on it.[85]

To strengthen the resolve of Highland gentlemen to come and stay in
Georgia, the Trustees made some large and unusual grants of land. Verelst
notified Dunbar on 30 August 1735 of land grants to Archibald MacGillivray
of 50 acres, 500 acres to Patrick Mackay and the "Heirs Male of his body
and in failure to Catherine his Daughter and the Heirs Male of her body,

500 acres to John Cuthbert and the Heirs Male of his body and in failure
to James Cuthbert [John's brother] and the Heirs Male of his body, and
500 acres to John Mackay and the Heirs Male of his body, And 500 acres to
Yourself and the Heirs Male of Your body & in failure to William your
Brother and the Heirs Male of His body."[86]

What is unusual is that, for the first time, the Trustees allowed the inheritance of the lands granted to go to someone other than the direct male issue
of the original grantee. Particularly significant is the grant to Patrick Mackay
of Cyder Hall in the county of Sutherland, whose 500 acres were to go to his
daughter Catherine if he died without sons.[87] This action by the Trustees
was in direct response to the method of land tenure in Scotland and aimed at
pacifying the concerns of the much-needed Highland gentlemen emigrants.
It also came at a time when both Mackay and Dunbar could use the information to entice additional recruits. It was indeed rare for women to inherit
entire land grants during the early years of the colony of Georgia. To placate
the first colonists, the Trustees had allowed widows to have their thirds of
the property as in England and they were entitled to the mansion house, but
they were not allowed to inherit the entire estate.[88] At times, however, upon
petition, the Trust allowed women to inherit real property but with the provision that subsequent inheritance would be tail male. So, in spite of policy,
a few women did inherit land during the Trustees' tenure. Grants showing
the same conditions as the one to Patrick Mackay were made to many other
Highland gentlemen, including George Dunbar and Hugh Mackay.[89]

Armed with the evidence of large land grants, Dunbar began his recruitment in Inverness-shire. He obtained the support of William Mackintosh of
Mackintosh, chief of Clan Chattan, for the venture. The possible reason for
support from "The Mackintosh" could be that several of his family were already in the Carolina and Georgia colonies. His brother, Æneas Mackintosh,
who was to later succeed him as chief, was already in Georgia in the service
of Oglethorpe. Also, he could not fail to see the opportunity available in
Georgia for his clan to regain some of their fortunes lost due to the forfeiture
of lands after the failed rising of 1715 and through the downturn of the economic situation in the Highlands.[90]

Dunbar found success among the various septs of the clan. Most of the
gentlemen going to Georgia were chosen for their leadership qualities, as
per the instructions of the Trustees' Common Council.[91] The most prominent among them was John Mohr Mackintosh, who had gone out to fight for
King James in the rising of 1715 with his uncle, Brigadier-General William

Mackintosh of Borlum.[92] He was called "Mohr" for his great size.[93] Among the emigrants were a number of Mackintoshes. Besides John Mohr Mackintosh of Borlum, there were also kinsmen John Mackintosh of Holme, John Mackintosh of Inverness, John Mackintosh of Kingussie, John Mackintosh of Dornes, John Mackintosh Bain, and John Mackintosh Lynvilge.[94] All of these above-mentioned men named John Mackintosh were gentlemen from Inverness-shire and paid their own passage to Georgia.[95]

Of course, not all of these gentlemen had ready money to pay for the trip. John Mackintosh of Holme, aged twenty-four, borrowed money from his relatives to finance himself and his sixteen-year-old cousin, Lachlan McGillivray of Dunmaglass, to go to Georgia. To help him start in the New World, his relative Mr. John Mackintosh, father of the Provost John Mackintosh of Inverness, assisted him, three years being the period within which it was thought the money could be repaid. A loan agreement was drawn up on 8 October 1735:

> Sir—Three years after this date pay to me, John Mackintosh senior, merchant in Inverness, on order at my shop Six pounds fourteen shillings sterlin money value given you by
> (signed) Jo: Mackintosh, Senr.
> To John Mackintosh, son to John Mackintosh of Holme accepts.(signed) John Mackintosh [96]

The young emigrant did not forget his benefactor. He seems to have thrived in Georgia and was careful to ask after old friends and relatives when he repaid his debt a year early. He writes:

> Dear Cos.
> I am not forgetful of the many favors you conferred upon me, particularly your act of benevolence at my departure from your place, and hopes, through devine assistance, to be in condition of making you an acknowledgement. I am ready to consign your money as you advise. I refer you to Sandy [McGillivray?] for description of this part of the world, and hopes you will use your interest with his father for servants and necessaries, since he is resolved to settle there. You will remember my kind service to your wife, your uncle Angus, and William and Angus, Lynvilg's sons. Dear Sir, your affect. cousin to serve you while
> (signed) John Mackintosh
> Darien, in Georgia, 3rd December, 1737.[97]

Along with Lachlan McGillivray, there were also other McGillivrays, Mackintoshes, MacBains, McDonalds, Grants, Frazers, MacLeans, Macphersons, and Macqueens from Clan Chattan land in and around Inverness.[98] Captain Dunbar had done well in his recruiting efforts among the renowned Jacobite strongholds, as Lieutenant Hugh Mackay had been successful among the Mackays, who had been staunch supporters of the Hanoverian government in 1715.

Both Dunbar and Mackay sent correspondence to the Trustees on 21 October 1735. Mackay wrote that on "Saturday the 18th Instant I shipped 86 heads of men, women, and children aboard the *Prince of Wales*, Captain Dunbar, the particulars are herewith enclosed."[99] Dunbar's letter was more explicit:

> We have on board One hundred sixty five Passengers whole heads Several of which pay their own passage by bills of their friends here all which I was fond of since it disburdened the Trust from Charge. One muster was over last night and our rolls are finished and will be on board either this night or tomorrow morning but the ship is falling down. . . . I'm obliged to send several on shore who pressed to be on board our muster day in hopes they might get over besides many of both freemen and servants who were in my offers.[100]

Many people, apparently overcoming their fear of being shanghaied to Jamaica, as Mackay had initially found in the Highlands, flooded to the docks where the *Prince of Wales* was berthed and tried to gain passage. The number exceeded that for which the Trustees had contracted and Dunbar had to remove them before the ship could leave Inverness. Obviously, the Trustees had found fertile ground for future settlers in Georgia.

Lieutenant Hugh Mackay and Captain George Dunbar had been successful in their recruitment of Scots from the Highlands. On 29 October 1735, the Earl of Egmont noted in his journal that "Captain George Dunbar of the *Prince of Wales* carried from Scotland 180 persons, of whom 130 were contracted to be at the Trustees' expense, but believed these last would be but 120."[101] Oglethorpe corrected that number by stating that three men were left behind. One man, he said, ran away. The other two men were put ashore because "they would neither pay their passage, nor indent as Servants of the Trust."[102] The first recruitment of Highland Scots for the Trustees was now complete. Mackay and Dunbar, with 177 Highland emigrants, left Scotland on 18 October 1735 aboard the *Prince of Wales* for the new colony of Georgia. It would be two years before the second venture for recruiting Highland Scots would be mounted and another four years before the last, but the Scots were coming to Georgia and they would make an important impact on Georgia's history.

CHAPTER 4

The Founding of Darien

To distant climes, a dreary scene, they go,
Where wild Altama murmurs to their woe,
Far different these from all that charmed before,
The various terrors of that distant shore . . .
—Oliver Goldsmith, *The Deserted Village*

THE MORNING OF 10 January 1736 launched a day filled with excitement, anticipation, and, no doubt, some trepidation for the newly arriving immigrants from the Highlands of Scotland. On board ship was a mixture of people preparing to make a new start in a new world: ardent Jacobites and strong supporters of the Hanoverian government, Episcopalians and Presbyterians, a mariner, a surgeon, three tailors, one joiner, one weaver, four men listed as gentlemen, twenty-five farmers, seventy men named as servants or laborers, a minister, and the complement of women and children that made up the families of this settlement on the British southern frontier in America.[1] As Savannah came into view, the *Prince of Wales*, commanded by Captain George Dunbar, sailed into the harbor at Tybee Roads on the coast of the colony of Georgia, after nearly three months on the wintry Atlantic.[2] As ordered, Lieutenant Hugh Mackay immediately set about sending the immigrants to Barnwell's Bluff on the Altamaha River, which was to become their new home.[3] Mackay left first with a detachment of the men in the periaguas[4] to take possession of the site and erect a shelter for the rest of the families, who were to follow later.[5]

The little flotilla sailed down the coast of Georgia and in less than a week reached the mouth of the Altamaha River. They then traveled through the low marshy islands that divided the broad river into narrow channels until the group landed at the foot of the first high ground. This had been the site of Fort King George, Britain's first attempt to defend the southernmost frontier of her continental colonies. It had been abandoned in 1727. Within a mile and a half of the fort's ruins, the Highlanders decided to make their stand and build their settlement.[6] They called the town Darien "at their own desire," certainly named after the failed attempt at a Scottish settlement in 1698 on the Isthmus of Darien in Panama.[7] That venture failed because of tropical illness and the efforts of the Spanish to eliminate the settlers. Choice of Darien as a name seems to have been a gesture of defiance on the part of these new immigrants against the Spanish in Florida.

The spot designated was situated on the mainland, about twenty miles northwest of St. Simons Island. The town was built on a branch of the Altamaha River on a bluff twenty feet high; the site was surrounded on three sides by woods.[8] The soil was sandy and black, with little to recommend it as fertile ground, but the site had not been chosen with agriculture in mind. The Spanish threat was to the south, which was the reason for the Highlanders' settlement at Darien.[9] Some of the Carolina people tried to persuade the Scots to settle in Carolina and not to antagonize the Spanish by settling on the Altamaha. They attempted to discourage the Scots at their landing by saying that the settlement would be so close to the Spanish fort that the Highlanders would be shot from within the Spanish houses. With typical Highland bravado, the Scots replied, "We will beat them out of their fort and shall have houses ready built to live in."[10]

Under Hugh Mackay's direction, the Highlanders immediately set to work to secure the site. The relatively mild temperature and clear sunny winter days in south Georgia, similar to the late spring and early summer of the Highlands, were an opportune time to do the heavy labor of clearing land out of a wilderness. The palmetto brush and scrub pine soon fell before axes, swords, and fire; within weeks Darien was taking shape. By the time General James Oglethorpe arrived on 22 February, the Scots had constructed a "battery of four pieces of cannon, built a guardhouse, a storehouse, a chapel, and several huts for particular people."[11] They had got so far as to build a house for the widow of one of their men who had died on the journey.[12]

The experiences of a new world were not without lighthearted predicaments. En route to visit the new Scots' settlement, Oglethorpe's party met a boat carrying Hugh Mackay and John Cuthbert, who were coming from Darien bound for Savannah. Mackay and Cuthbert returned with Oglethorpe to Darien. Along the way Cuthbert told Oglethorpe's group the story of an unidentified Highlander's first encounter with a persimmon tree loaded with of ripe fruit on one of the islands. The Scot could not climb the tree because it was too tall and thorny. Frustrated and not to be denied, the

Highlander cut down the tree and "gathered some dozens," not thinking of future harvests.[13]

As Oglethorpe arrived to view the new settlement and meet his southern-most defenders, they turned out under arms and presented a "most manly appearance with their Plaids, broadswords, targets, and firearms."[14] This was a proud moment for the Highlanders as they donned their plaids and carried their traditional weapons, perhaps for the first time since the carry-ing of weapons by clansmen had been outlawed in the Highlands in 1726.[15] The young men who had signed on for the adventure of the frontier and were hopeful at the prospect of fighting the Spanish must have felt a keen sense of exhilaration when the general's boat landed on the shore at the foot of their settlement.

Oglethorpe was well pleased with what he saw at this busy new frontier outpost. In honor of the Highlanders, he had come dressed in the Highland "Habit."[16] He must have looked comfortable and natural in it because Samuel Eveleigh, a member of Oglethorpe's party, reported later that when they arrived at Darien, several of the settlers cried out, "Mr. Oglethorpe, where's Mr. Oglethorpe?"—not being able to recognize him from the "rest of their brethren."[17] Further, when invited by Lieutenant, now Captain, Mackay to lie in his tent, where there was a bed with sheets—a rarity as yet in that part of the world—Oglethorpe excused himself. He chose rather to lie wrapped in his plaid at the guard fire, showing himself to be a soldier ca-pable of leadership, in the eyes of the rugged Highlanders.[18] Likewise, not to be seen as soft, Captain Mackay and the other gentlemen of Darien followed Oglethorpe's example and forsook the comforts of tent and bed, "though the night was very cold."[19]

Oglethorpe no doubt knew about the pride of place and the appearance of hardiness in leaders to the Highlandmen, and he did not want to disappoint them. He might have been familiar with the story of McDonald of Keppoch who, during a winter campaign against a neighboring clan over land posses-sion, gave orders for rolling a snowball to lay under his head during the night; "where upon his followers murmured, saying, 'Now we despair of vic-tory, since our leader is become so effeminate he can't sleep without a Pil-low.'"[20] This story may or may not be true; it is nevertheless an example of the expectations of Highland fighting men, and Oglethorpe much admired this hardiness. In a letter to the Trustees, he would later write, "The Indians and the Highlanders have behaved well with great courage, fidelity, and af-fection, and the English that came with me are not far behind with them."[21]

Before leaving Savannah for Darien, Oglethorpe had taken the precaution of sending Captain James McPherson and a group of his rangers overland to support the newly arrived Highlanders. McPherson, a South Carolinian, and his rangers had been transferred from Saltcatchers Fort at the head of the Combahee River on the Carolina frontier to the new colony of Georgia to "Cover and protect that Settlement from any insults" in 1733.[22] They were now to patrol the territory between Savannah and the new settlement of Darien. The company of rangers arrived in the fledgling compound during Oglethorpe's visit to Darien. The Highlanders felt a sense of relief and security with the troops' arrival from Savannah, knowing that they now had communication by land.[23]

The Yamacraw Indian chief and good friend of General Oglethorpe, Tomochichi, notified Oglethorpe that he had also sent a party of Indians to assist Captain Mackay and the new settlers at Darien. According to Francis Moore, secretary at Frederica and one of Oglethorpe's party, Tomochichi's Indians agreed "mighty well" with the Highlanders and "fetched" them venison.[24] The Highlanders' importance to the colony of Georgia was strongly evidenced by the support the settlement received.

To this distant outpost, communication was paramount. In order to connect the new settlement by direct land contact with the other Georgia colonists, Oglethorpe instructed Walter Augustine and Alexander Tolme to survey the country from Savannah to Darien for possible road routes.[25] Oglethorpe hoped that the road would have beneficial effects in Georgia just as General Wade's roads had brought to Scotland.[26] By the beginning of March the work was well under way on the road. Augustine and Tolme, with upward of a hundred men assisting, were building a cart road using a team of six horses to plough and clear the way. Hugh Mackay Jr., a ranger and nephew of Captain Hugh Mackay, was in command of a dozen rangers and protected the workers.[27] A group of Indians from Tomochichi's tribe and others from friendly camps found along the way were providing the food through hunting game. The road between Savannah and Darien would prove to be ninety miles long. Augustine and Tolme complained that if there were not two rivers to cross and some boggy places, the road might be seventy miles instead of ninety.[28]

While the work on the road was progressing, the people of Darien were busy clearing land and planting crops. House building had been postponed until the lands were cultivated, a sacrifice that was rewarded when the first harvest produced enough corn to meet the local needs, plus a surplus to sell.

The Earl of Egmont, chairman of the Georgia Trustees in London, was impressed with these newcomers to Georgia and with the priorities they set. He commented that the people in Darien were "extraordinary industrious" and that it "were to be wished the people of Savannah" had done the same.[29] This view contradicts the present opinion of such historians as Grady McWhiney, who posit the idea that Highlanders were inherently lazy and shunned farming at every opportunity.[30] John Brownfield, in a letter to the Trustees dated 6 March 1736, related how the Highlanders were "very forward in their settlement at Darien" and how everything to the southward went on "prosperously."[31] However, as noted, the sandy soil on the bluff around Darien was not ideal for cultivation and subsequent crops were not as good as the first efforts. Regardless, this did not deter the Highlanders' determination to continue in the New World and make Georgia their home.

Francis Moore's description of the land at Darien shows how the geography of Georgia surrounding the Scots' settlement determined the course of Darien's society. The physical characteristics of Georgia's environment played as much of a part in shaping the frontier society as did the geography of the Highlands in shaping Scottish society. He observed that the country behind Darien was high and healthy, and "very fit for cattle, tho' not so good for corn."[32] Land and climate were different in Georgia than in the Highlands, but this description was appropriate for both. Moore further stated that the timber upon the high land, behind the town, was "some of the best in Georgia."[33]

They had barely been able to subsist on the meager crops in the Highlands, and the ground around Darien was to prove even less adequate for farming. Provisions had to be imported from Savannah and other ports north, and during the first year they were often late. In the winter of 1736–37, the Highlanders in Darien had to kill some of their precious cattle for sustenance, and even then there were many anxious and hungry days. It was during this trying time that the settlers pulled together as a community with John Mohr Mackintosh[34] as their leader.[35] They would suffer through two more years of planting before they looked elsewhere for sustenance.

With good grazing ground and strong stands of timber in the vicinity, it was only natural for the Scots to turn to the same avenues of industry as in Scotland—cattle and timber. These clans had occupied some of the better-wooded glens in Scotland before their migration and were experienced sawyers. Some men of the Clan Chattan had perhaps worked for the York Buildings Company above Invergarry or supplied lumber for Ruthven Barracks and Fort Augustus in Inverness-shire. In Georgia, an obvious market for lumber existed for the building of houses and forts in the ever-expanding colony, and large herds of the Trust's cattle had been in Darien from the start.[36]

Benjamin Martyn, the secretary to the Trustees in London, described the economy of the Highlanders at Darien, recording that "they raised, at first, a considerable Quantity of Corn. They feed . . . great numbers of cattle, and have many good sawyers, who make an advantageous trade of lumber."[37] By July 1740, the Darien people were supplying five or six beeves a week to Oglethorpe's regiment stationed in the vicinity. They also sold butter and milk in large quantities to the soldiers. Cattle had become almost the sole source of income for the Darien settlers.[38]

As for the timber business, Oglethorpe was impressed with the advances made by the Scots. In a letter to the Trustees, dated 20 October 1739, Oglethorpe praised Darien as one of the settlements where the people had been "most industrious," as those in Savannah had been "most idle." He claimed that the Trustees had several servants who, under the direction of John Mohr Mackintosh, had not only earned their bread but had furnished the Trust with such quantities of "sawed stuff" as to have saved the Trust a great sum of money.[39]

Oglethorpe trusted and respected Mohr Mackintosh and felt it necessary to allow him to oversee the Trust's Highland servants because they were useful under "their own chiefs" and nowhere else.[40] Apparently the Scottish sawyers could speak only Gaelic, as Oglethorpe complained that the Highland servants could not be put under the direction of anyone at Frederica, nor of anyone who did "not understand the Highland language." Besides, according to Oglethorpe, "the woods fit for sawing are near Darien, and the Trustees engaged not to separate the Highlanders."[41] This intentional barrier by language and separation was designed by the Trustees to keep the Highlanders as a community on the southern frontier and to ensure that they lost neither their martial traditions nor their loyalty to the Trust. Oglethorpe also understood that a clan leader like Mohr Mackintosh could get more work out of the Highlanders than could any Englishman. To the Highlanders, cattle grazing and timber were less labor-intensive and time-consuming than crop cultivation on infertile and sandy soil, and as the tensions became more acute between British Georgia and Spanish Florida, the Highlanders would be called upon to perform as planned. Their raison d'être was to be frontier soldiers.

While the people of Darien were busy making a home for themselves on the frontier, the Spanish at St. Augustine had taken particular notice of the

Scots' arrival in Georgia and their encroachment upon land claimed by
Spain. From the first, Oglethorpe was keenly aware of possible reaction by
the Spaniards to the presence of a new settlement on the southern border,
and he immediately emphasized defense of the colony. After leaving the
Highland settlement on his first trip, he encamped on Cumberland Island,
so named by Tomochichi's nephew Toonahowi in gratitude to the Duke of
Cumberland, William Augustus, for a gold watch he had given the Indian
prince during a visit to London in 1734.[42] Little did anyone know the revul-
sion that many of the Scots would come to feel at the name of Cumberland
after the events on Culloden Moor in Scotland on 16 April 1746, when the
Jacobite hopes of a Stuart restoration were finally crushed and many relatives of the Georgia settlers were slaughtered. The Spanish called the island
San Pedro; the Scots would rename it "The Highlands."[43]

On the extreme western point of the island, which commands the passage
of boats from the south, Oglethorpe marked out a fort to be called St. Andrews and ordered Captain Hugh Mackay to build it.[44] Mackay had with him
thirty Highlanders, ten other men, a party of the Independent Company under the command of an ensign also named Hugh Mackay, a group of Indians,
tools for entrenching, and provisions. Oglethorpe left Cumberland Island
and continued down the coast to Amelia Island, named in memory of Prin-
cess Amelia of Great Britain. While Oglethorpe was gone from Cumberland,
Captain Mackay went to work on Fort St. Andrews. By the time Oglethorpe
returned on 25 March 1736, he was astonished at the progress of the
fortifications. The ditch had been dug, the parapet raised with wood and
earth on the landward side, and the brush cleared for fifty yards around the
fort. This was an extraordinary feat in that Mackay had no engineer with
him, nor any other such assistance except the directions originally given by
Oglethorpe.[45]

It was difficult to raise the works at St. Andrews because of the sandy soil,
so Mackay used the same method to support the ramparts as "Caesar mentions in the *Wars of Gaul*."[46] Mackay's men laid trees and earth alternately—
the trees prevented the sand from falling and the sand kept the wood from
possible fire. Oglethorpe was impressed, gave his thanks to the Highlanders,
and offered to take them back to Darien. In true Highland spirit, they replied that "whilst there was Danger" from the Spaniards "they desired Leave
to stay," though they should lose their next harvest. Only two of them, having
families in Darien, were ordered by Oglethorpe to go back with him.[47]

The Spanish, by June 1736, had begun to probe the defenses of the new
settlements in Georgia, keeping the settlers in a constant state of alarm. On

8 June a large boat filled with men and four pieces of cannon attempted to come into Jekyl Sound, about twenty miles south of Darien, without flying her colors. After being challenged by the guard on shore and seeing the British man-of-war *Hawk* anchored in the harbor, the boat ran out to sea, around Jekyl Sound, and southward into Cumberland Sound by Fort St. Andrews. When discovered and challenged by the Scots at the fort, the Spaniards "row'd away with the utmost precipitation"[48] and in "such haste that the same night they reached the Spanish out-guards on Saint John's River, near 60 miles distant."[49] On board the boat was Don Ignatio Cob with a detachment of the Spanish garrison and as many Indians as the launch could hold. When Cob arrived back in Spanish territory he had a conference with the commander of the Spanish horse guard, Don Pedro de Lamberto, who had come up by land with one hundred foot soldiers and fifty horses.[50]

Elsewhere, Oglethorpe and a contingent of Highland soldiers, under a flag of truce, were trying to meet the Spaniards at their outpost on the St. John's River. Apparently the guards had fled, leaving only their two horses "tied with hobbles among the sand-hills."[51] A young Scot named Frazer was sent forward to search the woods. In a short while the lad returned "driving before him a tall man with a musket upon his shoulder, two pistols stuck in his girdle and a long sword, and a short sword." Coming up to Oglethorpe, Frazer said, "Here, Sir, I have caught a Spaniard for you."[52] It turned out that the man was a messenger who had smuggled a letter out of St. Augustine from two Englishmen being held by the Spanish governor.

Meanwhile correspondence was going on between Oglethorpe and the Spanish governor of St. Augustine about the borders between the two provinces and the activities of the British-allied Indians attacking the Spanish. During the exchanges Oglethorpe was building more fortifications, moving troops in from Carolina, and arming patrol boats to cruise the inland passages between the inlets to stop possible infiltration by the Spanish and their allied Indians, while also preventing friendly Indians from crossing into Spanish territory.[53]

To complete his defense plans, Oglethorpe again turned to Darien to supply the needed soldiers for the frontier forts. Not only was Fort St. Andrews garrisoned by Darien's Highlanders but so was Fort St. George, sixty miles south of the Georgia land grant, on the St. John's River and across from the northernmost Spanish outpost.[54] This fort, built on the ruins of one constructed by Sir Francis Drake 150 years before,[55] was manned by sixty Scots who "desired that Post of Honor as most exposed to the Spaniards."[56] It would appear that the young men Captain George Dunbar recruited from

Scotland, who had signed on for the adventure of facing the Spanish and "would be disappointed on the Safe Side," were granted their wish.[57]

Oglethorpe had heard that the Spanish intended to regain the land that was Georgia up to the Edisto River in South Carolina. He was determined not give up a foot of ground that he believed belonged to Britain and vowed: "I will alive or dead keep possession of it 'till I have His Majesty's orders."[58] Knowing that Don Ignatio Cob and Don Pedro de Lamberto were approaching, Oglethorpe employed deceptive stratagems to make the Spanish believe "we were numerous" and more heavily fortified than they actually were. He had campfires lit along the coast at night to give the appearance of large numbers of troops encamped, and he had small cannons fire from the various forts in rapid succession when Spanish boats were in the area.[59] His ploy worked; the Spanish retreated to St. Augustine and determined that negotiation might be a better strategy to pursue.

The Spanish sent a delegation under a flag of truce to meet with Oglethorpe. The group consisted of Don Pedro de Lamberto, the English prisoner Charles Dempsey, and Don Manuel, secretary to the Spanish governor and adjutant of the garrison.[60] When Oglethorpe was advised of the approaching launch, he sent Ensign Hugh Mackay up to Darien to bring back "some of the genteelest Highlanders to be present at the conference."[61] On 19 June 1736, Oglethorpe welcomed the Spanish delegation aboard the British man-of-war *Hawk* with a detachment of the Independent Company in their regimentals lined up along one side of the ship, with bayonets fixed, and the Highlanders dressed in their plaids with "their targets and Broadswords drawn" lining the other.[62] The British commander intended to make the Scots' presence known.

Oglethorpe wanted to make an impression on the Spaniards of his military presence in the area, and he did. After dinner, toasts were offered to the health of the king of Great Britain and the king of Spain under the discharge of cannons from the ship. The salutes were answered by the batteries from the surrounding forts, as Oglethorpe had ordered. The Spaniards were duly impressed and surprised that there were so many forts within hearing distance of one another. At this Don Pedro smiled and said, "No wonder Don Ignatio made more haste home than out," referring to the hasty retreat eight days before.[63] The conference ended with the two parties agreeing to allow their governments in Europe to decide the boundaries between their respective countries.[64] However, Oglethorpe was determined to hold onto as much of the region for Britain as he could and he was confident that, as the saying goes, possession was nine-tenths of the law. In that supposition he was wrong.

After much haggling and many attempts to prove sovereignty over the debatable land, now south of the Altamaha, a treaty was concluded on 18 October 1736 in St. Augustine.[65] The Spanish were willing to concede the land within the Georgia grant, although they maintained the "ancient right of the Spanish King over the lands which Mr. Oglethorpe had peopled and fortified, he alleging they belong to the King of Great Britain."[66] Both sides were to restrain their people from further hostilities, and Fort St. George was to be "depeopled within fourteen days, the fort destroyed, the garrison withdrawn, and no further settlement to be made there by either side, without prejudice to Spanish claim to that territory."[67] This island was to be a no-man's-land or buffer zone between the two provinces, except that the agreement stipulated that Spanish ships putting into the island because of bad weather "should not constitute a breach of this treaty." Also, travel between Georgia and Florida was to be limited to individuals with permits from their own governments.[68] This respite would allow the people of Darien to return to the task of building their settlement; however, Oglethorpe kept the colony in a constant state of military preparedness. By the end of February 1737, the Trustees were advised that the Darien people had "entrenched themselves and are determined to defend themselves to the last extremity and not to quit their lands but with their lives."[69] This was exactly the attitude the Trustees had envisioned from the Highlanders when they were targeted for recruitment.

This drain of manpower from Darien began to take its toll on the settlement. More men were needed, and Oglethorpe was prevailed upon to allow Archibald MacBean, one of the Highland settlers, to return to Scotland and recruit forty more Highlanders for the Trust along with several indentured servants for individuals in Darien.[70] On 11 December 1736, MacBean was in London giving a report to the Earl of Egmont on the conditions in Georgia before he continued his journey to Scotland. He also made a present of a Georgia bear to the earl, which the earl declined, advising him to give it to the Trustees for display at the Georgia office.[71] MacBean wrote to Oglethorpe on 8 January 1737 informing him of the recruiting plans in Scotland:

I have a mind to let you know what passengers I can get at Inverness, all out of that shire and the next: the complement as I shall promise will be 100 people, 20 of them will be freeholders, 10 of them without families, and 20 young women, none of them whores nor transporters but to be indented servants, the rest the same. All this I will do and ship them aboard in a month's time. . . . I desire to get to Georgia as soon as possible. My cousin, Laughlin MacBean, will pay for twelve passengers.[72]

MacBean was not the only one in Scotland wanting to recruit emigrants for the Georgia colony. On 26 February the Trustees for Georgia received a letter from Daniel McLachlan, proposing to take a number of clansmen from the Highlands to the province. He promised that he would "carry over in two years enough men to more than double the present strength of Georgia without any expense other than proper utensils and first year's maintenance."[73] His reasoning to the Trustees for his proposal was that "this project would help civilize the Highland Clans, strengthen Georgia, and bring relief to people in a miserable starving condition."[74] He further declared that

> I desire no premium other than my expenses. If I cannot prevail upon all the clans at first I am sure to prevail upon our own and decoy the rest into happiness and plenty. The first detachment could be embarked about 1 August next. Our people are used to hardships: what they reckon comforts are very simple. If this project is kindly received I shall immediately apply myself to the prosecution thereof.[75]

McLachlan had applied to the Trust for sending Highlanders to Georgia once before. In May 1735, he had approached the Trustees but had been rejected because of a pamphlet he wrote entitled *An Essay upon Improving and Adding to the Strength of Great Britain and Ireland by Fornication.*[76] In retrospect, McLachlan called it "a ludicrous piece of humor upon fornication."[77] The Earl of Egmont had not forgotten the incident and declared, "I would not give my consent, he being the minister whose gown was stripped off his back for writing last year a pamphlet to justify that whoring is no sin."[78] "Besides," Egmont wrote in his diary, "we found that he expected those Scots should have a year's maintenance from our stores, which was not granted to persons who go over on their own account."[79]

McLachlan was not easily dissuaded. He appeared again on 6 April 1737 at the Trust office with a new proposal to carry over to Georgia "100 Scots at his own expense."[80] In a letter to James Oglethorpe, McLachlan wrote,

> To satisfy the Trustees that I have not amused them with any idle scheme I am resolved to settle these 100 men in Georgia who are in a capacity to transport and maintain themselves without being obliged to the Trustees for anything else than land. I beg no favor beyond approbation. I know that when the Trustees are satisfied they will reward me. If they take no notice of this proposal we shall settle in Carolina or some other part of America than Georgia. These people will set out by 1 August and wherever they plant themselves the rest of the clans will follow.[81]

Egmont again shunned the idea; but Oglethorpe, being present at the meeting, "was fond of accepting the proposal merely for strengthening the Colony."[82] Oglethorpe knew that these Scots were determined to leave the Highlands and that they might be persuaded to go to Georgia as readily as anywhere else. He argued that if they discouraged the Scots from going, they "should be in want of people to defend the Province and the reason for discouraging them would not be known."[83] It was decided to invite McLachlan to appear before the board and give account of himself. It was quite evident that Egmont did not like McLachlan and raised as many objections as he could. However, the rest of the board sided with Oglethorpe and stipulated that if McLachlan could settle his ecclesiastical problems, then the Trustees would consider his proposal. "So," notes Egmont in his diary, "we got rid of him for this time."[84]

While McLachlan was in London trying to persuade the Trustees of his sincerity, his clansman Lachlan McLachlan together with Donald Cameron sent a letter of inquiry to the Trustees "in the name and by the direction of several considerable families in the Highlands of Scotland who by the good encouragement their countrymen meet with in Georgia are inclinable to be of the number."[85] This group wanted to know in writing "what encouragements each particular rank of men may depend upon" and indicated that if they liked what they saw, they were "not only considerable but pretty numerous that are entered into an association to go."[86] Apparently news from Georgia had sounded good to the people back in Scotland. The letter was read before the Common Council of Georgia on 29 April 1737 and the Trustees resolved to send the terms "which the Trustees have settled for people going to Georgia at their own expense."[87]

At the 11 May 1737 meeting, Daniel McLachlan's proposal for sending over "100 Highlanders of the Cameron Clan at their own expense" was back before the council and this time it had the endorsement of his clansmen. It was passed with the agreement of an allowance of a one-time gift of twenty bolls or bushels of Indian meal and a musket and bayonet to each man.[88] Egmont was not happy with the arrangement because, he wrote, "the truth is we like not the fellow [Daniel McLachlan]"; however, he accepted it because "the proposal did not seem unreasonable."[89] It is more likely that Oglethorpe pushed through the proposal to answer the pressing need for soldiers in Georgia to face the increasing Spanish pressure, and he particularly liked Highlanders.

While McLachlan was busy recruiting among Clan Cameron, Archibald

MacBean had arrived in the Highlands to begin his work. He wrote to Harman Verelst from Inverness, on 26 March 1737, "I have begun to recruit Servants for the Trustees."[90] He also had the support and encouragement of John Hossack, provost of Inverness, in his endeavors.[91] The previous day Hossack had written to Verelst, stating that "gratitude had engaged all this country to express their regard to Mr. Oglethorpe for the noted favors he was pleased to do their friends" and that he would afford the "necessary credit to MacBean."[92] The Trust was in no doubt about the success of this venture in the Highlands.

On 18 April 1737 the Common Council contracted with the owners of the ship *Two Brothers,* Captain William Thomson master, to go to Inverness to take on board "40 men for Georgia at £5 per head."[93] As meticulous as always, the Trustees allowed 20 shillings per head for clothing and bedding.[94] Captain Thomson was to wait fourteen days at Inverness for the reception of the forty men. If they did not arrive within the set time, the ship was free to sail with the number of emigrants that were on board. Additionally, Thomson was ordered to deliver to Georgia on the same shipment "15 barrels of gunpowder for smallarms . . . 100 muskets and bayonets, 200 Indian arms, 3 cwt. of musket bullets, 3 cwt. of Indian gun bullets, 6 cwt. of lead, one pair of bullet moulds of 9 holes each for the musket bore, and two iron ladles."[95] The Trust was also careful to order "300 pairs of shoes made at four shillings per pair according to the pattern John Cox made . . . ordered 13 August 1735."[96]

Harman Verelst followed up the orders to Captain Thomson by sending John Hossack a letter on 23 April, informing him of the arrangements of the *Two Brothers* and requesting him to hire Archibald MacBean to secure the forty men.[97] The indentures were fairly standard. Persons of twenty years and upward were to serve four years and those under twenty were to be bound until the age of twenty-four. Hossack was to secure the indentures with the proper endorsements and signatures and send them to Thomas Causton in Georgia. He was also to make a list of the names and ages of each emigrant and forward it to the Trust.[98] The last instructions for Mr. Hossack were to "buy . . . for the Highlanders . . . 300 yards of Tartan at 12d sterling a yard for short Coats & short Hose & 1200 yards of Tartan at 14d sterling a yard for Plaids . . . [and] 12 Spinning Wheels with some Wool & Hemp or Flax for the Women to be employed in."[99]

With recruitment by both MacBean and McLachlan well under way in the Highlands, Verelst sent word to Thomas Causton in Georgia about the incoming Scots:

Capt. Thomson Sailed with the Ship *Two Brothers* on Saturday last for Inverness in Scotland to imbark 40 Men Servants which Mr. Hossack was wrote to engage for the Trustees. . . . These Servants are to be sent to Lieut. Moore Mackintosh at the Darien with a List of them,[100] and You are to Acquaint him that he is to offer to each Freeholder of the Darien that was there when Mr. Oglethorpe left the Place (beginning by the oldest) to take one of the said Servants and give Security by Bond for Repaying to the Trustees or their Order in Georgia the Sum of £8 Sterling in twelve months from that time. . . . the remaining Number of Servants sent by the Trustees Lieut. Moore Mackintosh is to Set to work in Sawing and Cutting up Timber on any ungranted Lands near the Darien for the use of the Publick. . . . You are to end up Provision to supply those remaining Servants with four pounds of Meat a Week each, a bushel of Corn and two pounds and a half of Butter a month each, and seven pounds of Cheese a Quarter each.[101]

While the Trust made preparations for the transport and settling of the new Scottish recruits, MacBean was facing unexpected difficulty. He wrote to Verelst from Inverness on 21 May 1737, complaining that negative newspaper reports prompted by Captain Hugh Mackay in Georgia "very much hurt the undertaking."[102] It is not known what Mackay's charges involved, but upon the arrival of the *Two Brothers* in Georgia on 16 November 1737, the new secretary for the Trust in Georgia, William Stephens, recorded in his journal:

> I learnt that Capt. Hugh Mackay had been very industrious in the Highlands to make bad impressions on the Minds of the people there, with relations to this Colony: a great deal Capt. Thompson complained of, and gave many instances; but from James Anderson (a carpenter) I got more Particulars, especially by a Letter which he shewed me he had received from one of the Magistrates of Inverness (Baylie Avis) who was his Friend and Kinsman, wherein I read abundance of malicious and false Reports, Spread by him to the Discredit of the Trust, and the great Discouragement of many who were otherwise well disposed to come over, and seek a livelihood here.[103]

However, at the time of MacBean's recruitment efforts, Hugh Mackay had the confidence of the Trustees. They responded to MacBean's charges in a letter to John Hossack by writing that "MacBean is very much to blame to take upon him to call Persons Names, & reflect upon Persons Capt. Mackay carried over with him. . . . You are desired to rebuke him for such Behavior, the Trustees having had no Complaints of any of those Persons Capt. Mackay took over with him, and they have been very pleased with his Services in

Georgia."[104] Although the letter rebuked MacBean, the matter was to come before the Trustees at their next meeting.[105]

MacBean was clearly having problems. It seems that Mackay's stories had caused a few of the new recruits to have second thoughts about going to Georgia. Near the end of May MacBean reported to Verelst that a few of the recruits had begun to mutiny and challenge the guards; he could not promise how long he could retain them.[106] In June Hossack confirmed MacBean's recruiting troubles to the Trustees. He praised MacBean, telling the Trust that "we could not propose a fitter person to recruit servants than MacBean: it is a very fatiguing task, some of them making their escape and others carried off by their friends who will not allow them to go abroad."[107]

Hossack's letter also sheds a little light on the controversy between Hugh Mackay and Archibald MacBean: "The reports which Lieut. Hugh Mackay gave of the colony has created some jealousies among the commons though it did not ascend higher. In the character which MacBean gave we think he [Mackay] meant to distinguish between his [Mackay's] and Captain Dunbar's recruits."[108] This explanation suggests that there may have been a power struggle or, at the least, some clan rivalry among the initial emigrants to Georgia. John Mohr Mackintosh was clearly in charge of the affairs in Darien and was given control of the militia in the settlement, while Mackay had a subordinate role in the running of Darien.[109]

Captain William Thomson, aboard the *Two Brothers,* arrived in Inverness on 21 June 1737, after a "tedious passage and bad weather."[110] Twenty of the menservants for the Trust came aboard on the 24 June and seventeen more were expected the next week; MacBean had gone to the country to retrieve them. Their efforts were being helped by several gentlemen who were trying to secure servants requested by their friends in Georgia, which Thomson hoped would facilitate their departure from Scotland.[111] He had found it "more expensive and troublesome to get servants here than he had imagined."[112]

Apparently MacBean was able to calm the fears of the contentious passengers. By 9 July, MacBean was in good spirits and again optimistic in his work. He confidently reported that "I have got now on board for the Trustees 33 servants and ashore 10 more. Besides I run a good chance next week in the two principal fairs that stand in this [Inverness] and another place four miles distance from it to make several servants and if possible a piper or two."[113] Hossack advised Harman Verelst on 15 July that Captain Thomson had lost no time in "raising his ship's deck and preparing conveniences for his passengers, how many there shall be cannot yet be concluded.

The friends of John Mackintosh of Leniwilg [Lynvilge] upon the river Altamaha are advised that he is much distressed by the death of the servants he carried over and his inability to purchase any in Georgia. They have therefore provided two or three to be sent him but doubt they can useful to him if he must pay for their passage."[114] He asked that Mackintosh's situation be referred to Oglethorpe and the Trustees for directions. The Trustees responded by allowing one servant to be transported to Georgia for Mackintosh of Lynvilge at their expense, "in lieu of a Servant he lost in the Trustees Service."[115]

The *Two Brothers* set sail from Inverness sometime in July and arrived on the coast of Georgia on Sunday, 13 November 1737.[116] Aboard the ship no less than twenty-six different clan names were represented among the passengers.[117] Hardship awaited them and Darien was in need of their arrival.

CHAPTER 5

War Comes to Darien: The Battle at Fort Mosa

With Lawless Force, and yet pretended Right,
They [Spain] search'd, seiz'd, plunder'd, and condemn'd at Sight:
The wretched TRADER's, doom'd to endless Fears
Of plunder'd Treasure, and the Loss of Ears.
    —Britannicus [Samuel Martin of Antigua?], "A Letter from Don Thomas
    Geraldino, in Answer to Don Blas de Lezo's, at Cathagene. Faithfully
    translated by Britannicus"

THE BEGINNING OF 1737 brought renewed fears of impending danger to the colony of Georgia and to the settlement of Darien. In February, reliable reports of Spanish preparations in St. Augustine "to invade and unsettle the colony of Georgia" were sent to Savannah from Lieutenant-Governor Thomas Broughton of South Carolina.[1] Additional information about the military buildup of the Spanish invasion forces from Cuba came to light when Governor Richard Fitzwilliam of New Providence, Bahama Islands, sent a letter, along with several dispositions from English seamen who were prisoners in Cuba, to the Duke of Newcastle.[2] The Spanish laid in "quantities of Corn and Provision" and additional firearms, and numbers of regular troops from Havana were sent to St. Augustine.[3] The proposed attack was to be led by John Savy, a former Indian trader from South Carolina who "styles himself Col. Wall," now in the service of the king of Spain.[4] The invasion was set for March.[5]

The colony of Georgia immediately busied itself in preparation for war. Efforts were made to ensure that the Indians in Georgia remained faithful allies, and the various settlements set about shoring up their fortifications. In a letter to Thomas Causton on 23 March 1737, Harman Verelst impressed upon the people in the province that "defense is the business of the inhabitants of Georgia."[6] This advice, along with the frequent alarms from other sources, according to Benjamin Martyn, "drew the People off from their Labor in the Sowing-Season, . . . and they were obliged to make Preparations for their Defense."[7]

The Highlanders at Darien built a fort and mounted twelve pieces of cannon.[8] Darien's inhabitants were determined to defend themselves while attempting to maintain some air of normality. Crops were planted and a sawing operation set up. The Scots were making the most of the poor soil around them.[9] However, Mohr Mackintosh was also vigilant in his duties as military leader. In a letter to Harman Verelst dated 15 November 1737, Mackintosh averred that "arms and ammunition are the soul of any place that wants to defend itself as we do" and requested more munitions along with a gunsmith for the settlement.[10]

The threatened Spanish invasion of Georgia never materialized in March and things were relatively quiet for Darien until the end of April, when the Spanish began forays into Georgia testing the defenses of the colony. Captain James Gascoigne, commander of the sloop *Hawk*, informed Oglethorpe that thirty Spaniards on board a launch had come to Amelia Island and had landed sixteen of their number. They were discovered and fired upon by the Highlanders garrisoned on the island. The Spanish immediately retreated to their boat.[11] Shortly after the incident, shots were fired at the outguards at Darien.[12] William Horton reported that "everyone of Mr. Mackintosh's people were within the fort at the time the sentries affirm they saw seven men, four of whom went under the cover of bushes one way and three another."[13] The Highlanders within the fort returned fire and one of the Scots told Horton that he thought he had wounded one of the intruders. They could not tell whether the snipers were white, Indian, or a combination of the two.[14] These encroachments kept the Scots in a constant state of alarm.

The Earl of Egmont, although hearing good reports of the progress of Darien, predicted that taking men from their farms to make soldiers of them would be damaging to the settlement.[15] Apparently he feared that the pressures of continual military preparedness combined with limited provisions could cause a civil revolt among the settlers, and that is exactly what happened. After a good harvest in the early spring of 1737, the weather turned so dry "as to burn up all that has been planted."[16] To add to the settlers' woes, as Mohr Mackintosh complained, "our being confined in such a small place as our fort brought a great number of rats and mice which have destroyed some corn."[17]

Supplies ran so low in the fall of 1737 that the people of Darien went en masse, with John Mohr Mackintosh leading them, to see Major William Horton, the Trustees' agent at Frederica, to demand relief. If he did not furnish the needed supplies, the Darien people threatened, they would go to Savannah and break open the Trustees' store there. Major Horton, although unable to supply them from Frederica, sent them to the *Hawk* and Captain Gascoigne, who was able to spare them stores from his ship.[18] This support pacified the Highlanders, and Mohr Mackintosh commended Horton for "sending us what he can spare us, and in a word doing everything to keep up good harmony between us and the other settlements."[19]

When William Stephens, the Trust's new secretary for the colony of Georgia, inspected Darien in February 1738, he was impressed by the "orderly behavior" of the Scots and their "real Diligence in Improvements; Having laid open a good tract of Land, . . . all of which they purposed to cultivate and plant this Season."[20] This comment by Stephens again dispels the notion of laziness and the aversion to farming attributed to the Highland Scots. The prospects for Darien were looking promising for 1738. The new servants that Archibald MacBean had recruited in the Highlands arrived in Darien and were put to work in the fields and as sawyers.[21] Mohr Mackintosh knew that the newly cleared land could produce crops and reported to Stephens that "the people [of Darien] were diligent and well content and that divers of them had 20 bushels of corn upon an acre in return for their labor."[22] These Scots knew how to get the most from poor soil from their past experience with the meager crops in the Highlands of Scotland. Stephens told the Trustees that the information was a "great encouragement especially when the crops of corn have so universally almost failed in all the neighboring provinces."[23]

By April 1738, Darien seemed to be settled and in good spirits. Despite renewed threats of Spanish intrigue, John Mohr Mackintosh could announce to the Trustees that the settlement "wants neither for provisions nor ammunition."[24] The enthusiasm for the Darien settlement was echoed in Stephens's report to the Trustees on 27 May (and noted in the Earl of Egmont's private journal), in which Stephens wrote that "the two settlements of Ebenezer and Darien ought indeed to take place of all others in the list of deserts, for they seem already to be near out of leading strings and want but little to stand alone."[25] However, the euphoric atmosphere was to be short-lived.

In June, personal tragedy struck Mohr Mackintosh and his family. Two of his young sons were swimming in the Altamaha River when they were attacked by an alligator. According to a report by William Stephens, one son escaped but the other, Lewis, was "snapt . . . and carried . . . quite off."[26] This was a terrible reminder of how dangerous frontier life in Georgia could be to the settlers from the Highlands. This incident was the first in a series of disasters for the settlement. The spring rains did not come and the seed for the corn crop was bad. Writing to the Trustees in July, Stephens lamented that the long continued drought should "teach us to think it well if we can secure half that abundance in a crop which we had eagerly conceived."[27] He went on to report that Frederica had lost their entire crop and Darien, "where we had expectations of plenty," was also "defeated."[28] William Horton in Frederica echoed Stephens's account by relating that "the crops of corn at both places [Frederica and Darien] are very bad, the seed was far from being good, and the season proving very dry it is generally parched up."[29]

The situation at Darien had changed drastically from the hopes and expectations of April to the desperate conditions in August. It was clear by the end of summer in 1738 that Darien's prosperity had rested on the fragile promise of cultivation, and the optimistic talk of self-sufficiency was replaced by universal defection. Other problems surfaced in Darien, perhaps for the first time. Many of the settlers complained of unfair and harsh treatment at the hands of Captain Hugh Mackay and John Mohr Mackintosh. One of the Scots, Alexander Monroe, was arrested for failing to sing out the words "all is well" while on guard duty. He claimed that he had a valid reason: all was not well—Indians had fired at the sentry on duty when he called out the night before.[30] The freeholders of Darien applied to General Oglethorpe for a court of justice to be established in Darien as in other towns; they received no response.[31]

Frustrated at the failure of their labors, the growing debts for supplies and servants, and the apparent brutal martial rule in Darien from both Mackay and Mohr Mackintosh, the freeholders, under the leadership of Benjamin Mackintosh, decided to send two of their number to Charles-Town to apply for a grant of land in Carolina. If accepted, the entire settlement, except John Mohr Mackintosh, would move to Carolina. The disaffected group decided to make Mohr Mackintosh and James Oglethorpe aware of their intentions and their reasoning before they sent the two men to Carolina. They asked John Mackintosh Lynvilge to make their case for them.[32] The Highlanders sought relief from the hardships of land tenure, the poverty of the soil, the absence of a market for their timber and cattle, and a lack of credit for support.[33] They wanted a public store set up for them in Darien.[34]

Apparently Mackintosh Lynvilge was convincing in his arguments because he returned with an answer from Oglethorpe, through Mohr Mackintosh, that they "should have credit for provisions, with two cows and their calves, and a breeding mare, if they would continue on their plantations."[35] This satisfied the Scots and "with a view of these Helps, and hoping for the further Favor and Countenance of the said Colonel [Oglethorpe] . . . [they] were willing to make another tryal."[36] Oglethorpe was no fool. He knew the value and importance of keeping his frontline soldiers satisfied to the best of his ability. He did not want to lose the Highlanders and he was willing to negotiate with them to keep them in Georgia.

William Stephens was surprised at the dissatisfaction of the Highlanders at Darien. To Stephens, these people had lived quietly, "not showing any discontent . . . intent upon cultivating their land."[37] Now they were making demands of Oglethorpe. The Highlanders wanted a public store set up for them and "to be allowed to make payments in lumber sawn, or in shingles, pipe staves and the like."[38] Stephens complained that if this were allowed, it would "unquestionably put an end to all the planting at once."[39] The secretary of Georgia was not ready to blame the Highlanders in Darien for this seeming betrayal of the interests in Georgia. He laid the responsibility squarely at feet of some disgruntled Lowland Scots in Savannah, whom he called "Malcontents."[40]

Oglethorpe was able to take advantage of the Darien demands. The Savannah settlers, under the leadership of these discontented Lowland Scots, had filed a petition of demands of their own. These malcontents were wanting to change the land inheritance laws and they wanted the use of "Negroes" in the colony.[41] These demands struck at the heart of the Trustees' plans for Georgia. The land restrictions and the prohibition of slaves were to secure the idea of Georgia as a colony of yeoman farmers and would remove the possibility of large-scale, idle landowners depending on the labor of others. The system was also designed to enhance the military defense of the Georgia colony by providing farmer-soldiers willing to protect their families and homes.

If the Highlanders at Darien would sign a counterpetition, Oglethorpe would see that they got their store, cattle, and a loan of money; at least, such was the charge made by several malcontents against Oglethorpe, and although the Earl of Egmont denied it, the evidence seems to support the charge.[42] Additionally, one of the malcontents, Alexander Monroe, claimed heavy-handed dealing by John Mohr Mackintosh to force support for the counterpetition. He complained later that he was threatened into signing the petition by being told that "if he did not, he would be ruined forever."[43]

Captain George Dunbar is identified as the author of the stirring statement to the Trustees, signed by eighteen of the leading Darien Highlanders, refuting the Savannah Petition.[44] All of the eighteen signers were men who had come to Georgia at their own expense except Hugh Morrison, a Trust servant and member of the Highland Independent Company. He immigrated on the Trust's account. The rest of the men were farmers—that is, gentlemen of the clans—except Ranald McDonald, John Mohr Mackintosh's servant.

In addition to indicating the immediate dangers to Georgia of Spanish-inspired insurrection among any slaves introduced into the colony, this document is of interest as one of the first antislavery petitions in American history, and in its text is found a portent of the coming horrors of the Civil War, 1861–65:

> It is shocking to human nature, that any Race of Mankind and their Posterity should be sentenc'd to perpetual Slavery; nor in Justice can we think otherwise of it, than that they are thrown amongst us to be our Scourge one Day or other for our Sins: And as Freedom must be as dear to them as to us, *What a Scene of Horror must it bring about!* and the longer it is unexecuted, the bloody scene must be the greater [emphasis mine; full text in appendix C].[45]

The Salzburgers at Ebenezer signed a similar appeal opposing the Savannah Petition and the introduction of slavery into Georgia.[46] The Trustees rejected the Savannah Petition, citing the Darien and Ebenezer settlers' opposition to it as an important part of their rationale, and slavery remained banned from Georgia until 1749.[47]

Oglethorpe kept his part of the bargain to the Scots; Darien got its store and a loan of £200 to buy cattle. This move by Oglethorpe changed the structure of Darien society as it moved from being agrarian based to becoming commercially dependent on the cattle and timber trade. The timber business was already in place and doing well. Oglethorpe argued that "by mere cultivating their lands, though they were very industrious, they [the Highlanders of Darien] would not be able to pay the debts already due to the Trust and clothe themselves, but that they understand taking care of cattle, which business they chiefly pursued in Scotland, and that it would be very beneficial to this province to have cattle slaughtered at Darrein for furnishing the Regiment and the men of war with fresh meat."[48]

It would seem that Oglethorpe's efforts to strengthen and, in essence, to underwrite the economy of Darien should have allayed the discontent there. They did not. New charges of arbitrary rule and of mismanagement in the

Trust store in Darien surfaced against Mohr Mackintosh. Claims were lodged with the Trust that he supplied the populace with bad corn and rotted cheese while he and his family enjoyed the best of the provisions; and that many of the Trust's servants, under Mohr Mackintosh's directions, were employed to build several buildings in Darien while receiving no pay.[49] Although the claims were rejected by the Trust, in September 1739, the inhabitants of Darien once again prepared to leave Georgia.[50] It was reported that they had sent a delegation to New York to see "if they could have lands in that province."[51] This time, however, war intruded on the Highlanders' plans.

The tensions that had been brewing beneath the surface of correspondence and feigned civility between the British and the Spanish finally boiled over. The settlement of Georgia and Oglethorpe's continued expansion south of the Altamaha River were reason enough to Spain for war. By the summer of 1739, the Spanish had already begun incursions into the lower Indian country in attempts to sway the Creeks away from their alliance with the British. Oglethorpe reported to the Earl of Egmont that Spanish priests were making inroads and finding some success.[52] Enough to encourage Oglethorpe's allies to invite him to a meeting of the Creek Nation in July in Coweta Town, five hundred miles west-northwest from Frederica, to decide whether they "will renew their assurances of fidelity to the King [George II] or go into the Spanish Interests."[53] His friends among the Creeks were confident that Oglethorpe's presence at that meeting would ensure their loyalty to the British.[54]

Oglethorpe notified Harman Verelst that the Indian chief Tomochichi advised him to go, informing Verelst that in addition to the Creek Nation, the Choctaws and Chickasaws would be represented, "so that 7000 men depend upon the event of this assembly. The Creeks can furnish 1500 warriors, the Chickasaws 500 and the Choctaws 500."[55] It was certainly in the interest of Georgia for these Indians to remain faithful because it was better to have them as allies than as enemies. On 8 July 1739, Oglethorpe left Frederica with an expedition composed of about twenty-five men, almost exclusively Highlanders and most from Darien, along with a number of Indians who served as hunters and guides.[56]

By 27 July, Oglethorpe's party had reached and crossed the Ogeechee River. The next day they continued westward, with the Indians supplying them with "plenty of deer and turkeys for our refreshment also several buffaloes," and passed into hillier country.[57] On the last day of July, from the top of one of the hills, Oglethorpe's men saw a column of smoke in the distance, which turned out to come from a party of Spanish horsemen. This was the proof Oglethorpe needed of the Spanish presence in the region. By the end of the first week of August, the party was near Coweta Town and found "Cakes and Bags of Flower" hung in the trees by the Indians to feed their British guests.[58]

The next night Oglethorpe's company camped near the Indian town and were presented a feast of venison, watermelons, potatoes, squashes, and fowls. In the morning Oglethorpe was escorted, with ceremony, into Coweta to meet the king, who held a British flag as a sign of friendship.[59] After an evening banquet, several days of talks continued until 21 August, when the Indians reaffirmed their allegiance with the British and signed an agreement. Along with James Oglethorpe's name were the signatures of ten Highland Scots: Lieutenant George Dunbar, Adjutant Hugh Mackay, Æneas Mackintosh Esq. Brother to the Laird of Mackintosh, John Cuthbert of Draikes, Mr. Robert McPherson Brother to Thomas McPherson Esq. of Dobradie, Mr. John Mackintosh son of John Mackintosh of Holmes, Mr. James McQueen son of James McQueen of Corribrough, Mr. Kenneth Baillie son of John Baillie of Ballrobart, Mr. John Mackintosh, and Mr. George Cuthbert.[60] Although Oglethorpe confirmed the Indians' loyalty to the British, he did not gain their support for raids into Florida. Instead they promised neutrality.[61] With a sense of security for the west and southwest backcountry, he could now turn his attention to the south. He arrived back in Frederica on 8 November 1739, just five days before war broke out with Spain in Georgia.[62]

A relatively minor incident was the stimulus for a declaration of war by the British government. An English smuggler named Robert Jenkins was caught by the Spanish *guarda costas* for plying his trade in Spanish territory. The Spanish from St. Augustine and Havana had been boarding British ships and impressing seamen since the settlement of Georgia. To teach Jenkins a lesson and as a warning to other smugglers, the authorities punished him by cutting off his ear. Jenkins preserved the ear and, during testimony, displayed it before an outraged British Parliament. The War of Jenkins' Ear, as the conflict came to be called, was officially declared by Parliament on 23 October 1739.[63]

The war was a prelude to the War of the Austrian Succession and was fought primarily on the Georgia frontier. The active war with Spain in Georgia began with the killing of two unarmed Highlanders from Darien garrisoned on Amelia Island. Before dawn on 13 November 1739, about a dozen Spanish-allied Indians landed on Amelia and concealed themselves in the brush near the small fort. The two young Scots, John Mackay and Angus MacLeod, were ambushed in a hail of musket fire. One of the British scout boats heard the reports of firearms and rushed to the scene, only to find the two men's bodies beheaded and mutilated, with the enemy nowhere to be seen.[64] The response by Oglethorpe and the people of Georgia was immediate.

Every able-bodied man in Darien who was not already in the Highland Company of Foot or the Highland Rangers was called to arms in defense of the colony. John Mohr Mackintosh declared that the love of king and country compelled the Scots in Darien to enlist.[65] Oglethorpe was inspired at the prospect of finally going to war. He wrote to the Trustees, on 16 November 1739, that the "French have attacked the Carolina Indians and the Spaniards have invaded us. . . . We are resolved to die hard and will not lose one inch of ground without fighting."[66] He regretted the fact that the colony was under-supplied with weapons and stores, so the best expedient was to "strike first" and form a siege at St. Augustine.[67] Oglethorpe appealed to Carolina for troops and supplies.

South Carolina was open to Oglethorpe's request to join him in his attack on St. Augustine. The Carolinians had just suffered a slave rebellion on the Stono River. It was quickly put down, but they claimed it had been brought on by a Spanish proclamation in the spring of 1738. This document prom-ised that all slaves fleeing South Carolina or any other English colony would be granted freedom and would be given land and protection in Florida.[68] At first, the invitation had little effect; however, word spread among the slaves and the number of runaways increased. The number escaping to Florida was enough for the governor of St. Augustine to settle them in their own village at Fort Mosa.[69] It was here that the Darien Highlanders would fight the de-cisive battle of the St. Augustine Expedition of 1740.

Oglethorpe began marshaling his forces immediately. In addition to his request for troops and supplies from Carolina, he sent George Dunbar and Captain Æneas Mackintosh to Fort Augusta to enlist the aid of an indepen-dent band of Chickasaws, numbering less than thirty. These Indians lived separately from the rest of their tribe and were noted as being "daring and bold" warriors, "pickt men led by experienced Chiefs."[70] Oglethorpe es-teemed these men "more than equal to a hundred common men."[71] He also sent Thomas Eyre into Cherokee country to gain that nation's support. Eyre returned with the assurance of the chiefs that "all of their young men should come down to our assistance in two months."[72] With war declared, troops as-sembling, and hostilities started, Oglethorpe was anxious for action and de-clared that he was on his way to "annoy the Spaniards."[73]

By December 1739, Oglethorpe had already begun sallies into Spanish Florida. These initial incursions were intended to harass the Spanish and to gather information on the strength of the enemy forces. During their reconnaissance the British located several new Spanish fortifications. Besides the fort at St. Augustine, they found Fort San Francis de Pupo, Fort Picolata, Fort San Diego, Fort Rossa, Fort Chiketo, Fort Pinion, and "a new one of stone, called Moosa [Mosa], to protect the Plantations they had granted to runaway Negroes."[74] The blacks were armed and officered in order to garrison the fort. Oglethorpe reported that "on my first inroad, the Spaniards quitted Moosa and drew off the Negroes."[75]

On 7 January 1740 a detachment of Oglethorpe's regiment (the Forty-Second Foot, which arrived in Georgia mid-1739), the Highland Rangers, and a strong body of Chickasaw, Uchee, and Creek Indians launched an attack on the Spanish fort Picolata. By daybreak the fort was taken and burned. Two hours later the troops moved against Fort St. Francis de Pupo. The Indians and the Highland Rangers, commanded by Adjutant Hugh Mackay, led the attack, while the regular troops under the command of Captains Hugh Mackay and Albert Desbrisy, Lieutenant George Dunbar, and Ensigns Mackay, Sutherland, and Maxwell began their artillery barrage. The battle began at 10:00 A.M. and lasted the entire day. The fort was taken at sunset; the Spanish surrendered their munitions and the forces inside became prisoners of war.[76] After these first skirmishes, Oglethorpe returned to Frederica to plan his attack and siege of St. Augustine.

The British campaign was successful in the beginning against Florida; however, times were not going as well for the inhabitants left behind in Georgia. Most of Darien's men had been recruited to serve under John Mohr Mackintosh in the Highland Independent Company of Foot,[77] while the others served in the mounted Highland Rangers under Captain Hugh Mackay. They wore their colorful tartans and were armed with their traditional weapons—broadswords, dirks, muskets, and targets or targes—to go into battle,[78] but there were few men left behind in Darien to wear their work clothes into the fields to plant.

The Reverend George Whitefield, while traveling through the colony in 1740, commented that he had been to Frederica and Darien, as well as Savannah, and did not know which settlement was worse. Very few people in the colony, according to Whitefield, intended to plant any corn; further, while in Darien he "scarce saw a garden with any thing in it through the whole town."[79] He reported to the Earl of Egmont that the people of Darien were "dispirited."[80] The Reverend John MacLeod, minister of Darien, rejected Whitefield's proposal to build a church for the people because he said that it was "uncertain whether the people would continue there or not."[81] This fear would be compounded after the disastrous battle at Fort Mosa in Florida.

While Oglethorpe was planning the next expedition into Florida, an event occurred in the Highlands of Scotland that would have a direct effect on one of the Scots in his command. Captain Æneas Mackintosh, commander of Fort Palachicola, received word that William Mackintosh, his brother and "Chieftain of that Clan, was dead, or near dying; and Whom, as next Heir, he [Æneas] was to succeed in Title and Estate."[82] Captain Mackintosh, now the new chief of Clan Mackintosh and the powerful Clan Chattan, came to Savannah to clear his accounts and to inform Oglethorpe of his leaving. He was to return to Scotland at the "first opportunity."[83] Before leaving for Moy Hall in Inverness-shire to assume his place in Scotland, Mackintosh went back to Palachicola to "surrender the Command of that Fort to his Brother, whom the General had given the Commission to succeed him."[84] Æneas's younger brother John, a Palachicola ranger since at least 1737, was promoted to captain and assumed command of the garrison.[85]

In the first week of May, the British forces left Georgia on their campaign into Florida.[86] They captured and occupied Fort San Diego before moving to within six miles of St. Augustine.[87] On 9 June 1740, General Oglethorpe ordered a "flying force" composed of lightly armed men from several different units to march to Fort Mosa the next day. The troop of Highland Rangers, commanded by Captain Hugh Mackay, took ten men on the mission. The troop of English Rangers, under Lieutenant Robert Scroogs, numbered eight men. The troop of Carolina Rangers, recruited and paid by Oglethorpe, mustered nine men. Captain William Palmer, son of Colonel John Palmer, commanded the Carolina group. Captain John Mohr Mackintosh's Highland Independent Company of Foot brought fifty-seven men. Forty Indians, including Uchee, Yamacraw, and Creek, served under Thomas Jones. The contingent was rounded out with a sergeant and twelve privates from the red-coated Forty-Second Regiment of Foot. The party consisted of 137 men of all ranks, with the operational command given to Colonel John Palmer of Carolina.[88]

Disputes arose between the Carolina commanders and the Highlanders. It appears that the Highlanders would take commands only from their own officers. The Scots felt justified in their complaint in that of the ninety-seven whites who were in the detail, sixty-seven were Highlanders. Add to this the fact that most of the Scots spoke only Gaelic. In the Highlands the feeling of "us" against "them" was between clans or the followers of the Stuarts and the supporters of the House of Hanover; but in the palmetto fields in the Florida brush, it was the Highlanders from Georgia united against the English from Carolina. This conflict proved to be fatal.

The flying party had specific orders from Oglethorpe to keep mobile and "take great care not to engage yourselves in suspicious places for fear of being surprised, nor to camp two nights in one place, but to keep to the thickets in the nights and the plains in the daytime."[89] From this point on, there are differing versions as to what actually happened at Fort Mosa—Georgia and the Highlanders on one side and the English from Carolina on the other—each group disguising their own mistakes while exposing the mistakes of the other group.[90] The truth probably lies somewhere in between, and there is blame in both camps.

On arriving at Fort Mosa on 10 June, all but the English Rangers moved into the fort and built temporary huts of palmetto leaves. Whether this had been ordered by Colonel Palmer or was at the direction of Captains Mackay and Mackintosh was hotly debated in the aftermath, but regardless of whose idea it was, the Highlanders moved into the fort and the English Rangers camped in the dry moat outside.[91] At this point the struggle for authority began in earnest between the two factions. Disagreements over the placing of sentries and the conduct of their missions ended with Palmer's orders being, if not disobeyed, merely ignored by Mackay and, apparently, Mohr Mackintosh. Initially, Mackay wanted to abandon the vicinity of Fort Mosa and camp in the thickets, according to Oglethorpe's commands; however, Palmer did not believe that the Spaniards would dare attack his force and thought St. Augustine could be monitored more easily if the troops remained "at, or in sight of, Fort Mosa."[92]

If the Scots' account is true, then Mackay and Mackintosh felt that if they were to stay in the area of Fort Mosa, they might as well stay inside. Colonel Palmer was incensed at the refusal of the Highlanders to remove their men from the fort and at the apparent laxity of security within. He told them that "the Spaniards from the Castle could count their Number almost to a Man and that they would have their Throats cut."[93] With typical Highland bravado, the Scots replied that "there they had encamped and that they would not move, if the enemy came, they must fight."[94] This attitude led to daily arguments between the officers, in front of the men. It appeared to the troops that no one was in charge. In his dismay, Colonel Palmer often complained aloud before his men that "they were left a Sacrifice by him [Oglethorpe]."[95]

The flying party had been daily harassing the Spaniards by burning the houses outside the fort at St. Augustine and firing on the town "to alarm" the people while Oglethorpe's artillery bombarded the fortifications from the shore.[96] The siege was having an effect on the inhabitants of St. Augustine. By 14 June 1740, Spanish Governor Montiano proclaimed that "it is impossible to express the confusion of this place. . . . we must all indubitably perish."[97] Drastic action had to be taken for St. Augustine to survive. A daring raid before daybreak was planned with Captain Antonio Salgado selected to lead. The attack force consisted of three hundred Spanish troops along with a detachment of Yamassee Indians. The target—Fort Mosa.

The Spanish raiding party slipped out of St. Augustine about eleven o'clock that night and made their way by stealth toward the unsuspecting British forces at Fort Mosa. Around 1:00 A.M. on the morning of 15 June, some Highland Rangers who had been out to burn down a house at St. Augustine returned and informed Colonel Palmer that they had heard "the Spanish Indians dancing a War Dance."[98] Colonel Palmer, an experienced Indian fighter of the Yamassee War in Carolina in 1715, knew that they could expect a "brush" before day and told everyone to get some sleep while they could.[99] He did not have to wait long for the attack.

About three o'clock that morning, Colonel Palmer roused his men to arms. The majority of the Rangers outside the fort got up immediately and stood ready while Palmer entered the fort to stir the Highlanders to action. He warned them of the impending danger of a Spanish attack but, as usual, "not regarding him, most of them lay down again."[100] This infuriated Palmer, who was certain an assault on the fort would come. He turned and left the fort, again muttering to himself aloud that "the General had sent them there for a Sacrifice."[101] Meanwhile, the Spanish raiding party had been moving closer and took up a position within one hundred yards of the fort.

At the first light of dawn, a Carolina sentry spotted the advancing Spanish forces and ran into camp crying the alarm.[102] Colonel Palmer and Thomas Jones were standing in the gateway of the fort when they heard the warning. Palmer is reported to have ordered: "Stand to your Arms! Not a Man of you fire, but receive their first Fire; then half of you fire and fall back, making room for the rest to come up, and we will kill them like Dogs."[103] Not known for patience and in a state of alarm, the Highlanders on the wall opened fire and the enemy responded by pouring in "a large Volley."[104] Captain Hugh Mackay reported that the Spanish opened fire first and that the Highlanders responded "very warmly."[105] In the heat of battle it mattered not who fired first; the enemy had been engaged.

Colonel Palmer commanded his men into the moat while Jones ran inside the fort to organize his Indians' response. Inside the fort, Jones found confusion and chaos—some men were dressed, others not, but most were in disarray searching for their clothes and their weapons. Captain Mackay—dressed only in a shirt, a pair of linen breeches, and stockings and carrying a small sword and musket—ordered his officer of the guard, Cornet Baillie, to "seize and defend the gate." [106] The Spaniards forced their way through the gate, only to be repulsed twice by supporting fire from Colonel Palmer in the trench and from two flanks inside the fort. [107] On the third assault, the Spanish attacked from three sides, coming through the gates and over the breaches in the wall. The bulk of the remaining Spanish forces flooded into the fort. "Here was the greatest part of the slaughter." [108]

The Highlanders inside the fort were vastly outnumbered by the Spaniards and were paying dearly for leaving their bayonets and targets behind at Fort San Diego. [109] Having only their broadswords and no shields, the Scots were no match for the trained Spanish soldiers with bayonets. Seeing that the battle was lost, Captain Mackay, sword in hand, jumped on top of a parapet and "call'd out to as many as were alive to draw off" and follow him. [110] Taking Mohr Mackintosh's fourteen-year-old son William with him, Mackay jumped into the moat below and "cut [their] way through the enemy." [111] Mohr Mackintosh, still inside the fort, had no option but to surrender under the watching eyes of the remaining British forces outside. [112]

Some managed to escape, but sixty-three men of the company were killed, including Colonel Palmer. The Spanish took twenty prisoners, including Captain John Mohr Mackintosh, along with about a dozen men from the Highland Independent Company of Foot, Cornet Baillie, Quartermaster James McQueen, and "one MacDonald who has a family in Georgia." [113] Of the slain, at least thirty-five were Highlanders from Darien. [114] Of the sixty-seven Highlanders from Darien who had accompanied Oglethorpe to Florida, fifty-one were either killed or captured at Fort Mosa. This defeat at Mosa was the turning point of Oglethorpe's invasion in Florida, and the consequences would have disastrous effects on the remaining population of Darien.

On 4 July 1740, Oglethorpe ordered the British forces to withdraw. [115]

CHAPTER 6

Darien and the Aftermath
of Fort Mosa, 1740–1748

1740—This affair destroyed the Settlement of Scotchmen and people in Whom Oglethorpe had complete confidence.
—Governor Don Manuel de Montiano to Don Juan Francisco de Güemes y Horcasitas, 28 July 1740

1742—The Darien settlement flourishes exceedingly . . . a return of the improvements
in the Southern part of this province which are really wonderful considering the situation and opposition.
—James Oglethorpe to the Trustees, 28 May 1742

AFTER THE SMOKE OF BATTLE had lifted, the bodies of the dead had
been buried, and the survivors had gone, the scene left behind at Fort Mosa
was one of total defeat for the British forces in Florida. Captain John Mohr
Mackintosh, now a prisoner of the Spanish, spent three months in close
confinement in St. Augustine before being sent to Havana, Cuba, and eventually to San Sebastian, Spain.[1] He contacted his "friend and namesake,"
Alexander Mackintosh of Lothbury, a year later from his prison cell in Spain,
expressing his concern for his family left behind in Darien: "You are to know
that I left a wife and seven children in Georgia for ought I know starving, for
all my servants was listed to make up the company [Highland Independent
Company of Foot]."[2] He had good reason for his concerns.

After Mohr Mackintosh was taken prisoner at Fort Mosa, his family was
left destitute. William, the oldest child, who had fought and escaped from
Mosa, remained with Oglethorpe.[3] Lachlan, the second oldest, and his sister
Anne were sent to George Whitefield's orphanage at Bethesda. The other
children remained with their mother, who was forced to leave Darien and
seek refuge with her kinsman, Captain John Mackintosh, brother to Mackin-

tosh of Mackintosh, at Fort Palachicola on the Savannah River.[4] Mrs. Mackintosh and the remaining children stayed at the fort nearly two years before returning to Darien. Only by the aid that William Stephens provided were they able to survive the ordeal.[5] Other families did not fare as well.

Oglethorpe's expedition into Florida and the fiasco at Fort Mosa were blamed for "putting an end to the settlement of Darien; for there are now in that place not one quarter part of the number who settled there at first, and that is made up mostly of women and children."[6] In October 1740, by the account of the Malcontents,[7] of the approximately 250 persons who originally settled at Darien, only fifty-three remained. Of that fifty-three, over two-thirds were women and children, "besides eleven of the Trustee Servants inlisted as Soldiers."[8]

The news coming out of Darien continued to be dismal. In August, Thomas Hawkins wrote to Benjamin Martyn that he had "no better intelligence from these parts. . . . the number of widows are much increased at Darien by their husbands being killed or taken at the late expedition to St. Augustine."[9] Thomas Causton of Savannah echoed Hawkins's sad report, relating that Darien "being almost depopulated of its first inhabitants," the remaining widows and broken families were a "melancholy object."[10] The sadness of widows in Darien was compounded by the fact that some were newlyweds who had barely had time for a honeymoon before losing their husbands at Mosa.

In December 1738, some of the Highland soldiers had asked Oglethorpe for his permission to marry women who were in the service of the Trust in Darien. Oglethorpe consented.[11] His reasoning was threefold: first, a married man would be more likely to defend his home than would a single, hired soldier. Second, marriage brought families and families built communities. He hoped these communities would build Georgia. Third, by marrying, the women concerned would be released from the Trustees' charge, which would save the colony money.[12] Perhaps Oglethorpe was correct in his assumptions; however, the events at Fort Mosa would stop any hope of proving them. These Highlanders who had come to Georgia with inflated hopes, but no illusions, were paying a dear price for the move.

By October 1740, a few of the remaining Scots in Darien decided to leave the colony and move to South Carolina. John Mackintosh of Holmes left that month for Charles-Town, along with Benjamin Mackintosh.[13] In May 1741, the Reverend John MacLeod abandoned the colony to accept a pastorate in Edisto, South Carolina.[14] Thus, in addition to the loss from Darien of those dead or captured, the town was becoming deserted through defections to

Carolina for safety. Others, such as Lachlan McGillivray,[15] left Darien to enter the Indian trade with kinsmen from Carolina.[16]

Despite the turmoil, despair, and continued Spanish threat in Darien, the survivors would find assistance from the Trustees in London. On 13 April 1741, the Trustees decided to turn again to Scotland for recruits to replenish the sagging numbers in Georgia.[17] They determined that twenty-five men and fifteen women should be sent in support to Darien.[18] The Trustees met with James Grey, a Highlander recruiting in Scotland, on 24 April and discussed the costs of securing and transporting the forty Highlanders to London.[19] Grey said it would cost "£50 to engage and clothe them, 6d. a day to maintain them till put on board a vessel to carry them to Gravesend, 20 Shillings a head to the Captain who should carry them from Scotland thither, and 6d. to keep them till Captain Thompson should take them on board for Georgia."[20] The next day the Trustees contracted with Grey, with the assistance of their former recruiter in the Highlands, Captain Hugh Mackay, to "find the proper persons" and bring the secured Highlanders to London, where they would be escorted on to Darien.[21] This was the opportunity for Mackay to reestablish his influence on the population makeup and clan control in Darien.

Accordingly, the Trustees informed John Hossack in Inverness of Mackay's and Grey's coming and asked Hossack to advance Mackay fifty pounds sterling upon his arrival.[22] The recruiters for Georgia were successful in their venture in the Highlands. On 23 July 1741, Grey advised Harman Verelst that he had "thirty-six full heads and nine children."[23] The emigrants embarked for the Thames the next day and arrived at Gravesend on 13 August. The Trustees chartered the *Loyal Judith*, Captain John Lemon master, to carry the Highland emigrants to Georgia, and on 15 September 1741, the Earl of Egmont recorded that forty-three Highlanders, only two of whom spoke English, were aboard ship (see appendix D).[24] James Grey would not accompany the group to Georgia; instead John A. Terry, the Trustees' new secretary at Frederica, would be their escort.[25]

The Trustees, in their usual meticulous manner, made all provisions for the new settlers to Darien. The cargo list for the *Loyal Judith* marked "Highlanders" contained:

> 2 Grindstones Loose. 1 Parcel containing 18 Shovells, & 1 cask & 1 Bundle containing 18 New England Axes, 18 narrow Hoes, 18 Broad Hoes, 18 Helved Hatchets, 2 Axale Trees & Winches, 2 Whip-Saws handled and sharpt, 1 cross Cutt Saw Do., 6 Pitt saw Files, 3 three square Do., 3 Hand Saws, 3 Tennent

Do., 3 Frame Do., 3 carpenters Hammers, 12 Gimblets sorted, 3 Drawing
Knives, 4¾ Inch Augers, 4 Inch Do., 2 Inch ¼ Do. & 2 Inch ½ Do., 3 pair
Pinchers, 3 pair Compasses, 2 smoothing Planes fixt, 2 Jack Do., 2 Fore Do.,
2 Long Do., 1 m 20d Nails, 1 m 10d Nails, 1 m 8d Nails & 1 m 6d nails.

In addition to the implements for timber work and for building, each Highlander was to receive a "Musquet 3 feet 10 Inches clean bored Barrel," with
musket flints, bullets, gunpowder, and cleaning supplies. These men were
obviously being sent as soldiers and to work in the Trustees' timber lands
while rebuilding the town of Darien. The passengers' comfort needs were
not overlooked by the Trust. For the voyage, the Highlanders' refreshments
included "5 Cwt. of Potatoes, 30 Bushels of Carrotts & 48 Gallons of English
Brandy" to be used "when the beer is out." The foodstuffs provided for the
new immigrants on their trip would be unfamiliar to them since potatoes
had not yet been introduced to the Highlands of Scotland. The bedsteads
and bedding which the passengers used during the voyage were to go with
them for their use in Darien.[26]

The significance of this recruitment effort in Scotland as distinct from the
two previous ventures lies in the land grants to each man over twenty-one
years of age.[27] They were to be settled as "Freeholders,"[28] and as Verelst informed Oglethorpe on 18 September 1741, they were to receive "Fifty Acre
Lots to hold in *Tail General*" (emphasis mine) rather than in tail male, as had
been the case until then.[29] The importance of the Highlanders to the continued survival of Georgia and to Darien had effectively changed the land policy of the Trustees in Georgia by 1741.[30] This change would certainly be welcomed by everyone in the province since land tenure had been a major point
of contention from the start, especially among the malcontents. One other
change of importance was the payment of money for their first-year maintenance instead of the Trust supplying foodstuffs and clothing, which, as has
been seen, had previously proven contentious.[31] The Trustees were learning
from their earlier mistakes and were attempting to remedy past failings, in
part because of the importance of the Highlanders to Georgia.

If is interesting to note that in the letter Verelst wrote to Oglethorpe, he
pointed out that "Captain Mackay was consulted on this occasion and assisted in sending them from Scotland."[32] Mackay's influence is evident in
the list of passengers from Scotland. Of the forty-three emigrants from the
Highlands, twelve were surnamed Mackay and two other men, who had families, were connected directly to the Mackay clan through marriage.[33] Almost half of the new emigrants were known Mackays and the other names

represented included MacDonald, Munroe, Douglas, and Grant. It seems
that the political makeup of Darien would have shifted from predominantly
Jacobite sympathizers to supporters of King George II. Whether this was intentional is only a guess; however, it can be assumed that this was a consideration on the part of the Trustees.

The *Loyal Judith,* conducting the newest settlers from the Highlands of
Scotland to Georgia, arrived on 2 December 1741.[34] William Stephens
would not allow the Highlanders to disembark until a periagua was arranged
to take them directly to Darien. He feared that "our Secret workers of Mischief [the malcontents]" would persuade the newcomers that Darien was a
"place of Misery" and entice them to desert the colony.[35] To ensure that the
arriving Highlanders would feel more stable, the Trustees ordered bailiff
Henry Parker to pay them a half-year's allowance in advance.[36]

Although the War of Jenkins' Ear continued and the threat of invasion
hung in the air, by the fall of 1741, the situation for the Scots of Darien improved. The reports that more settlers were on their way from Scotland to
help revive the community had to be encouraging. By October that year, the
remaining people of Darien, wrote Egmont, expressed themselves to be
"very easy and contented, and but one or two families deserted to Carolina."[37] The changes the Trustees had made for the newcomers and the infu-
sion of money into Darien had apparently quelled the discontent of the majority of Highlanders and encouraged those remaining to stay. The cattle
business was proving to be productive since the soldiers were stationed close
by and provided a ready market for beef, butter, and milk.[38] The situation
might not be ideal, but it was better than it had been. In May 1742, Oglethorpe was expressing his delight at how well the Darien settlement flour-
ished, "considering the opposition and situation."[39]

The "situation," as Oglethorpe called it, was the constant military preparedness in which the settlement remained. Although there were no major
invasions in 1741, both the Spanish and the British military commanders
sent units into each other's territories on hit-and-run missions to terrorize
the populace and harass the enemy. On 18 March 1741 a party of Yamassee
Indians from Spanish Florida had raided the plantation of a Scottish gentleman, Mark Carr, killing four men and wounding several others. While the
Indians pillaged the property and burned the outbuildings, they locked the
women and children in the cellar of the main house. They loaded their booty
into a large canoe to escape back to Florida. British scout boats caught the
intruders and, in the ensuing battle, regained the stolen property. The invading Indians fled from the scene.[40]

Oglethorpe retaliated by sending his own war party of Creek Indians under the command of the war captain Accouclauh to St. Augustine during the night to gather intelligence and to raise the alarm in the town. They attacked a party of Spanish horse troops and took a prisoner before returning triumphantly to Frederica.[41] No doubt everyone's nerves were on edge on both sides of the St. John's River.[42]

In late December 1741, just as the new Highland Recruits were starting to settle, Oglethorpe mounted a larger incursion into Florida. He assembled two well-armed vessels with two hundred soldiers, "besides Mariners," and set out on a "secret Expedition" against the Spaniards.[43] After putting out to sea, the enterprise immediately ran into trouble in the form of winter storms that continued into January, not allowing the ships to make any progress. Apparently the deluges threatened the survival of the boats, as people "were forced to throw their Guns overboard to Save their Lives."[44] The attack plans were abandoned. On 8 January 1742, the British troops returned to Frederica without having engaged the enemy.

Back in Frederica, Oglethorpe set about rebuilding his forces and planning his strategy for the new year. To the south, the Spanish governors of St. Augustine and Havana were doing the same.[45] On 20 October 1741, King Philip V of Spain had ordered Governor Juan Francisco de Güemes y Horcasitas of Cuba to organize an invasion to devastate Georgia and South Carolina.[46] It was important that after carrying out their destruction of the countryside, the Spanish forces were to withdraw quickly to Cuba and Florida before British reinforcements could arrive.[47] The Spanish were confident that once the invasion of the British southern colonies was under way, the slaves of the English in Carolina would join the Spaniards and revolt.[48] The fear of Spanish intrigue among the slaves to revolt was one of the most persuasive arguments against the introduction of slavery into Georgia.[49]

Governor Manuel de Montiano of St. Augustine was appointed commander of the invasion forces in May, with Major-General Don Antonio de Arrendondo as second in command.[50] Arrendondo was familiar with the Georgia coast and with dealing with Oglethorpe. He had been the man who made the case for the Spanish claim to the debatable land in 1736 and was passionate in his determination to recover that claim.[51] The Spaniards' principal target for the invasion was St. Simons Island. After securing the island, the expedition was to move north into Carolina, destroying all British settlements in Georgia along the way.[52]

On 21 May 1742, a small fleet of ten ships left Havana sailing for St. Augustine.[53] The British man-of-war *Flamborough*, Captain Hamar master,

while on reconnaissance for Oglethorpe off the Florida coast, intercepted
the Spanish fleet before it reached St. Augustine. During the ensuing battle,
two Spanish ships were run aground. Some of the British seamen attempted
to board one of the ships but were captured by Spanish soldiers from one of
the beached vessels. Outnumbered and seeing their comrades captured, the
men of the *Flamborough* retreated to Charles-Town.[54] The British lost eighteen men in the action, one of them being "a brother of Captain Mackay."[55]
The Spanish convoy resumed its journey to St. Augustine.

On 20 June 1742, the invasion fleet from St. Augustine joined the approaching convoy from Havana and set sail for the Georgia coast.[56] The
long-awaited Spanish invasion of Georgia had begun. The fleet consisted of
fifty-two men-of-war—schooners, sloops, galleys, half-galleys, periaguas,
and other small craft, with 1,950 officers and men on board.[57] The next day,
21 June, contact was made. A strong wind forced a contingent of the Spanish
ships to seek shelter in Cumberland Sound. The fourteen vessels were
greeted with cannon fire from the eighteen-pounders at Fort William and
from the coast guard schooner *Walker,* with fourteen guns and ninety men
commanded by Captain George Dunbar.[58] The British guns fired "so briskly
on them that they sheered off as fast as they could."[59] The Spanish then
sailed north into St. Andrews Sound and anchored out of reach of the cannon at Fort St. Andrews.[60]

Upon hearing reports of the battle at Fort William, Oglethorpe immediately set out by horseback to Fort St. Simons, where from the mast of Captain Thompson's ship, *Success,* the Spanish flotilla could be seen in the distance in St. Andrews Sound.[61] Oglethorpe sent for reinforcements from
Frederica to support Fort St. Simons and sent Captain Horton over to land
Indians and troops on Cumberland Island, where he expected a major Spanish attack.[62] On Thursday, 24 June, Oglethorpe left St. Simons Island with a
detachment of troops in three boats headed for Cumberland. He left orders
for Major Heron and most of the regiment to follow. As his advance party
crossed the sound, they were sighted by the Spanish ships, which immediately started in pursuit. The Spanish vessels had the wind in their sails and
the tide in their favor, so they soon overtook Oglethorpe's group.[63]

In his report to the Duke of Newcastle, Oglethorpe recounted that he
was "attacked in the sound by 14 sail but with two boats fought my way
through."[64] The third boat, mastered by Lieutenant Tolson, Oglethorpe
complained, "quitted me in the fight and run into a river where he hid himself 'till the next day."[65] Tolson, convinced that the first two boats had been
sunk by the Spaniards, reported the next day that Oglethorpe had been

lost.[66] However, Oglethorpe and his men made it through the Spanish vessels and Tolson was later arrested for cowardice.[67] The Spaniards withdrew to St. Augustine and Oglethorpe removed his forces from Fort St. Andrews to reinforce Fort William.[68]

On 25 June 1742, the Highland Independent Company of Foot at Darien received an order to come down directly, "with all the assistance they could get."[69] The Highlanders responded immediately. As they prepared to move south to meet the enemy, the women and children were evacuated to Fort Argyle, about twenty miles west of Savannah, for their safety.[70] The Scots were anxious for an opportunity to avenge their kinsmen who had fallen at Fort Mosa. They would not have to wait long and they would not be disappointed.

The main body of the Spanish invasion fleet appeared off the coast of Georgia on 28 June and dropped anchor. High winds and feints by Oglethorpe's vessels kept the Spanish ships on the open seas until 5 July when, running out of water and now finding favorable winds, they decided it was time to attack.[71] Oglethorpe blockaded the entrance to St. Simons Sound to prevent the Spaniards from finding safe harbor to land their army; however, with "36 sail of Spanish vessels," the enemy ran the blockade in line of battle.[72] Oglethorpe reported of the incident: "We cannonaded them very hotly from the shipping and batteries. They twice attempted to board Captain Thom[p]son but were repulsed."[73] The Spanish overran the blockade and passed into the sound beyond the batteries of Fort St. Andrews. By six o'clock that evening, the Spaniards began disembarking their troops, and by the next morning the entire invasion force was ashore.[74]

Knowing that he had been outflanked, Oglethorpe immediately set about abandoning Fort St. Simons and moving quickly to defend Frederica before the arrival of the Spanish forces. He ordered all remaining provisions, vessels, and artillery at the fort destroyed so as to keep them from falling into the hands of the enemy.[75] He arrived at Frederica the morning of 6 July, about the same time as the Spanish army occupied Fort St. Simons. The Spanish bivouacked at the fort that night in preparation for their attack on Frederica the next day.

Wednesday, 7 July 1742, is a day long remembered in the history of Georgia and, in particular, in the history of the Highlanders of Darien. The morning began with the dispatching of two detachments of Spanish soldiers in search of the trail to Frederica. After becoming confused in their exploration, the two units joined forces and continued toward the British settlement.[76] They came to within a mile and a half before they were discovered by a party of rangers on patrol. A skirmish ensued between the small patrol and the larger Spanish force. The rangers broke off and retreated back to Frederica to inform Oglethorpe of the advancing enemy.[77]

Upon hearing the news, Oglethorpe wasted no time in mounting a horse and ordering the Highland Company, the rangers, and a group of Indians out to meet the oncoming Spanish. He ordered the troops of the Forty-Second Regiment to follow. It was imperative for Oglethorpe's men to engage the Spaniards in the woods, before they reached the open ground to form ranks.[78] With his Chickasaw, Tomotohetaw, and Creek warriors, along with "six Highland men who outrun the rest," Oglethorpe did not hesitate: he mounted what could only be termed a full Highland charge.[79] Larry Ivers, in his account of the meeting, wrote that for these men, "all warlike by tradition, the charge represented life at its best."[80] The intensity of the charge completely demoralized the Spanish as the first line crumbled under the onslaught and the main body, caught by surprise and terrified, turned and fled into the surrounding woods. The British troops gave pursuit for two to three miles to a broad opening before pausing to wait for the reinforcements to arrive.[81] Oglethorpe, in his report to the Duke of Newcastle, proudly boasted that "we entirely routed the first party."[82] The Spaniards lost thirty-six men in the encounter, while one Highlander died from heat exhaustion.[83]

Expecting the Spanish to regroup and counterattack, Oglethorpe posted the three newly arrived platoons, consisting of about sixty regulars of the regiment, in the woods on one side of the road facing the marshes. He then placed about fifty Highlanders in the thickets on the other side. Oglethorpe knew that the Spanish must pass on the road along the edge of the opening to get to Frederica.[84] After his men were posted for their ambush, Oglethorpe returned to Frederica to rouse additional troops for support. In the meantime, the Spanish commander, Montiano, ordered Captain Antonio Barba and three companies of grenadiers numbering between 150 and 200 men to counter the seeming British advance and to protect the retreat of the remaining Spanish troops of the first party.[85]

According to the Spanish accounts, as they approached the woodlands, the advance party, who had been with the earlier group, noticed some logs and "some brush-wood arranged like a parapet" that had not been there before.[86] Upon investigation, the Spaniards realized they had walked into an ambuscade. It was too late. The English, Indians, and Highlanders opened fire from their cover in the woods, catching the enemy in an impossible situation. The Spaniards were being showered with musket balls without being able to see more than muzzle flashes.[87] They were nevertheless able to return fire, which caused three platoons of the regiment to turn and flee the scene of battle. However, one platoon of the regiment, under the command of Lieutenant Patrick Sutherland and Sergeant John Stewart, and the Highland Company under Lieutenant Charles Mackay stood fast and continued their volleys.[88] Oglethorpe reported that the Spaniards fired "with great spirit" but without effect, because thanks to the cover of the woods, "none of their shot took place, but ours did."[89]

Oglethorpe, hearing the sounds of gunfire, sped down the road from Frederica toward the action. About two miles from the battleground, he met the three platoons who had left the field. They claimed that the entire British force had been routed, but Oglethorpe, still hearing the sounds of battle, ordered them to rally and return to face the enemy.[90]

They arrived to find that they were not needed. The Spanish had fallen back under the constant pressure of the combined forces of Englishmen, Highlanders, and Indians. Oglethorpe rewarded Lieutenant Sutherland by promoting him to brigade-major and Sergeant Stewart to second-ensign.[91] For Oglethorpe and the Highlanders of Darien, their reward was the satisfaction of knowing they had secured their revenge for Fort Mosa. In a letter to Mary Mathews on 20 July 1742, Oglethorpe wrote, "We have some Satisfaction for the Blood at Moosa. The white people[,] Indians, and the Highlanders all had their share in the Slaughter."[92]

Although the battle was not more than a heated skirmish in which less than a dozen Spanish soldiers were killed, in the broader view of the war between Spain and Great Britain, the victory at the place now known as Bloody Marsh was important in that it gave the Georgians much needed confidence and it broke the morale of the Spanish leadership in North America. The tide of the war on the southern frontier now shifted in favor of the British. This battle was the last exchange of any importance between the British defenders and the Spanish invaders in Georgia during the War of Jenkins' Ear.

The Spanish retreated to their camp at the southern tip of St. Simons Island. A few days later they became so alarmed at the appearance of five ships on the horizon that they hurriedly embarked their troops and headed for St. Augustine. It was not the five sails on the horizon that precipitated the Spaniards' hasty retreat but the fear of the unknown number of ships that might lie just beyond.[93] The war between Great Britain and Spain would not end until 1748, with the Treaty of Aix-la-Chapelle; however, the war in Georgia was essentially over. The Spanish threatened another invasion in

1743, but Oglethorpe struck first. In March, he advanced on St. Augustine and used every device to decoy the enemy into an ambush; he failed even to provoke the garrison to respond.[94] Oglethorpe returned to Frederica without the loss of a man. Georgia would continue to be threatened by Spain and France in the backwoods over the Indian trade until the final victory of the British in 1763, but for now the colony could get on with the business of establishing itself.

In July 1743, Oglethorpe was recalled from Frederica to England, never to visit his beloved Georgia again. As Oglethorpe was preparing to leave for England to settle money matters, to answer charges from a subordinate officer,[95] and because of rumors of invasion by the young pretender Charles Edward Stuart, he found hidden in the hold of one of his ships two young Highlanders from Darien. The young men were members of his regiment and the sons of John Mohr Mackintosh. According to a family story, William and Lachlan Mackintosh also had heard the rumors and were anxious to return to Scotland to follow the Stuart banner as their father had done in 1715. Oglethorpe, himself the product of staunch Jacobite parents, ordered the two youths to his cabin and persuaded them that the Stuart cause was hopeless and that their future lay in Georgia.[96]

Following the failed Spanish invasion of Georgia, the sense of impending doom lifted from the inhabitants of Darien as the settlers began to drift back. John Mohr Mackintosh's wife, Marjorie, returned with most of her children from Fort Palachicola in August 1742.[97] Lachlan, their son, stayed with Oglethorpe's regiment and remained in Darien with his family. John Mohr Mackintosh returned from his imprisonment in Spain sometime in the summer of 1743 and resumed his command of the Highland Company of Foot.[98] James McQueen and Ranald MacDonald came with Mohr Mackintosh from Spain and both returned to their families in Darien.[99] A handful of Scots who had left Darien to enter the Indian trade with their kinsmen in Carolina returned to the settlement as prosperous citizens. They were ready to take up land grants given to them by the Trust years before and establish themselves in the community. There continued to be alarms of attacks by Spanish- and French-allied Indians along the frontier around Darien, but the Highland Rangers constantly patrolled the backcountry.[100]

In 1743 the population of Darien received another boost by the addition of thirty-eight mutineers and their families who were transferred from Britain to Georgia from the Forty-Third Highland Regiment of Foot, known as the Black Watch.[101] These men were all Highlanders who had joined the Black Watch on the premise that they would serve only as a police force in their native glens of Scotland. In this they were mistaken. The regiment was ordered to London on the pretext of being reviewed by King George II when the real purpose was to send them to Flanders for action against the French. Upon hearing that they were being sent abroad and believing they were going to the West Indies, 120 soldiers deserted in London and started back for the Highlands.

The mutineers surrendered to authorities about one hundred miles north of the capital. One man died during the attempt, twelve escaped, and 107 men were brought to trial for desertion. Among the prisoners were thirteen MacGregors, thirteen from Clan Cameron, ten MacDonalds, eight Frasers, some Stewarts, MacLeans, and MacIntyres, and twenty-six from Clan Chattan, of whom seventeen were McPhersons.[102] Three of the five executed as leaders of the revolt were from Clan Chattan: Samuel and Malcolm MacPherson and Farquhar Shaw. The remaining prisoners were divided into three groups to be billeted abroad. The first group of twenty-six men went to Gibraltar; the second, consisting of thirty-eight men, was indeed sent to the dreaded West Indies. The final contingent of thirty-eight went to Georgia to help replenish Oglethorpe's Highland Company in Darien.[103]

By 1745, while their kinsmen in the Highlands of Scotland were enmeshed in the contest over the throne of Great Britain between the Hanovers and the Stuarts, the Scots in Darien could at last begin to relax from their military obligations and settle into becoming full-fledged citizens of Georgia. The regiment, Highland Company, and Highland Rangers would continue to be garrisoned in and around Darien, thereby ensuring protection and a stable economy for the area until the war against the Spanish ended in 1748.[104]

CONCLUSION

THE COLONY OF GEORGIA owed a debt of gratitude to this determined group of Highlanders. They had been recruited as a community to secure the southern frontier of Georgia against her enemies and had performed that duty with distinction. After 1748 the unique trustee period of Georgia's infancy came to an end and Georgia became a royal colony. The significant contributions of the Highland community gave way to the individual efforts of the Highland Scots themselves. The Highlanders at Darien could set aside their broadswords and turn their energies to cattle farming, the timber industry, Indian trade, mercantilism, rice plantations, and politics. In all of these areas they made a vital impact on Georgia's growth and stability.

The Trustees for Establishing the Colony of Georgia in America sought a particular type of people who were rugged and would loyally serve as the front line of defense in the New World. For their colony to survive, it had to be protected and secure. After the dismal experiences with the first group of settlers, English and Lowland Scots, the Trustees reasoned that they must look for colonists made of sterner stuff. The hardy Highlanders seemed the ideal choice. To entice the Scots to leave their homes in the Highlands and venture to the wilds of Georgia, the Trustees offered free land and provisions for the first year. For Scots who were barely surviving on leased lands and subsistence farming, this was an offer too good to refuse. For a few emigrants such as John Mohr Mackintosh, who had lost his inheritance due to forfeitures following the Rising of 1715, this was an opportunity to regain lost fortunes. Some young gentlemen of the clans came just for the adventure while others, after their initial fears and reluctance had been allayed, came to find a new home on the frontier of the new province.

The Highland Scots traditionally lived in a society that was in a constant state of military preparedness. Benjamin Martyn correctly echoed the Trustees' choice when he proclaimed that "Highlanders were sent to the Colony: these, being accustomed to hardship, and labor, were not afraid of it in Georgia, and they live by it very comfortably." [1]

Could these people hold the frontier against the Spanish in Florida, the French in Mississippi, and the Indians in the backcountry? The answer is a resounding yes. Although at times there were discontent and conflict among the ranks of the Scots, they never shied away from their responsibility as soldiers and protectors of the colony. Life was hard on the frontier in the pine barrens of Georgia and some Highlanders found it too much to endure. These people moved to Carolina, which seemed out of harm's way. At the time they could also own slaves in Carolina to do the manual labor for them, which was not the case during the Georgia colony's first two decades. The idea of slavery did not fit into the Trustees' design for a yeoman colony where men and women lived by the products of their own labors and did not rely on the work of others. The constant threat of Spanish invasion and complicity in slave revolt also served to keep slavery from entering Georgia until 1750, after the War of Jenkins' Ear.

Those Highlanders who remained in Georgia did not shirk their duty but adapted to the rigors of colonial frontier life. Obviously, they knew the benefit of hard labor and did not fit the stereotypical picture of Celtic peoples as lazy and averse to farming. Time and time again James Oglethorpe, the Earl of Egmont, William Stephens, and others in authority praised the labor and industry of these sturdy frontiersmen and women. Whether or not they lived comfortably is another question. There is no record that the town of Darien suffered any epidemic or widespread sickness during its colonial days. During the Trustee period the settlement persevered, survived, and eventually obtained a measure of prosperity in spite of the hardships.

The fact that the land surrounding Darien was not viable for effective cultivation of staple crops did not deter the Highlanders from making a success of their experience in America. The Scots turned initially to the familiar life patterns to which they were accustomed in the Highlands. Their society was structured around clan leaders, in this case John Mohr Mackintosh and Captain Hugh Mackay, who acted traditionally as decision makers and adjudicators. An early Savannah newspaper said of John Mohr Mackintosh during the first years of Darien that "many of these new Emigrants, being all together, never learned the English language, and the whole lived in the greatest simplicity and harmony, having neither Lawyers nor Courts, but their differences all amicably settled by the decisions of their good old Captain."[2] Darien in the Trustee period was a self-contained Scottish society, separated from the rest of the inhabitants of the colony by design and, more important, by language. Gaelic was the language of the people of Darien and the plaids of the Highlands were their attire. As Samuel Johnson remarked, "they change nothing but their abode, and of that change they perceive the benefit."[3]

Darien was a military settlement and life was conducted accordingly. The settlers ventured into cattle raising and timber production, to both of which they brought previous experience from the Highlands of Scotland. The lumber business would continue to be a mainstay in Darien's industry until the American Civil War in the 1860s. In effect, the Scots transferred their experiences and culture from Scotland and adapted them to the frontiers of Georgia.

These warlike colonists became the military crutch upon which James Oglethorpe depended. He made sure that Highlanders accompanied him on each military expedition, not only in the border clashes between British Georgia and Spanish Florida but also during tense negotiations with the Indian nations in the backcountry. The presence of the Highland Rangers and the Highland Independent Company of Foot brought assurance throughout the colony. Although many of the Trustees' decisions about the new colony were faulty, the correctness of this choice was clear. The Highlanders were capable of filling the ranks and assisting the military forces sent to secure the province and protect it from danger.

While the Spaniards provided external problems for the colony, the band of disgruntled colonists called the Malcontents were the major cause of internal turmoil. This group complained to the Trustees from the beginning about the authorities in Georgia and about land tenure, and they called adamantly for the introduction of slaves. Many of these men were Lowland Scots from Edinburgh and Glasgow with friends and family who owned slaves and property in Carolina. They wanted large estates and slaves to work their plantations, as the Carolinians and settlers in Barbados had. To the Trustees, for Georgia as a military colony and a buffer against Spanish and French incursions into British colonies in America, this policy was not acceptable. It was the Highlanders in Darien who helped maintain the Trustees' policies and plans for the colony in both of these situations. Although all this was to change with the advent of royal control, the Scots' military presence, their support of Oglethorpe, and their petition against slavery helped the Trustees contain both internal and external threats.

The protection afforded by the Scots during the early years came at a great price to the Highland settlers of Darien in terms of men and family life; however, their contributions to the continued existence of Georgia cannot be overstated. Although the settlement was threatened by war in 1740 and 1742, and by famine in 1736 and 1739, it endured. Many young

Highland men, after their arrival in 1736–43, found the adventure they had sought. Others lost their lives or were taken captive by the Spanish during the conflicts on Georgia's frontiers. Still, the Scottish role in turning back the Spanish invasion of 1742 was a key one. There would be small skirmishes after that encounter, but the tide had turned against the Spanish and they would never again be a serious threat to the security of Georgia.

There is little evidence of settlers returning to Scotland after making their home in Darien. As mentioned in the last chapter, the two young Mackintosh lads, William and Lachlan, attempted to return for the Jacobite Rebellion of 1745 but found their fortunes in Georgia instead. Archibald McGillivray did return in 1744, leaving his Indian trade business to his kinsman Lachlan McGillivray, who had arrived in 1736. Lachlan McGillivray returned to his native glens in Scotland after his lands were confiscated during the American War of Independence in 1781. McGillivray had remained a loyalist[4] while most of the Darien Scots rebelled.[5]

After 1748, when the War of Jenkins' Ear ended, Parliament's military aid to Georgia was cut off. Oglethorpe's Forty-Second Regiment was disbanded.[6] Each man of the regiment was offered fifty acres of land and support for him and his family for a year. Many accepted the offer.[7] The province suffered a depression and the Highlanders in Darien were left without the economic base of the military presence. They now had to fend for themselves. Lachlan Mackintosh, taking his younger brother George with him, left Darien in 1748 to go to Charles-Town to find his fortune. The two would return to Darien after Georgia became a royal colony in 1754 and would claim several thousand acres of land for themselves and their families.[8]

Other major changes occurred in the colony during the next few years. Since the threat of war was removed with the Peace of Aix-la-Chapelle in 1748, the foundation to the Trustees' argument against slavery vanished. Slavery was introduced into Georgia on 15 August 1750.[9] Darien and the rest of Georgia would never be the same. Along with the admission of slavery came large-scale rice cultivation, and the people of Darien, despite having opposed slavery in 1739, became heavily involved with both. The marshlands that had been unviable for staple crops were ideal for labor-intensive rice cultivation using slaves. By the 1760s many Highlanders' rice plantations were thriving and as a result, Darien as a town suffered. As the plantations grew, families moved out of town. However, there was renewed interest in the town and in 1767 the governor and Council of Georgia ordered a new town laid out where "the Old Town formerly stood."[10] On the eve of the American Revolution, many of the largest local land and slave owners came from the ranks of the Darien Scots, and this would continue to be the case until the middle of the nineteenth century. Again, the Scots' resilience and determination to survive and their practical sense for land use were sufficient to carry them through difficult times. Of all the smaller settlements of the 1730s and 1740s, Darien is one of the few that still exists.

The impact of this first band of Highland settlers on Georgia was marked. After being almost completely depopulated in 1740, the Darien settlement rebounded and survived. These Scots pushed on to new frontiers. As noted, the Darien youth Lachlan McGillivray received his Indian trading license in 1744 and went on to make important contributions in the government's Indian affairs and to the economy of Georgia.[11] Likewise, Lachlan Mackintosh, the second son of John Mohr Mackintosh, only eight years old when he arrived in Darien, became one of the largest rice planters in the region and was instrumental in the politics of Georgia during the remainder of the colonial period and during the infancy of the new United States.[12]

The departure of the settlers in this study, these first three groups of Highland immigrants to Georgia, had minimal impact on life in the Highlands of Scotland. These few people did not represent a large manpower drain on the Scottish economy, but they were a major influence on the survival of the infant colony of Georgia. Although little information exists about correspondence between families in Georgia and Scotland, these people were the pioneers for the mass migration from Scotland after 1763. There is no evidence of any large-scale migrations to Georgia, but there continued to be a steady stream of new Scottish immigrants. David Dobson claims that the Register of Emigrants for the period 1773 to 1775 indicates that two-thirds of those who migrated directly from Great Britain to Georgia had been born in Scotland.[13]

While society was changing in the Highlands, traditional bonds remained in force for some time among the settlers in Georgia. The Scots of Darien brought with them the determination to survive and the hard experiences of life in the Highlands to effect that determination. They were able to adapt and thrive on the rugged frontier of Georgia more readily than were most other early settlers. That ability would carry them into every niche of colonial society. Scottish names are to be found throughout Georgia's continuing history in the ranks of politics and place-names. Government rolls are replete with names such as Bulloch, Graham, Houston, McDonald, and others. Counties named Forsyth and McIntosh, the towns of Glasgow, Culloden, Cuthbert, St. Andrews, and Inverness, and estates called Ashantilly, Borlum, and Glenmore are all found on Georgia's maps. These Highlanders may scarcely have been missed in the glens and mountains of Scotland, but in Georgia they made a difference. Their impact is recorded on historical plac-ards and memorials, and their influence and culture persist in the town of Darien, where some two hundred present inhabitants out of a population of 1,788 claim direct descent from the original settlers and still celebrate their Scottish heritage.[14]

So it was that these first Highlanders, long neglected by most Georgia his-tories and relegated to the shadows in others, helped establish and secure the life of Georgia from its English beginnings and subsequently con-tributed to the state's history out of all proportion to their numbers.

List of Jacobite Prisoners
Sent to South Carolina, 1716

THE SCOTS HIGHLANDERS listed below were captured at the Battle of Preston in the failed Jacobite rising of 1715. They were banished to the plantations in America and were shipped from the port at Liverpool in 1716. Of a total of 608 Jacobite prisoners sent to the colonies, 150 were exiled to the colony of South Carolina. The list is divided into two sections: those who were transported on the *Wakefield* and those transported on the *Susannah*. One prisoner was carried to South Carolina aboard the *Hockenhill*.

One third of those banished were from the Highland Clan Chattan.

The list is compiled from David Dobson's *Directory of Scots Banished to the American Plantations, 1650–1775* (Baltimore: Genealogical Publishing Company, 1983). Numbers in parentheses denote page numbers in Dobson's book.

Wakefield, Master Thomas Beck. Sailed from Liverpool 21 April 1716.

Clark, James (233)
———, Thomas (233)
Cowson, William (234)
Croft, David (234)
Cunningham, George (235)
Dunlop, James (236)
Dysart, George (236)
Ferguson, Finlay (236)
Flint, James (237)
Fraser, John (237)
Guthrie, John (237)
Henderson, William (74)
Kennedy, Malcolm (87)

Lyon, Philip (93)
McBean, Lachlan (95)
McCoy, Donald (100)
————, John (100)
McDonald, Coll (238)
————, Donald (238)
————, John (107)
McGillivray, Alexander (238)
————, James (114)
————, John (114)
————, Loughlan (114)
————, Owen (114)
————, William (238)
McIntosh, Alexander (238)
————, Donald (238)
————, Duncan (120)
————, James (120)
————, John (121)
————, John (238)
————, William (122)
McKenzie, William (134)
McLean, Alexander (137)
————, John (139)
McLeod, John (143)
McPherson, Alexander (148)
————, Donald (148)
McQueen, Alexander (150)
————, Alexander (150)
————, David (150)
————, Duncan (150)
————, John (151)
McQuin, Alexander (152)
Moor, Miles (239)
Nicholson, John (172)
Rankin, John (182)
Ross, Charles (191)
Shaw, John (196)
————, John (196)
Sinclair, Patrick (200)
Smith, Donald (201)
Songster, Andrew (204)
Stewart, Donald (207)

Strachan, Charles (213)
Wilkie, James (226)
Wilson, James (227)

Susannah, Master Thomas Bromhall. Sailed from Liverpool 7 May 1716.

Cameron, Donald (232)
———, John (232)
Cameron, John (232)
Chambers, Joseph (233)
Clark, Hugh (233)
Cornell, George (233)
Cousins, John (233)
Creighton, James (234)
Crockett, John (234)
Dalgetty, Alexander (235)
Dalziel, William (235)
Davidson, Donald (235)
Doctor, David (235)
Duff, Donald (41)
———, Thomas (236)
Eggoe, John (236)
———, William (236)
Forbes, George (237)
Fotheringham, John (237)
Frazer, Duncan (237)
———, Hugh (237)
———, William (54)
Gill, Henry (57)
Grant, Ludovick (66)
Guild, Thomas (69)
Guthrie, John (70)
———, Robert (70)
Hammond, George (72)
Herd, John (74)
Johnston, John (84)
Lemon, John (91)
Leslie, Alexander (91)
McBean, Elias (95)
McCallum, Donald (96)
———, Duncan (96)

——, John (96)
McCoy, Donald (100)
McDonald, James (106)
——, John (107)
——, Rory (110)
——, William (110)
McGilliveray, Donald (114)
McGillivray, Fergus (114)
McGregor, Duncan (116)
——, Malcolm (117)
McInnes, John (118)
McIntosh, Duncan (120)
——, Ewan (120)
——, James (120)
——, John (121)
——, John (121)
——, John (121)
——, William (122)
McKeels, Daniel (126)
McLaren, John (137)
——, Patrick (137)
McNaughton, Duncan (146)
McPherson, Angus (148)
——, Donald (148)
——, Duncan (149)
——, John (149)
McQuin, John (152)
McVane, John (153)
——, Malcolm (153)
Matthewson, John (158)
Newton, Jonathan (172)
Rae, John (181)
Reid, Malcolm (182)
Robertson, Donald (186)
——, James (187)
Robinson, John (190)
Ross, Thomas (193)
Shaw, Donald (196)
——, Ewan (196)
——, John (196)
——, Peter (197)
——, William (197)

Shuttard, Bernard (198)
Simson, James (199)
Smith, David (201)
——, Donald (201)
——, Patrick (203)
Stewart, Alexander (206)
——, Duncan (207)
——, Hugh (208)
——, John (209)
——, Neil (210)
——, Neil (210)
——, Patrick (211)
Swinhoe, James (215)
Yeaman, Francis (230)

Hockenhill, Master Hockenhill Short. Sailed from Liverpool 25 June 1716.

Gardner, Patrick (55)

List of Scottish Settlers
to Georgia to 1741

THIS LIST WAS COMPOSED from Egmont's list of settlers found in *A List of the Early Settlers of Georgia*, edited by E. Merton Coulter and Albert B. Saye. The list is divided into two parts, using Egmont's division of those persons who went to Georgia at the Trustees' charge and those who went to Georgia on their own account. The selection of names was based on three criteria: (1) obvious Scottish name, (2) date of arrival and ship's name, and (3) Egmont's notation that they were Scots.

Part A: Persons Who Went to Georgia at the Trustees' Charge

Bain, Jo. of Lochain—Age 45; Tr. servant; embark'd on 20 Oct. 1735; arrived 10 Jan. 1735–6.

Calder, Will.—Age 20; Tr. servt. for 4 years; embark'd 20 Oct. 1735; arrived 10 Jan. 1735–6. Made by Col. Oglethorpe at the expiration of his service a soldier of the Highland Independt. Compy. & as such returned on 6 May 1741.

Cameron, Jannet—Age 26; servt. for 4 years; embark'd on 19 Nov. 1737; arrived 14 Jan. 1737–8. Hired & carry'd at Capt. Thompson the owners risk, but the Planters unable to pay for her, Mr. Causton without orders took her on the Trustees Acct. and certified the same which made us lyable to the charge.

Cameron, Jo.—Age 18; Tr. servt.; embark'd 24 June 1737; arrived 20 Nov. 1737.

Cameron, John—Age 20; Tr. servt.; embark'd 24 June 1737; arrived 20 Nov. 1737. Made a Ranger by Col. Oglethorpe at the expiration of his service, and as such return'd living 6 May 1741.

Cameron, John—Age 27; servt. for 4 yrs.; embark'd 19 Nov. 1737; arrived 14 Jan. 1737–8. Hired & carry'd at Capt. Thompson the owners risk, but the Planters unable to pay for him, Mr. Causton without orders took him on the Trustees Acct. and certified the same which made us lyable to the charge.

Campbell, Jo.—Age 24; wood cutter; Scotch; embark'd on 21 Sept. 1741; arrived 2 Dec. 1741.

Cleaness, Alexr.—Age 24; Tr. servt.; embark'd 24 June 1737; arrived 20 Nov. 1737. Living at Darien, & still a servant 6 May 1741.

Coguch, Jo.—Age 33; labourer & Cow heard; Scotch; embark'd 21 Sept. 1741; arrived 2 Dec. 1741.

————, Anne Mackay, w.—Scotch.

————, Angus, son—Age 7; Scotch.

————, Christiana, d.—Age 16; Scotch.

————, Isabel, d.—Age 13; Scotch.

————, William, son—Age 11; Scotch.

Cotton, Anne—Age 23; single woman; Scotch; embark'd on 21 Sept. 1741; arrived 2 Dec. 1741.

Denune, Jo.—Age 26; Tr. servt.; embark'd 20 Oct. 1735; arrived 10 Jan. 1735–6.

Douglass, Geo.—Age 28; labourer; Scotch; embark'd on 21 Sept. 1741; arrived 4 Dec. 1741.

————, Marg. Monro, w.—Age 29.

————, Isabel, d.—Age 2.

Frazer, Anne—Age 35; servt. for 4 years; embark'd 19 Nov. 1737; arrived 14 Jan. 1737–8. Hired & carry'd at Captn. Thompson the owners risk, but the Planters not able to pay for them, Mr. Causton without order paid the acct. and by certificate charged the Trustees therewith.

————, Cath.—Age 16; servt. for 4 years; embark'd on 19 Nov. 1737; arrived 14 Jan. 1737–8. The same case hers.

————, Henrietta—Age 16; servt. for 5 years; embark'd on 19 Nov. 1737; arrived 14 Jan. 1737–8. The same case hers.

————, Hugh—Taylor; embark'd 15 June 1733; arrived 29 Aug. 1733; lot 97 in Savannah. Fyn'd 20 shill. for retailing strong liquors without lycense 16 Sept. 1734. Lot I suppose vact. Dead Jan. 1738–9.

————, Hugh—Age 19; servt. for 5 years; embark'd 19 Nov. 1737; arrived 14 Jan. 1737–8. Hired & Carry'd at Captn. Thompson the owners risk, but the Planters not able to pay for them, Mr. Causton without order paid the acct. and by certificate charged the Trustees therewith.

————, Jannett—Age 18; servt. for 4 years; embark'd on 19 Nov. 1737; arrived 14 Jan. 1737–8. The same case hers. Alive at Darien 6 May 1741.

————, John—Age 21; Tr. servt.; embark'd 24 June 1737; arrived 20 Nov. 1737. Living at Darien still a servant 6 May 1741.

————, John—Age 28; Tr. servt.; embark'd 24 June 1737; arrived 20 Nov. 1737; out of his time.

————, Margaret—Alive at Darien 6 May 1741.

Gaddis, Ja.—Age 21; servt. for 4 yrs.; embark'd 19 Nov. 1737; arrived 14 Jan. 1737–8. Hired & carry'd at Capt. Thompson the owners risk but the Planters not being able to pay for him, Mr. Causton without orders took him, and so certified, which made the Trustees lyable to the charge.

————, John—Age 20; servt. for 4 yrs.; embark'd 19 Nov. 1737; arrived 14 Jan. 1737–8. His was the same case.

Graham, Cath.—Age 24; servt. for 5 years; embark'd on 19 Nov. 1737; arrived 14 Jan. 1737–8. Hired & carry'd at Capt. Thompson the owners risk but the Planters not being able to pay for her Mr. Causton without orders took her, and so certified, which made the Trustees lyable to the charge.

Grant, Christian—Age 16; servt. for 5 years; embark'd on 19 Nov. 1737; arrived 14 Jan. 1737–8. His was the same case.

————, Gilbert—Age 9; servt. 10 yrs. & ½; embark'd on 19 Nov. 1737; arrived 14 Jan. 1737–8. His was the same case. Return'd by Col. Oglethorpe to be a soldier in the Highland Independt. Compy. 6 May 1741.

————, Jo.—Age 19; Tr. servt; embark'd 24 June 1737; arrived 20 Nov. 1737.

————, Jo.—Age 15; servt. 9 yrs.; embark'd 19 Nov. 1737; arrived 14 Jan. 1737–8. Hired & carry'd at Capt. Thompson the owners risk but the Planters not being able to pay for him Mr. Causton without orders took him, and so certified, which made the Trustees lyable to the charge. Return'd by Col. Oglethorpe to be a soldier in the Highland Independt. Compy. 6 May 1741.

————, Jo.—Age 22; labourer; Scotch; embark'd 21 Sept. 1741; arrived 4 Dec. 1741.

————, Peter—Age 18; servt. 5 years; embark'd 19 Nov. 1737; arrived 14 Jan. 1737–8. Hired & carry'd at Capt. Thompson the owners risk but the Planters not being able to pay for him Mr. Causton without orders took him, and so certified, which made the Trustees lyable to the charge.

————, Will.—Age 14; servt. 10 yrs.; embark'd 19 Nov. 1737; arrived 14 Jan. 1737–8. His was the same case.

Gray, Margt.—Age 24; single woman; Scotch; embark'd on 21 Sept. 1741; arrived 4 Dec. 1741.

Grey, Jo.—Age 50; servt. 3 yrs.; embark'd 19 Nov. 1737; arrived 14 Jan. 1737–8. Hired & carry'd at Capt. Thompson the owners risk but the Planters not being able to pay for him Mr. Causton without orders took him, and so certified, which made the Trustees lyable to the charge.

Jolliffe, Mary—Age 22; single woman; Scotch; embark'd on 21 Sept. 1741; arrived 4 Dec. 1741.

Macannon, Margt.—Age 21; servt. for 4 yrs.; embark'd on 19 Nov. 1737; arrived 14 Jan. 1737–8. Hired & carry'd at Capt. Thompson the owners risk, but taken by Mr. Causton as on the Trustees Acct. & by him so certifyed, tho without order, which made us lyable.

Macbean, Archibald—Indian trader; arrived 16 Jan. 1737–8. He came to Engl. to carry over Servt. and therefore the Trustees paid his passage back.

————, Elizabeth—Age 40; servt. 4 years; embark'd on 19 Nov. 1737; arrived 14 Jan.

1737–8. Hired & carry'd at Capt. Thompson the owners risk, but recd. by Mr. Causton as on the Tr. Acct. which made us lyable.

———, Margaret—Age 13; servt. for 7 years; embark'd on 19 Nov. 1737; arrived 14 Jan. 1737–8. In the same case.

Macbean, Will.—Age 27; Tr. servt.; embark'd 20 Oct. 1935; arrived 10 Jan. 1735–6. Living at Darien, still a servt. 6 May 1741.

———, Will—Age 17; Tr. servt.; embark'd 24 June 1737; arrived 20 Nov. 1737. Living at Darien still a Tr. Servant 6 May 1741.

———, Will—Age 21; Tr. servt.; embark'd 24 June 1737; arrived 20 Nov. 1737.

Macdonald, Alexr.—Alive at Darien 6 May 1741 but an invalid.

———, Archibald—Age 22; Tr. servt.; embark'd 24 June 1737; arrived 20 Nov. 1737.

———, Christian—Age 21; servt for 4 years; embark'd on 19 Nov. 1737; arrived 14 Jan. 1737–8. Hired & carry'd at Capt. Thompson the owners risk, but recd. by Mr. Causton as on the Tr. Acct. which made us lyable.

———, Donald—Age 16; Tr. servt.; embark'd 24 June 1737; arrived 20 Nov. 1737.

———, Dugald—Age 40; Tr. servt.; embark'd 24 June 1737; arrived 20 Nov. 1737.

———, Eliz.—Age 19; servt. for 4 yrs.; embark'd 19 Nov. 1737; arrived 14 Jan. 1737–8. Hired & carry'd at Capt. Thompson the owners risk, but recd. by Mr. Causton as on the Tr. Acct. which made us lyable; alive at Darien 6 May 1741 but named Hellen.

———, Florenica—Age 20; servt for 1 yr.; embark'd on 19 Nov. 1737; arrived 14 Jan. 1737–8. In the same case; alive at Darien 6 May 1741.

———, Geo.—Age 19; of Tar.; labour. Tr. servt; embark'd 20 Oct. 1735; arrived 10 Jan 1735–6.

Macdonald, Geo.—Age 21; labourer; highlander; embark'd on 21 Sept. 1741; arriv'd 2 Dec. 1741.

———, Hugh—Age 37; of Tar. labour.; Tr. servt.; embark'd 20 Oct. 1735; arrived 10 Jan. 1735–6.

Macdonald, Jo.—Age 32; hunter; highlander; a late freeholder of Savannah; embark'd 20 Oct. 1741; arrived 2 Dec. 1741.

———, Marian Cadach, w.— Age 29; dead 5 Aug. 1742.

———, Donald, son—Age 2.

———, Elizabeth, d.—Age 6.

———, William, son—Age 4.

Macdonald, Norman—Age 32; labourer; Highlander; embark'd 21 Sept. 1741; arrived 2 Dec. 1741.

———, Eliz. Mackay, w.—Age 29.

———, Catherine, d.—Age 9.

———, John, son—Age 6.

Macdonald, Rachel—Age 19; servt. for 4 yrs.; embark'd on 19 Nov. 1737; arrived 14 Jan. 1737–8. Hired & carry'd at Capt. Thompson the owners risk, but recd, by Mr. Causton as on the Tr. Acct, which made us lyable.

MacEever, Evander—Age 22; Tr. servt.; embark'd 24 June 1737; arrived 20 Nov. 1737.

———, Rodorick—Age 22; servt. for 4 yrs.; embark'd on 19 Nov. 1737; arrived 14 Jan. 1737–8. Hired and carry'd at Capt. Thompson the owners risk, but Mr. Causton recd. such servants on the Trustees acct. and certifyed the same which made us lyable.

Macgilivray, Duncan—Age 24; Tr. servt; embark'd 24 June 1737; arrived 20 Nov. 1737.

Macgregor, Gregy.—Age 18; servt. for 5 yrs.; embark'd on 19 Nov. 1737; arrived 14 Jan. 1737–8. Hired and carry'd at Capt. Thompson the owners risk, but Mr. Causton recd. such servants on the Trustees acct. and certifyed the same which made us lyable.

Macgruer, Alex.—Age 30; Tr. servt.; embark'd 24 June 1737; arrived 20 Nov. 1737.

———, Anne—Age 4; servt. for 20 yrs.; embark'd 19 Nov. 1737; arrived 14 Jan 1737–8. Hired and carry'd at Capt. Thompson the owners risk, but Mr. Causton recd. such servants on the Trustees acct. and certifyed the same which made us lyable.

———, al[ia]s. Frazer, Jo.—Age 24; Tr. servt.; embark'd on 24 June 1737; arrived 20 Nov. 1737.

Mackany, Rodorick—Age 20; Tr. servt.; embark'd 24 June 1737; arrived 20 Nov. 1737.

Mackay, Alexr.—Age 26; of Lange; labourer; Tr. servt.; 20 Oct. 1735; arrived 10 Jan. 1735–6.

———, Angus—Age 19; of Tonge; Labourer; Tr. servt.; embark'd 20 Oct. 1735; arrived 10 Jan. 1735–6.

———, Angus—Age 28; of Andratichlis; Tr. servt.; embark'd 20 Oct. 1735; arrived 10 Jan. 1735–6.

———, Angus—Age 21; taylor; Highlander; embark'd on 21 Sept. 1741; arrived 2 Dec. 1741.

———, Bain Donald—Age 39; of Tar.; labourer; Tr. servt.; embark'd 20 Oct. 1735; arrived 10 Jan. 1735–6.

———, Catherine.

———, Catherine—Daughter to widow Christian Lossley; embark'd 21 Sept. 1741; arrived 2 Dec. 1741.

Mackay, Donald—Age 32; labourer; Highlander; embark'd on 21 Sept. 1741; arrived 2 Dec. 1741.

———, James, son—Age 8.

———, Margaret, d.—Age 12.

Mackay, Donald—Age 21; labourer; Highlander; embark'd on 21 Sept. 1741; arrived 2 Dec. 1741.

———, Elizabeth—Age 20, single woman; Highlander; embark'd 21 Sept. 1741; arrived 2 Dec. 1741.

———, George—Age 20; of Tar.; labourer; Tr. servt.; embark'd 20 Oct. 1735; arrived 10 Jan. 1735–6.

———, Geo.—Age 20; cow herder.; Highlander; embark'd on 21 Sept. 1741; arrived 2 Dec. 1741.

———, Isabel—Age 18; single woman; Highlander; embark'd 21 Sept. 1741; arrived 2 Dec. 1741.

———, John—Age 22; of Tonge; labourer; Tr. servt.; embark'd 20 Oct. 1735; arrived 10 Jan. 1735–6. Out of his time.

———, Jo.—Age 25; servt. to Joseph Stanley; embark'd on 6 Nov. 1732; arrived 1 Feb. 1732–3. He left neither wife nor child. Dead 25 July 1733.

———, Marian—Age 16; single woman; Highlander; embark'd 21 Sept. 1741; arrived 2 Dec. 1741.

———, als. Morison, Robt.—Age 23; Tr. servt.; embark'd 24 June 1737; arrived 20 Nov. 1737.

———, Neil—Age 40; of Tar.; Tr. servt.; embark'd on 20 Oct. 1735; arrived 10 Jan. 1735–6. Living at Darien still a servt. 6 May 1741 but said to be then but 23 years old.

———, Will.—Age 24; of Tar.; Tr. servt.; embark'd on 20 Oct. 1735; arrived 10 Jan. 1735–6.

———, Will.—Age 18; of Tar.; cooper; Tr. servt.; embark'd 20 Oct. 1735; arrived 10 Jan. 1735–6.

———, Will.—Age 19; Tr. servt.; embark'd 24 June 1737; arrived 20 Nov. 1737. Liv.

———, Will.—Age 21; cow heard; Highlander; embark'd on 21 Sept. 1741; arrived 2 Dec. 1741.

Mackensie, Alexr.—Age 24; Tr. servt.; embark'd 24 June 1737; arrived 20 Nov. 1737.

———, Andrew—Age 24; servt. for 5 yrs.; embark'd on 19 Nov. 1737; arrived 14 Jan. 1737–8. Hired & carry'd at Capt. Thompson the owners risk, but taken by Mr. Causton as on the Trustees Acct. & by him so certifyed tho without order, which made us lyable. Dead about June 1738.

———, Donald—Age 22; Tr. servt.; embark'd 24 June 1737; arrived 20 Nov. 1737.

———, Jo.—Age 29; Tr. servt.; embark'd 24 June 1737; arrived 20 Nov. 1737.

———, Tho.—Age 23, Tr. servt.; embark'd 24 June 1737; arrived 20 Nov. 1737. Living at Darien still a servt. 6 May 1741.

———, Will.—Age 17; Tr. servt.; embark'd 24 June 1737; arrived 20 Nov. 1737. Living at Darien still a servt. 6 May 1741.

Mackintosh, Adam—Age 22; of Lange; labourer; Tr. servt.; embark'd 20 Oct. 1735; arrived 10 Jan. 1735–6.

———, Cath. Monro, w.—Age 25; embark'd 20 Oct. 1735; arrived 10 Jan. 1735–6.

———, Donald—Age 22; servt. for 5 yrs.; embark'd 19 Nov. 1737; arrived 14 Jan. 1737–8. Hired & carry'd at Capt. Thompson the owners risk, but taken by Mr. Causton as on the Trustees Acct. & by him so certifyed, tho without order, which made us lyable.

————, Isabel—Age 18; servt for 4 yrs.; embark'd 19 Nov. 1737; arrived 14 Jan. 1737–8. In the same case; alive at Darien 6 May 1741.

————, Jo.—Age 21; of Inverness; labourer; Tr. servt.; embark'd 20 Oct. 1734; arrived 10 Jan. 1735–6. Kill'd or taken prisoner; I believe at Moosa June 1741, leaving a widow and 3 children.

————, Mary—Age 20; servt. 4 yrs.; embark'd 19 Nov. 1737; arrived 14 Jan. 1737–8. Hired & carry'd at Capt. Thompson the owners risk, but taken by Mr. Causton as on the Trustees Acct. & by him so certifyed, tho without order, which made us lyable.

Mackintyre, Hugh—Age 18; servt. for 7 yrs.; embark'd on 19 Nov. 1737; arrived 14 Jan. 1737–8. In the same case.

Maclain, Alexr.—Age 36; Tr. servt.; embark'd 24 June 1737; arrived 20 Nov. 1737.

Maclean, Jo.—Age 30; servt. 4 years; embark'd 19 Nov. 1737; arrived 14 Jan. 1737–8. Hired & carry'd at Capt. Thompson the owners risk, but taken by Mr. Causton as on the Trustees Acct. & by him so certifyed, tho without order, which made us lyable.

Macleod, Alexr.—Age 19; Tr. servt.; embark'd 24 June 1737; arrived 20 Nov. 1737.

————, Angus—Age 17; of Apint.; labourer; Tr. servt.; embark'd 20 Oct. 1735; arrived 10 Jan. 1735–6. Of the Highland Independt. Company & so return'd by Col. Oglethorpe 6 May 1741.

————, Cath.—Age 19; servt. for 4 years; embark'd on 19 Nov. 1737; arrived 14 Jan. 1737–8. Hired & carry'd at the owner Capt. Thompson's risk, but taken by Mr. Causton as on the Trustees acct. without order, and so certified, which made us lyable.

————, Evan—Age 16; Tr. servt.; embark'd 24 June 1737; arrived 20 Nov. 1737.

————, Jo.—Age 35; fisherman; Highlander; embark'd on 21 Sept. 1741; arrived 2 Dec. 1741.

————, Roderick—Age 24; Tr. servt.; embark'd 24 June 1737; arrived 20 Nov. 1737. Of the Highland Independt. Company, & so return'd by Col. Oglethorpe 6 May 1741.

————, Rodorick—Age 26; Tr. servt.; embark'd 24 June 1737; arrived 20 Nov. 1737.

Macpherson, Jo.—Age 20; Tr. servt.; embark'd 24 June 1737; arrived 20 Nov. 1737.

————, Jo.—Age 20; Tr. servt.; embark'd 24 June 1737; arrived 20 Nov. 1737.

Monro, Donald—Age 16; servt. 7 yrs.; embark'd 19 Nov. 1737; arrived 14 Jan. 1737–8. Hired & carry'd at the owner Capt. Thompson's risk, but taken by Mr. Causton as on the Trustees acct. without order, and so certified, which made us lyable. Dead about June 1738.

————, Hector—Age 19; of Tonge.; labourer; Tr. servt.; embark'd 20 Oct. 1735; arrived 10 Jan. 1735–6.

————, John—Age 15; servt. 7 yrs.; embark'd 19 Nov. 1737; arrived 14 Jan. 1737–8. Hired & carry'd at the owner Capt. Thompson's risk, but taken by Mr. Causton as on the Trustees acct. without order, and so certified, which made us lyable.

Morrison, Hugh—Age 22; of Tonge.; labourer; Tr. servt.; embark'd 20 Oct. 1735; arrived 10 Jan. 1735–6. Of the Highland Independt. Company, & so return'd by Col. Oglethorpe 6 May 1741.

Munro, Ja.—Age 33; cow heard; Highlander; embark'd 21 Sept. 1741; arrived 2 Dec. 1741.

Murray, Alexr.—Age 26; of Rogart; labourer.; Tr. servt.; embark'd 20 Oct. 1735; arrived 10 Jan. 1735–6.

————, Anne—Age 18; single woman; Highlander; embark'd 21 Sept. 1741; arrived 2 Dec. 1741.

————, Christian—Age 18; servt for 4 yrs.; embark'd 19 Oct. 1737; arrived 14 Jan. 1737–8. Hired and carry'd at Capt. Thompson the owners risk, but taken by Mr. Causton as on the Trustees acct. and so certified, tho without orders, which made us lyable. Alive at Darien 6 May 1741.

Ross, Daniel—Age 16; servt. for 6 years; embark'd 19 Nov. 1737; arrived 14 Jan. 1737–8; Hired & carry'd at Capt. Thompson the owners risk, but the Planters not being able to pay for such servt. Mr. Causton without orders took him as on the Trustees Acct. & so certified, which made us lyable. Dyed at Darien. Dead 1738.

————, Will.—Age 32; Tr. servt.; embark'd 24 June 1737; arrived 20 Nov. 1737.

————, Will.—Age 25; Tr. servt.; embark'd 24 June 1737; arrived 20 Nov. 1737.

Stewart, Donald—Age 24; Tr. servt.; embark'd 24 June 1737; arrived 20 Nov. 1737; drownd 1741.

————, Donald—Age 30; servt. for 4 years; embark'd on 19 Nov. 1737; arrived 14 Jan. 1737–8. Hired & carry'd at Capt. Thomas the owners risk; but the Planters not being able to pay for such servt. Mr. Causton took him as on acct. of the Trust without orders, & so certified, which made us lyable. Shot by accidt. 6 Aug. 1741.

————, James—Age 27; Tr. servt.; embark'd 24 June 1737; arrived 20 Nov. 1737. Of the Highland Company of Rangers, & so return'd by Col. Oglethorpe 6 May 1741. Out of his time.

Stronach, John—Age 28; servt. for 3 yrs.; embark'd on 19 Nov. 1737; arrived 24 Jan. 1737–8. Hired & carry'd at Capt. Thomas the owners risk: but the Planters not able to pay for such servt. Mr. Causton without orders did it for them and by certificate charged the Trustees with the expence. An invalid (at Darien May 6, 1741).

————, Cath., w.—Age 35; servt. for 3 yrs. Her case the same. Alive at Darien 6 May 1741.

————, Pricilla, d.—born in Georgia. Alive at Darien 6 May 1741 & then 3 months old.

————, Will, son—Born in Georgia. Alive at Darien 6 May 1741 then about 4 years old.

————, Michl.—Age 16; Tr. servt.; embark'd 24 June 1737; arrived 20 Nov. 1737.

Sutherland, Robt.—Age 35; of Leath.; labourer; Tr. servt.; embark'd 20 Oct. 1735; arrived 10 Jan. 1735–6.

Sutherland, Robt.—Age 21; labourer; Highlander; embark'd 21 Sept. 1741; arrived 4 Dec. 1741.

Taylor, Joseph—Age 25; servt. for 4 yrs.; embark'd on 19 Nov. 1737; arrived 14 Jan. 1737–8. Hired at Capt. Thompson the owners risk & carry'd but the Planters not being able to pay for such servants, Mr. Causton did it & so certified to the Trustees, which made them lyable.

———, Cath., w.—Age 23; servt. for 4 yrs. Her case the same.

Taylor, Will.—Age 17; servt. for 4 yrs.; embark'd 19 Nov. 1737; arrived 14 Jan. 1737–8. His case the same.

Part B: Persons Who Went to Georgia on Their Own Account

Anderson, Hugh. Esq.—Arrived 27 June 1737; lot 178 in Savannah. This gentleman went over with a large family of servants as well as children, and was made Inspector Genl. of the Publick garden and mulberry plantations.

———, Eliz., w.

———, Alexr., son.

———, Cath., d.

———, Moore, son.

Anderson, Ja.—Age 25; joyner; embark'd 20 Oct. 1735; arrived 10 Jan. 1735–6. Lot 235 in Savannah. He was possest of his lot 1 May 1737, but neglects it & lives on his br. John's lot in Savannah No. 190, which John was not arrived in 1738.

———, (?), w.

———, James, son—Born in Georgia; dead 1740.

———, John—Lot 190 in Savannah. Not arrived 1738. But James his brother improves on his lot, and built a good house.

Baillie, James, servt. to Kenneth Baillie—Age 33; embark'd 20 Oct. 1735; arrived 10 Jan. 1735–6.

Baillie, John—Arrived 1 Aug. 1734. He had a grant of 400 acres 18 Oct. 1733.

Baillie, John of Fortrose—Farmer; embark'd 20 Oct. 1735; arrived 10 Jan. 1735–6. Dead April 1737.

Ballie, Kenneth—Age 20; farmer; embark'd 20 Oct. 1735; arrived 10 Jan. 1735–6. Ensign to the Darien Company, taken by the Spaniards at Moosa and made his escape from St. Sebastian to England Jany. 1741–2 and return'd to Georgia March 1741–2.

Ballie, Martha—D. of John Ballie, Smith; born in Georgia 22 Oct. 1738.

Bain, Kenneth—Age 18; servt. to Alex. Tolmie; embark'd 20 Oct. 1735; arrived 10 Jan. 1735–6.

Bain, Will., of Thuso—Age 19; taylor; embark'd 20 Oct. 1735; arrived 10 Jan. 1735–6.

Burges, Joseph—Embarked 20 Oct. 1735; of Darien: Slayn at the seige of Augustine

June 1740, & left a wife & child at Darien living 6 May 1741. Dead June 1740.

————, Margt., w.—Margt. Burges widow of Joseph. Resident at Darien 6 May 1741.

————, James, son—Born in Georgia. James Burgess their son 4 years & 3 months old 6 May 1741.

Burnes, John—Servt. to Hugh Anderson.

Burnes, Robt.—Servt. to Patrick Tailfer.

Cameron, Alexr.—Embark'd 20 Oct. 1735. Of Darien: slayn at the seige of Augustine June 1740, & left only a widow of Darien 6 May 1741. Dead June 1740.

————, (?), w.—Wid. of Alexr. In Darien I suppose 6 May 1741.

Cameron, Margt.—Servt. to Abrm. Minas.

Campbell, Colin. gent.—Age 27; embark'd 20 Oct. 1735; arrived 10 Jan. 1735–6.

Campbell, James—Lot 221 in Savannah. He ran away with the Revd. Mr. John Wesley 3 Dec. 1737. This lot formerly belong'd to Will Cookey who resign'd it for lot 9 being swamp and overflow'd. An idle fellow & in debt. He return'd and was in Georgia 7 Jan. 1740–1 and was employd to read prayers for want of a minister. Run away for debt but returned.

Chisholme, Alexr. of Invernes—Age 26; servt. to Farqr. Mcgilivray; embark'd 20 Oct. 1735; arrived 10 Jan. 1735–6; run away to Carolina Aug. 1742.

Chisholme, Alexr. of Dornach—Age 17; servt. to Mr. Mackay of Scourie; embark'd 20 Oct. 1735; arrived 10 Jan. 1735–6.

Chisholme, Margt.—Age 22; servt. to J. Sinclair; embark'd 20 Oct. 1735; arrived 10 Jan. 1735–6.

Clark, Donald—Age 23; of Dorris. Farmer; embark'd 20 Oct. 1735; arrived 10 Jan. 1735–6.

Clark, Donald—Age 42; of Tongie; embark'd 20 Oct. 1735; arrived 10 Jan. 1735–6. Slayn at Augustine June 1740 and left a wife & 4 children living at Darien 6 May 1741.

————, Barbara Grey—Age 40; w. Resident at Darien 6 May 1741.

————, Alexr., son—Age 15; dead as suppos'd.

————, Angus, son—Age 5. Living at Darien 6 May 1741.

————, Barbara, d.—Age 2; dead I suppose.

————, Geo., son—Age 13; dead I suppose.

————, Hugh, son—Age 12. A soldier in the highland Independt. Company, and return'd as such 6 May 1741.

————, Will., son—Age 8. Living at Darien 6 May 1741.

Clark, Elias—Son of Hen. & Anne; born in Georgia 13 Mar. 1732–3; dead 28 Oct. 1733.

Clark, Eliz.—Child. servt. to Will. Bradley.

Clark, Henry—Son of Hen. & Anne; born in Georgia 17 Sept. 1733; dead 9 Sept. 1733 (sic).

Clark, Hugh—Age 21; of Dorris. Farmer; embark'd 20 Oct. 1735; arrived 10 Jan.

1735–6. A soldier in the highland Independt. Company, and return'd as such 6 May 1741. is Serjt. of ye Compy.

Clark, Hugh—Born in Georgia.

Clark, Hugh—3 years 3 months old 6 May 1741.

Clark, John—Born in Georgia; lot 53 in Savannah.

Clark, Jo.—3 years 9 months old 6 May 1741. Dead —.

Clark, Will.—Born in Georgia. 2 years 6 months old 6 May 1741.

Clarke, John.—Lot 73 (or 93) in Savannah. He marry'd the widow Dearn and lives on her Lot 29. Appointed Secy. for the Indian affairs 3 May 1738. He went over with Col. Oglethorpe 1738. Died at Frederica. Dead —.

Crookshanks, Rob.—Servt. to Farqr. Mcgilivray; embark'd 20 Oct. 1735; arrived 10 Jan. 1735–6. Col. Oglethorp writes July 1739 that he was grown blind in the Trustees service and therefore he allow'd him 5 pence a day subsistence: But he went from Scotland a Servt. to Farquar Macgilivray not on the Trustees acct. and how he came to fall upon the Trust or when I know not. Alive at Darien 6 May 1741.

Cross, Thomas—Soldier; lot 22 in Savannah. Marry'd the widow Judith Clark 29 June 1734. He was in Independt. Compy. Soldier at St. Simons Fort, and run away Dec. 1738. In the Colony the end of the year 1746.

———, Judith Clark—Wid. his wife; arrived 29 June 1734.

Cuthbert, Geo.—of Inverness. Farmer; embark'd 20 Oct. 1735; arrived 10 Jan. 1735–6. Settled at Darien. I find him a cattle hunter with 6 servants from 18 Sept. 1738 to 18 June 1739 at the annual expence of 174£ and Mr. Oglethorp writes that it is absolutely necessary to continue this charge.

Cuthbert, Jo.—Run away to Carolina Aug. 1742.

Cuthbert, Jo.—Age 31; of Draikes, gent.; embark'd 20 Oct. 1735; arrived 10 Jan. 1735–6. Grant of 500 acres made him 3 Sept. 1735, which he took up at Josephstown, but afterwards abandon'd, and settled at Darien or new Inverness. In 1736 Mr. Oglethorp made him Comander of Fort St. Andrews. Dead 16 Nov. 1739.

———, (?), w.—embark'd 24 June 1737; arrived 20 Nov. 1737.

Douglass, David—Lot 170 in Savannah. His lot was granted to him in 1736. Cost in auction of 50£ sterl. debt due to Ja. Muier for 2 years rent 7 July 1737. A factious man: & went to Carolina for fear of the Spaniards 30 Aug. 1740. Quitted 30 Aug. 1740.

———, Jannet, his sister.

Douglass, Willm.—Servt. to Patrick Tailfer; arrived on 1 Aug. 1734.

Drisdale, James—Servt. to Hugh Anderson.

Dunbar, George, Capt.—He had a grant of 500 acres which he took up at Josephstown: but afterwds. quitted it to settle at Darien. Now Lieut. in Oglethorp's Regiment.

Dunbar, John—Age 36; of Inverness. Farmer; embark'd 20 Oct. 1735; arrived 10 Jan. 1735–6; dead 1740.

Dunbar, John—Lot 181 in Savannah. He went to England about Dec. 1737. Went to England Dec. 1737.

Dunbar, Margt.—Servt. to Will. Bradley.

Duncan, John—Servt. to Patrick Houston; arrived 1 Aug. 1734. Servt. at first to Patrick Houston, but afterwards bought by A. Johnson 21 Jan. 1734–5.

Ferguson, Tho.—Servt.; arrived 8 June 1737.

Ferguson, Will.—Master of the Scout boat.

Forbes, Hugh—Servt. to Will. & Hugh Sterling; embark'd on 20 Oct. 1735; arrived 10 Jan. 1735–6.

Forbes, John—Age 26; Servt. to Jo. Cuthbert of Draikes.

Frazer, Donald—Servt. to A. Johnson; arrived 7 May 1734. Sentenc'd 30 lashes for assault 1734.

Frazer, Donald of Abercour—Servt. to Patrick Grant; embark'd 20 Oct. 1735; arrived 10 Jan. 1735–6.

Frazer, Donald, of Inverness—Age 20; Servt. to Alexr. Mackintosh; embark'd 20 Oct. 1735; arrived 10 Jan. 1735–6.

Frazer, Donald of Ditto—Age 22; Servt. to Jo. Cuthbert of Draikes; embark'd 20 Oct. 1735; arrived 10 Jan. 1735–6.

Frazer, Donald of Kingussie—Age 25; servt. to Jo. Mackintosh; embark'd 20 Oct. 1735; arrived 10 Jan. 1735–6.

Frazer, Thomas—Servt. to Patrick Houston; arrived 1 Aug. 1734. In the colony the end of the year 1746. Out of his time.

Frazer, Will.—Servt. to A. Johnson; arrived 7 May 1734.

Fyffe, Rachl.—Servt. to Patrick Houston; arrived 1 Aug. 1734.

Gordon, Margt.—Servt to Cha. Pury.

Gordon, Phil.—Servt. to Jo. Penrose.

Gordon, Robert—Servt. to Tho. Young.

Graham, Patrick—Apothecary; lot 189 in Savannah. He neglects his own lot and rents lots 137 [and] 211. On 19 May 1736 a grant of 100 acres was past to him. Marry'd Capt. Cuthberts sister 6 March 1739–40.

Grant, John—Age 18; servt. to Patrick Grant; embark'd 20 Oct. 1735; arrived 10 Jan. 1735–6.

Grant, Lodowick—A trader in the Cherokee nation.

Grant, Margaret—Alive at Darien 6 May 1741.

Grant, Peter—Servt. to Tho. Causton.

Grant, Patrick—Age 24; of Aberlour. Farmer; embark'd 20 Oct. 1735; arrived 10 Jan. 1735–6; lot 166 in Savannah. A grant of 100 acres was granted him same year, but he neglects both, & has taken 2 other lots in the town at rent from the owners. Tything man 1738 and a pert sawcy fellow. Kill'd in duel 1740.

Grant, Sarah—Born in Georgia. Alive at Darien 6 May 1741 & then 2 years old.

Grey, Will.—Agent with the Chickesaw & Utchea Indians.

Gun, Will.—Age 30; Servt. to Mr. Mackay of Scourie; embark'd 20 Oct. 1735; arrived 10 Jan. 1735–6; out of his time.

Houston, Patrick—Gent. 1740 took a lot in Frederica by mar. to Capt. Dunbars sister; arrived 1 Aug. 1734; lot 3S. in Frederica. Fyn'd 1.0.0 for selling rum 17 July 1735. Convicted of not supplying his servants with necessarys 21 Oct. 1735. A lot of 500 acres was granted him 1 Aug. 1733. But not set out till June 1737. In Oct. 1738 Col. Oglethorp lent him on the Trustees acct. 100£ to enable him to set up a boat to furnish provision cheap to the Colony.

————, (?), Dunbar, w.

Kennedy, Will.—Age 22; Taylor. Servt. to Jo. Cuthbert of Draikes; embark'd 20 Oct. 1735; arrived 10 Jan. 1735–6. A tailor. Out of his time. Run away with his family to Carolina Aug. 1742.

————, Eliz., w.—Age 24; servt. to Ditto.

————, (?),—Child of above; born in Georgia; run away.

————, (?),—Child of Ditto; born in Georgia; run away.

Macbane, Lachlans—Indian trader. On 14 June 1736 Mr. Oglethorp order'd him a lot of 500 acres & a house in Fort Augusta. In the Colony at the end of the year 1746.

Macbean, Archibald—Age 26; of Aberlaur. Farmer; embark'd 20 Oct. 1735; arrived 10 Jan. 1735–6. Returned Dead 1740.

————, Cath. Cameron, w.—Age 21.

————, Alexandr., son—Dead 1740.

Macbean, Duncan—Age 21; servt. to Jo. Mackintosh, Holmes son; embark'd 20 Oct. 1735; arrived 10 Jan. 1735–6.

Macbean, McWillie, Jo.—Age 27; servt. to Jo. Spence; embark'd 20 Oct. 1735; arrived 10 Jan 1735–6.

Macbride, Ant.—Servt. to Will & H. Sterling; arrived 1 Aug. 1734.

Macbride, Hen.—Servt. to Will & H. Sterling; arrived 1 Aug. 1734.

Macdermot, Barrow—Tr. Servt.; arrived 10 Jan. 1733–4.

Macdonald, Donald—Age 22; embark'd 20 Oct. 1735; arrived 10 Jan. 1735–6. Living at Darien. Still a servant 6 May 1741.

————, Alvine Wood, w.—Age 20. Alias Winwood Macdonald. Alive at Darien 6 May 1741.

Macdonald, Donald—Born in Georgia. Alive at Darien 6 May 1741 and then 6 months old.

Macdonald, Ja.—Servt. Fynd 19.0.0 for enticing and carrying away servants 23 June 1734.

Macdonald, Jo.—Born in Georgia. Alive at Darien 6 May 1741 & then 2 years 3 months old.

Macdonald, Jo.—Servt. to Jo. Baily; arrived 1 August 1734. At first servt. to John Baily: afterwards to Andrew Grant.

Macdonald, John—Age 19; servt. to Donald Macdonald.

Macdonald, Mary—W. of Alexr; a Soldier; embark'd 16 August 1737; arrived 31 Oct. 1737.

Macdonald, Rachel—Servt. to Will Stephens, Esq.

Macdonald, Rainold—Age 18; Servt. to Jo. Mackintosh of Kingussie junr.; embark'd 20 Oct. 1735; arrived 10 Jan. 1735–6. Of Darien of the highland company of Rangers 6 May 1741. There was one of both names kill'd or made prisoner at Moosa June 1740 who left a wife & 4 children at Darien 6 May 1741. Qy if this be he.

Macer, Alexr.—Servt. to Hugh Anderson.

Macferline, Danl.—Servt. to Will & H. Sterling; arrived 1 Aug. 1734.

Macgilivray, Archibd.—Age 15. He had a grant of 50 acres made him 3 Sept 1735, and on July 9 same year a town lot in Savanah but I believe he took it not.

Macgilivray, Farquar—Age 30; servt. to J. Cuthbert of Draikes; embark'd 20 Oct. 1735; arrived 10 Jan. 1735–6.

Macgilivray, Lachlan—Age 16; servt. to Jo. Mackintosh, Holmes son; embark'd 20 Oct. 1735; arrived 10 Jan. 1735–6.

Macgowran, Pet.—Tr. servt; arrived 10 Jan. 1733–4.

Macgragor, Jane—Servt. to Will. & H. Sterling; arrived 1 Aug. 1734.

Mac-Inver, Murdow—Servt. to J. Cuthbert of Draikes; embark'd 20 Oct. 1735; arrived 10 Jan. 1735–6.

Mackay, (?)—of Scourie. Gent.; embark'd 20 Oct. 1735; arrived 10 Jan. 1735–6.

Mackay, (?)—of Strothie. Gent.; embark'd 20 Oct. 1735; arrived 10 Jan. 1735–6.

Mackay, Cha.—Age 17; of Tar; embark'd 20 Oct. 1735; arrived 10 Jan. 1735–6. Ensign to the Highland Independt. Company, & so returnd by Col. Oglethorpe 6 May 1741.

Mackay, Hugh, Lt.—Now Capt. in Oglethorps Reg. He had a grant of 500 acres made him 24 July 1735. He quitted the Colony and Regiment upon not being promoted to Major of the Regiment 1740. Quitted 1740.

———, Hellen, w.—Embark'd 14 Oct. 1735; arrived Feb. 1735–6.

Mackay, Hugh—Born in Georgia. Alive at Darien 6 May 1741 & then 1 year old.

Mackay, James—Age 17; of Tar; embark'd 20 Oct. 1735; arrived 10 Jan. 1735–6. Of Darien; Slayn at the Seige of Augustine June 1740.

Mackay, Ja.—Age 40; of Durnes. Farmer; embark'd 20 Oct. 1735; arrived 10 Jan. 1735–6. Slayn or made prisoner at Moosa June 1740. Left a wife & 4 children.

———, Barbara McLeod, w.—Age 36. Alive at Darien with her 4 children 6 May 1741.

———, Barbara, d.—Age 17. Alive at Darien 6 May 1741 but said then to be only 11 years old.

———, Donald, son—Age 9. Alive at Darien 6 May 1741.

———, Jeanne, d.—Age 6.

Mackay, John—Age 56; of Durnes. Farmer; embark'd 20 Oct. 1735; arrived 10 Jan. 1735–6.

————, Jannet, w.—Age 32.

————, Eliz., d.

————, Hugh, son—Age 18.

————, John, son—Age 3.

————, Mary, d.

————, Will., son—Age 6.

Mackay, John, Esq.—Arrived 1 Feb. 1732–3. He had a grant of 500 acres made him 3 Sept. 1735, & took it at Josephstown, but dying, that settlement in a little time disperst. Dead 25 July 1736.

Mackay, Jo.—Age 50; of Lairg; embark'd 20 Oct. 1735; arrived 10 Jan. 1735–6.

————, Jannet Mackintosh, w.—Age 40. Alive at Darien 6 May 1741.

————, Donald, son—Age 6.

————, Jeanne, d.—Age 2.

————, Patrick, son—Age 7.

Mackay, Patrick—Fled Scotland for Felony. He had a grant of 500 acres made him 3 Sept. 1735, and keeps servts. on it: But has also a plantation on Carolina side of the River Savannah, on which he keeps Negroes, which is of bad example to our Planters.

————, (?), w.—Mrs. Montagut—She was wid. of Mr. Montagut & remar. 1740.

————, Will., son—Arrived 1 Feb. 1732–3; lot 55 in Savannah. Took possession of his lot 21 Dec. 1733 his father quitting Josephstown his country grant, lives here with his son. Abs[ent]. 24 Feb. 1736–7.

Mackay, William—Age 18; servt. to Mackay, (?) of Strothie.

Mackay, Will.—Age 21; of Lavig; servt. to Mackay, (?) of Scourie. A Soldier in the Independent Company of highlanders & so return'd by Col. Oglethorp 6 May 1741.

Mackdonald, Georgia—Born in Georgia. Alive at Darien 6 May 1741 and then abt. 6 years old.

Mackdonald, Janet—Born in Georgia. Alive at Darien and then 2 years old.

Mackenzie, Cath.—Servt. to Noble Jones.

Mackimmie, Alexr.—Age 50; labourer; embark'd 20 Oct. 1735; arrived 10 Jan. 1735–6.

Mackintosh, Anne—Born in Georgia. Living at Darien and then 4 years old.

Mackintosh, Benj.—Age 50; of Dorris. Farmer; embark'd 20 Oct. 1735; arrived 10 Jan. 1735–6.

————, Cath., w.—Age 45. Alive at Darien 6 May 1741.

————, Eliz., d.—Age 20.

————, Jannet, d.—Age 18.

————, Lachlan, son—Age 12. Living at Darien 6 May 1741 but said to be only 13 years old at that time.

Mackintosh, Donald—Age 17; servt. to John Mackintosh of Inverness. Living at Darien still a servt. 6 May 1741.

Mackintosh, Donald—Age 20; of Inverness. Servt. to Alexr. Mackintosh; embark'd 20 Oct. 1735; arrived 10 Jan. 1735–6.

Mackintosh, Eneas—Capt. at Fort St. George. Afterwards at Fort Polachocolas. Capt. at fort St. George at 37.10.0 *p. ann.* till 16 May 1739. He was Capt. of 10 Rangers, which Col. Oglethorp reduced 16 Dec. 1738. But continued him ¼ a year longer to hunt up the Trustees wild cattel, which is generally done in May. He afterwards was Comandr. at Fort Palachocolas, but in Feb. 1739–40 return'd to Scotland where an estate fell to him. Quitted 27 Feb. 1739/40.

Mackintosh, Geo.—Age 21; of Durnes; taylor; embark'd 20 Oct. 1735; arrived 10 Jan. 1735–6.

Mackintosh, Geo.—Born in Georgia. Two years old May 1741.

Mackintosh, Hugh—Born in Georgia. Alive in Georgia 6 May 1741 & then 2 years old.

Mackintosh, Jo.—Age 50; Senr. of Dornes. Farmer; embark'd 20 Oct. 1735; arrived 10 Jan. 1735–6. Alive at Darien 6 May 1741.

————, Cath., w.—Age 47.

————, Alexr., son—Age 8. Living at Darien 6 May 1741.

————, Beatrix, d.—Age 5. Living at Darien 6 May 1741.

————, Will., son—Age 12. Of the highland Compy. of Rangers & so return'd by Col. Oglethorpe 6 May 1741.

Mackintosh, Jo.—Age 15; farmer; embark'd 20 Oct. 1735; arrived 10 Jan. 1735–6. Of the Highland Company of Rangers, and as such return'd by Col. Oglethorpe 6 May 1741.

Mackintosh, Jo.—Age 21; of Dorris. Farmer; embark'd on 20 Oct. 1735; arrived 10 Jan. 1735–6.

Mackintosh, Jo. Holmes went to settle in Carolina. Dec. 1740. Quitted Dec. 1740.

Mackintosh, John—Age 24; of Inverness. Farmer; embark'd 20 Oct. 1735; arrived 10 Jan. 1735–6. Son of Holmes. One of both names was killd at Moosa, or made prisoner June 1741. Qy. if this be he. The man left a wife & child at Darien 6 May 1741.

Mackintosh, Jo.—Age 36; Junr. of Kingussie Farmr.; embark'd 20 Oct. 1735; arrived 10 Jan. 1735–6.

————, Margt., w.—Age 30. Alive at Darien 6 May 1741.

————, John, son—Age 8. Alive at Darien 1741.

————, Lachlan, son—Age 9.

————, Margt., d.—Age 18.

————, Phineas, son—Age 3. Alive at Darien 1741.

————, Will., son—Age 10.

Mackintosh, John—Age 50; of Dornach; embark'd 20 Oct. 1735; arrived 10 Jan. 1735–6.

Mackintosh, Moor Jo.—Gent.; Chief of Darien. See his family [above: Margt., John, Lachlan, Margt., Phineas, and Will]. Keeper of the Store at Darien 1739. Taken at

Moosa in 1740 & now a prisoner in Spain Nov. 1741, where if he dies he will leave a widow & 6 children in Darien. At the seige of Augustine Col. Oglethorpe made him Capt. of the Highland Company. Has a wife & 6 children at Darien 6 May 1741.
——, (?), w.—Resident at Darien with her 6 children 6 May 1741.

Mackintosh, Lachner—Age 26; servt. to Benj. Mackintosh.

——, Margt., w.—Age 23; servt. to Benj. Mackintosh.

Mackintosh, Lachlan—Ranger at Fort Arguile the middle way between the Darien & Savannah. When Col. Oglethorp dismist the 15 Rangers there he was obliged as he writes to keep on two at 24£ *p. ann.* each. They were paid by him till 19 April 1739, but thinks to reduce them also when the German servants have got in their crop. He had the charge of Fort Arguile in 1740.

Mackintosh, Robt.—Servt. to Saml. Davison. Employ'd in the Scout boat 1738 and another servant promised Davison in his room.

Mackintosh, Robt. of Moy—Age 20; servt. to Ja. Maqueen; embark'd 20 Oct. 1735; arrived 10 Jan. 1735–6.

Mackintosh, Roderick—Age 19; farmer; embark'd 20 Oct. 1735; arrived 10 Jan. 1735–6. Of the Highland Company of Rangers, & so return'd by Col. Oglethorpe 6 May 1741.

Mackintosh, Sarah—Servt. to David Douglass.

Macintyre, Will.—Servt. to Will & H. Sterling; arrived 1 Aug. 1734.

Maclean, Allan—Age 21; of Inverness. Farmer; embark'd 20 Oct. 1735; arrived 10 Jan. 1735–6.

Maclean, Alexr.—Age 32; of Inverness. Farmer; embark'd 20 Oct. 1735; arrived 10 Jan. 1735–6; dead Mar. 1739/40.

Maclean, George—Age 30; of Ardelack. Farmer; embark'd 20 Oct. 1735; arrived 10 Jan. 1735–6.

Maclean, John—Age 19; of Inverness. Servt. to Allan Maclean. Of the Highland Company of Rangers & so return'd by Col. Oglethorpe 6 May 1741.

Maclean, John—Age 20; servt. to Robt. Macpherson of Alvie; embark'd 20 Oct. 1735; arrived 10 Jan. 1735–6.

Maclean, Simon—of Inverness; servt. to Allan Maclean.

Macleod, Angus of Hawnick—Age 17; weaver; servt. to Mackay of Strothie; embark'd 20 Oct. 1735; arrived 10 Jan. 1735–6.

Macleod, Donald of Tar—Age 18; labourer; servt. to Mackay of Strothie; embark'd 20 Oct. 1735; arrived 10 Jan. 1735–6. Of the Highland Independt. Company, and so return'd by Col. Oglethorpe 6 May 1741.

Macleod, Donald of Tar—Labourer; servt. to Mackay of Strothie; Embark'd 20 Oct. 1735; arrived 10 Jan. 1735–6.

Macleod, George—Age 17; labourer; servt. to Mackay of Strothie; embark'd 20 Oct. 1735; arrived 10 Jan. 1735–6.

Macleod, Hugh [John]—Scots Minister at Darien; embark'd 20 Oct. 1735; arrived 10 Jan. 1735–6. A grant of 300 acres to him & his successors as ministers at the

Darien for religious uses was made out 1739. Quitted the Colony 1741 [*sic*].

Macleod, Hugh—Age 21; labourer; servt. to Mackay of Strothie; embark'd 20 Oct. 1735; arrived 10 Jan. 1735–6. Of the Highland Independt. Company, & so return'd by Col. Oglethorpe 6 May 1741.

Macleod, Hugh—Age 18; labourer; servt. to Mackay of Strothie; embark'd 20 Oct. 1735; arrived 10 Jan. 1735–6. Of the Highland Independt. Company & so return'd by Col. Oglethorp 6 May 1741.

Macleod, John—Age 18; labourer; servt. to Mackay of Strothie; embark'd 20 Oct. 1735; arrived 10 Jan. 1735–6. Of the Highland Company of Rangers and so return'd by Col. Oglethorpe 6 May 1741.

Macleod, Mary—Servt. to Tho. Causton.

Macmurrwick, Alexr.—Age 20; servt. to Colin Cambel; embark'd 20 Oct. 1735; arrived 10 Jan. 1735–6.

Macoul, Alexr.—Servt. to Mr. Mackay of Scourie; embark'd 20 Oct. 1735; arrived 10 Jan. 1735–6.

Macpherline, Duncan—Servt. to Will. & H. Sterling; arrived 1 Aug. 1734.

Macpherson, Ja.—A minor; son of Capt. Patrick; arrived 1 Feb. 1732–3; lot 61 in Savannah. He went to Carolina, and is with his Father. Abs[en]t. 29 Feb. 1736–7.

Macpherson, Norman—Age 24; labourer; embark'd 20 Oct. 1735; arrived 10 Jan. 1735–6.

Macpherson, Robt.—Age 24; of Alvie; farmer; embark'd 20 Oct. 1735; arrived 10 Jan. 1735–6.

Macqueen, Ja.—Age 19; of Inverness; embark'd 20 Oct. 1735; arrived 10 Jan. 1735–6.

Macqueen, James—Age 19; his servt.; embark'd 20 Oct. 1735; arrived 10 Jan. 1735–6.

Main, Geo.—Age 23; servt. to Donald Steward; embark'd 20 Oct. 1735; arrived 10 Jan. 1735–6.

Malcome, Jane—Servt. to A. Grant; arrived 1 Aug. 1734.

————, (?),—Her child.

Miller, David—Age 26; servt. to Mackay of Strothie; embark'd 20 Oct. 1735; arrived 10 Jan. 1735–6. Of the highland Independt. Company, & so return'd by Col. Oglethorpe 6 May 1741.

Miller, James—Age 18; servt. to Ja. Anderson; embark'd 20 Oct. 1735; arrived 10 Jan. 1735–6.

Miller, Jo.—Private storekeeper. A private store keeper at Augusta.

Miller, Michl.—Arrived 11 Mar. 1733–4. Mostly at Tybee.

Miller, Richd.—Arrived 11 Mar. 1733–4. Settled at Tybee, and in possession of his lot there 2 April 1734.

Monro, Alexr.—Age 30; of Inverness; farmer; embark'd 20 Oct. 1735; arrived 10 Jan. 1735–6. Return'd dead 1740.

————, Margt., w.—Age 27.

————, Isabel, d.—6 m. old.

Monro, Alexr.—Age 24; of Dornoch; labourer; embark'd 20 Oct. 1735; arrived 10 Jan. 1735–6; dead 1740.

Monro, Donald—Age 45; of Alnit Rossit; labourer; embark'd 20 Oct. 1735; arrived 10 Jan. 1735–6.

Monro, John—Age 16; of Alnit Rossit; labourer; embark'd 20 Oct. 1735; arrived 10 Jan. 1735–6.

Monro, John—Age 21; of Kiltairn; labourer; embark'd 20 Oct. 1735; arrived 10 Jan. 1735–6.

Monro, Robt.—Age 17; of Dornoch; labourer; embark'd 20 Oct. 1735; arrived 10 Jan. 1735–6.

Monro, Will.—Age 12; of Dornach; labourer; embark'd 20 Oct. 1735; arrived 10 Jan. 1735–6.

Monro, Will.—Age 40; of Durnes; farmer; embark'd 20 Oct. 1735; arrived 10 Jan. 1735–6. Of the Highland Company of Rangers and so return'd by Col. Oglethorpe 6 May 1741.

————, Eliz., d.—Age 17.

————, Margt., d.—Age 14.

Murray, Alexr.—Age 17; labourer; embark'd 20 Oct. 1735; arrived 10 Jan. 1735–6.

Murray, Jo.—Age 25; servt. to Mackay of Scourie; embark'd 20 Oct. 1735; arrived 10 Jan. 1735–6; out of his time.

Ross, Hugh of Drenack—Age 36; servt. to Mr. Mackay of Scourie; embark'd 20 Oct. 1735; arrived 10 Jan. 1735–6. Living at Darien still a servant 6 May 1741 but said to be 54 years old.

Ross, James—Servt. to Patrick Houston; arrived 1 Aug. 1734.

Ross, James—Miller; of Waffin; embark'd 20 Oct. 1735; arrived 10 Jan. 1735–6.

Ryley, Alice—Servt. to Ri. Cannon; arrived 10 Jan. 1733–4. An Irish Transport. Condem'd for the murder of Will. Wise her master 1 Mar. 1733–4. Hang'd 20 Jan. 1734–5.

Sinclair, Archibald—Servt. to Patrick Houston; arrived 1 Aug. 1734.

Sinclair, John—Servt. to Jo. Mackintosh of Dorres; arrived 10 Jan. 1735–6.

Spence, John—Age 36; Servt. to Jo. Cuthbert of Draikes; arrived 10 Jan. 1735–6.

Stephens, Donald—Age 53; of Lange; labourer.

Sterling, Hugh—Gent.—Arrived 1 Aug. 1734. 14 Nov. 1733 he had a grant of 500 acres. Hugh & William settled at Sterlings Bluff on the Ogykee river, but after some years cultivation abandon'd their improvmts. to live in Savannah, where they wasted their substance; they quitted before Sept. 1737. Dead 1740.

————, Will.—Gent.; arrived 1 June 1734. 14 Nov. 1733 he had a grant of 500 acres. On 26 May 1739 he & Andrew Grant wrote they had lost 906.2.9 by cultivating with white servants and desired consideration for it. Went to Carolina for fear of ye Spaniards. Quitted 30 Aug. 1743.

Steward, Donald—Age 48; of Inverness; mariner; embark'd 20 Oct. 1735; arrived 10 Jan. 1735–6; Lot 207 in Savannah. Master of a sloop. Drowned in sailing within Portroyal Sound. Drown'd April 1740.

———, Jeanne, w.—Age 35.

———, (?). son—Age 8.

———, Anne, d.—Age 8.

———, Isabel, d.—Age 5; born in Georgia.

———, John, son—Age 11.

Steward, Donald—Age 23; servt. to Donald Steward of Inverness.

Steward, Tho.—Boy.

Stewart, Anne—Alive at Darien 6 May 1741.

Stewart, Anne—Alive at Darien 6 May 1741 and then 8 years old.

Stewart, David—Age 23; of Cromdale; surgeon; arrived 10 Jan. 1735–6.

Sutherland, Alexr.—Age 30; servt. to Mr. Mackay of Scourie; embark'd 20 Oct. 1735; arrived 10 Jan. 1735–6.

Tailfer, Patrick—Surgeon; arrived 1 Aug. 1734. Settled at first on the river Nese, but quitted to practice surgery in Savannah. He had a grant of 500 acres 18 Oct. 1733. A proud saucy fellow and a Ringleader for allowance of Negroes & change of tenure. Went away to Carolina for fear of the Spaniards 31 Aug. 1740 (*sic*).

Todd, Andrew—Servt. to Will. & H. Sterling; arrived 1 Aug. 1734.

Tolmie, Alexr.—Age 36; Farmer; embark'd 20 Oct. 1735; arrived 10 Jan. 1735–6. Lot vacant he died without heirs. Dead 16 Nov. 1736.

Wade, John—Servt. to Hugh Frazer; arrived 10 Jan. 1733–4.

Watson, Hugh—Age 18; servt. to Tho. Baillie; embark'd 20 Oct. 1735; arrived 10 Jan. 1735–6; murd. at sea June 1739.

Petition of the Inhabitants
of New Inverness to
His Excellency General Oglethorpe

THE FOLLOWING MATERIAL can be found in Egmont Papers, vol. 14203, 368–69, University of Georgia Library.

We are informed that our Neighbors of Savannah have petitioned your Excellency for the Liberty of having Slaves: We hope, and earnestly intreat, that before such Proposals are hearkened unto, your Excellency will consider our Situation, and of what dangerous and bad Consequence such Liberty would be of to us, for many Reasons.

1) The Nearness of the Spaniards, who have proclaimed Freedom to all Slaves who run away from their Masters, makes it impossible for us to keep them, without more Labor in guarding them than what we would be at to do their work.
2) We are laborious, & know a White Man may be, by the Year, more usefully employed than a Negroe.
3) We are not rich, and becoming Debtors for Slaves, in Case of their running away or dying, would inevitably ruin the poor Master, and he become a greater Slave to the Negroe-Merchant, than the Slave he bought could be to him.
4) It would oblige us to keep a Guard Duty at least as severe as when we expected a daily Invasion: And if that was the Case, how miserable would it be to us, and our Wives and Families, to have one Enemy without, and a more dangerous one in our Bosoms!
5) It is shocking to human Nature, that any Race of Mankind and their Posterity should be sentenc'd to perpetual Slavery; nor in Justice can we think otherwise of it, than that they are thrown amongst us to be our Scourge one Day or other for our Sins: And as Freedom must be as dear to them as to us, what a Scene of

Horror must it bring about! And the longer it is unexecuted, the bloody Scene must be the greater.

We therefore for our own Sakes, our Wives and Children, and our Posterity, beg your Consideration, and intreat, that instead of introducing Slaves, you'll put us in the Way to get some of our Countrymen, who, with their Labor in Time of Peace, and our Vigilance, if we are invaded, with the Help of those, will render it a difficult Thing to hurt us, or that Part of the Province we possess. We will forever pray for your Excellency, and are with all Submission, & c.

New Inverness Formerly   John Mackintosh-Moore
named Darien 3 Jan.   John Mackintosh-Linvilge
1738–9   John Mackintosh-Son to L.
                          John Mackintosh-Bain
                          Jo. Cuthbert
                          James Mackay

Archibald McBain, his mark AMB
Ranald Macdonald
John Macdonald
John Macklean
Jos. Burges, his mark BE
Donald Clark—first
Alex. Clark, Son of the above
Donald Clark—second
Donald Clark—third, his mark X
Hugh Morrison, his mark HM
Alex. Munro
Will Munro

List of Highlanders on the
Loyal Judith, 17 September 1741

THE FOLLOWING MATERIAL can be found in Candler et al., *Colonial Records of the State of Georgia,* 30: 197–99.

John Cogach, a Labourer and Cowherd Aged 33 & Anna Mackay his Wife Aged 30, his two sons William Aged 11 and Angus Aged 7 and his two Daughters Christian Aged 16 and Isabell Aged 13.

Norman MacDonald, a Labourer Aged 32, Elizabeth Mackay his Wife Aged 29, John his Son Aged 6, and Katherine his Daughter Aged 9.

John MacDonald, a Labourer & Hunter Aged 32, Marion Cadiach his Wife Aged 29, his two Sons William Aged 4 & Donald Aged 2, his Daughter Elizabeth Aged 6.

Donald Mackay, a Labourer Aged 32, his Son James Aged 8, and his Daughter Margaret Aged 12.

Donald Mackay, a Labourer Aged 21.

George MacDonald, a Labourer Aged 22.

Elizabeth Mackay, a Single Woman Aged 20.

George Douglas, a Labourer Aged 28, Margaret Munro his Wife Aged 29, and Isabell his Daughter Aged 2.

James Munro, a Cowherd Aged 33 and Jannet MacLeod his Wife Aged 26.

John Grant, a Labourer Aged 22.

William Robertson, a Cowherd Aged 21.

John MacLeod, a Fisherman Aged 35.

George Mackay, a Cowherd Aged 20.

Ann Murray, a Single Woman Aged 18.

Margaret Gray, a Single Woman Aged 24.

Christian Lossly, a Widdow Aged 30 and Katherine Mackay her Daughter Aged 6.

Isabell Mackay, a Single Woman Aged 18.

Robert Sutherland, a Labourer Aged 21.

William Mackay, a Cowherd Aged 21.
Angus Mackay, a Taylor Aged 21.
Marrian Mackay, a Single Woman Aged 16.
John Campbell, a Wood Cutter Aged 24.
Ann Cotton, a Single Woman Aged 23.
Mary Jolliffe Do, Aged 22.
————, Aged ————. [passenger unknown]

Summons to Disarm
to the Mackintosh Clan in the
Highlands of Scotland, 1725

THE FOLLOWING MATERIAL can be found in Fraser-Mackintosh Collection, Scottish Record Office 128/38.4, Edinburgh.

To all of the name of Mackintosh, and their tribes and followers, in the Parishes of Dunleckity, Doors, Moy, Dallaricie, Croy, and Petty, and to all others of them inhabiting the four Parishes of Badenoch—viz., Inch Alvy, Kinghuizie, and Laggan, in the Shire of Inverness, and to those of the Parish of Calder, in the Shire of Nairn: BY George Wade, Esq., Major-General and Commander-in-Chief of all His Majesty's forces, castles, forts, and barracks, in North Britain, &c.: In His Majesty's name, and in pursuance of the power and authority to me given by His Majesty under his royal sign manual, by virtue of an Act of Parliament, intitled An Act for More Effectual Disarming of the Highlands in That Part of Great Britain called Scotland, and For Better Securing the Peace and Quiet of that Part of the Kingdom, I do hereby strictly require and command you and every of you on (or before) Saturday, the 18th day of this instant September, to bring or send to Inverness all your broadswords, targets, poynards, whinzars or durks, side pistol or side pistols, guns, or any other warlike weapons, and then and there to deliver up to me, or the Governor of the said town, as is above mentioned, all and singular your arms and warlike weapons for the use of His Majesty, his heirs and successors, and to be dispossed of in such manner as His Majesty, his heirs and successors, shall appoint; and by doing so you will avoid the pains and penalties by the said Act directed to be inflicted on all such person or persons who shall presume to refuse or neglect to pay a due obedience to the same.

Given under my hand and seal at Inverness this 6th day of September, 1725.

(signed) George Wade.

Executed by (signed) Edmund Burt.

ABBREVIATIONS

CGHS	*Collections of Georgia Historical Society.* 20 vols. to date. Savannah: Published by the Society, 1840–.
CO	Colonial Office, Public Record Office, London
CRG	Allen D. Candler, Lucian Lamar Knight, Kenneth Coleman, and Milton Ready, eds. *The Colonial Records of the State of Georgia.* 32 vols. to date. Atlanta and Athens: various printers, 1904–1916, 1976–.
CRG, Ms	Typescript Colonial Records of Georgia, Georgia Department of Archives and History, Atlanta
CSP, A&WI	*Calendar of State Papers, Colonial Series, America and the West Indies.* London: His Majesty's Stationary Office, 1899.
Egmont Diary	John Percival, First Earl of Egmont. *Manuscripts of the Earl of Egmont: Diary of the First Earl of Egmont (Viscount Percival).* 3 vols. London: His Majesty's Stationary Office, 1923.
Egmont Journal	Robert McPherson, ed. *The Journal of the Earl of Egmont: Abstracts of the Trustees' Proceedings for Establishing the Colony of Georgia, 1732–1738.* Athens: University of Georgia Press, 1962.
GHQ	*Georgia Historical Quarterly*
GHS	Georgia Historical Society, Manuscript Collection no. 532, William Mackenzie Papers, folder 1
Oglethorpe Letters	Mills Lane, ed. *General Oglethorpe's Georgia: Colonial Letters 1733–1743.* 2 vols. Savannah: Beehive Press, 1975.
PRO	Public Record Office, London

St. Augustine Report	John Tate Lanning, ed. *The St. Augustine Expedition of 1740: A Report to the South Carolina General Assembly.* Columbia: South Carolina Archives Department, 1954.
SRO	Scottish Record Office, Edinburgh
Stephens Journal	E. Merton Coulter, ed. *The Journal of William Stephens, 1741–1743, 1743–1745.* 2 vols. Athens: University of Georgia Press, 1958.
Steuart's Letter-Book	William Mackay, ed. *The Letter-Book of Bailie John Steuart of Inverness, 1715–1752.* Edinburgh: University Press by T. and A. Constable for the Scottish Historical Society, 1915.

NOTES

Preface

1. *Egmont Diary; Egmont Journal;* William Stephens, *A Journal of the Proceedings in Georgia Beginning October 20, 1737: To Which Is Added, a State of That Province, as Attested upon Oath in the Court in Savannah, November 10, 1740*, 2 vols. (1742; New York: Readex Microprint, 1966); *Stephens Journal.*

2. *Oglethorpe Letters.*

Introduction

1. *CRG*, 3: 387.

2. Albert Sidney Britt Jr. and Lilla Mills Hawes, eds., *The MacKenzie Papers* (Savannah: Society of Colonial Wars in the State of Georgia, 1973), 11.

3. *CRG*, 3: 373.

4. *CRG*, 3: 387.

5. J. P. MacLean, *An Historical Account of the Settlements of Scotch Highlanders in America Prior to the Peace of 1783 Together with Notices of Highland Regiments and Biographical Sketches* (Cleveland: Helman-Taylor Company, 1900); *GHQ* 20 (1936).

6. Harvey H. Jackson, *Lachlan McIntosh and the Politics of Revolutionary Georgia* (Athens: University of Georgia Press, 1979); Edward Cashin, *Lachlan McGillivray, Indian Trader: The Shaping of the Southern Colonial Frontier* (Athens: University of Georgia Press, 1992).

7. David Dobson, *Scottish Emigration to Colonial America, 1607–1785* (Athens: University of Georgia Press, 1994); Edna Sue Bailes, "The Scottish Colonization of Georgia in America, 1732–1742" (Ph.D. dissertation, University of Edinburgh, 1977).

8. Bernard Bailyn, *Voyagers to the West: A Passage in Peopling of America on the Eve of the Revolution* (New York: Vintage Books, 1986).

9. David Hackett Fischer, *Albion's Seed: Four British Folkways in America* (Oxford: Oxford University Press, 1989).

10. Grady McWhiney, *Cracker Culture: Celtic Ways in the Old South* (Tuscaloosa: University of Alabama Press, 1988).

11. Dobson, *Scottish Emigration*, 89; Duane Meyer, *The Highland Scots of North Carolina, 1732–1776* (Chapel Hill: University of North Carolina Press, 1957), 27.

Chapter 1. Discovery, Exploration, and First Contests in the
Debatable Land Called Georgia

1. Herbert Eugene Bolton and Mary Ross, *The Debatable Land: A Sketch of the Anglo-Spanish Contest for the Georgia Country* (Berkeley: University of California Press, 1925).

2. T. Frederick Davis, "History of Juan Ponce de León's Voyages to Florida," *Florida Historical Quarterly* 14, 1 (July 1935): 1–49; Louis De Vorsey Jr., "Early Maps and the Land of Ayllón," in *Columbus and the Land of Ayllón: The Exploration and Settlement of the Southeast,* Jeannine Cook, ed. (Darien, Ga.: Darien News, 1992), 6.

3. Phinizy Spalding, "Spain and the Coming of the English," in *A History of Georgia,* 2nd edition, Kenneth Coleman, et al., eds. (Athens: University of Georgia Press, 1991), 9.

4. David B. Quinn, ed., *New American World: A Documentary History of North America to 1612* (New York: Arno Press and Hector Bye, 1979), 1: 231–33.

5. David B. Quinn, *North America from Earliest Discovery to First Settlements: The Norse Voyages to 1612* (New York: Harper and Row, 1975), 140.

6. De Vorsey, "Early Maps," 7, 11n; see also L. D. Scisco, "The Track of Ponce de León in 1513," *Bulletin of the American Geographical Society* 45, 10 (1913): 725, and Douglas T. Peck, *Reconstruction and Analysis of the 1513 Discovery Voyage of Juan Ponce de León* (Bradenton, Fla.: Privately printed, 1990), 5.

7. Paul E. Hoffman, *A New Andalucia and a Way to the Orient: The American Southeast during the Sixteenth Century* (Baton Rouge: Louisiana State University Press, 1990), 17–20, 34–36; Paul E. Hoffman, "Lucas Vásquez de Ayllón," in *Columbus and the Land of Ayllón: The Exploration and Settlement of the Southeast,* Jeannine Cook, ed. (Darien, Ga.: Darien News, 1992), 30–31. The grant is translated in appendix F of Paul Quattlebaum's *The Land of Chicora: The Carolinas under Spanish Rule with French Intrusions 1520–1670* (Gainesville: University Presses of Florida, 1956). On the Ayllón expedition it is useful also to see Woodbury Lowery, *Spanish Settlements within the Present Limits of the United States 1513–1561* (New York and London: G. P. Putnam's Sons, 1901). Most chronological evidence comes from Peter Martyr, *De Orbo Novo: The Eight Decades of Peter Martyr d'Anghera,* translated by Francis M. MacNutt, 2 vols. (New York: G. P. Putnam's Sons, 1912), 1: 254–68, and Gonzalo Fernández de Oviedo y Valdés, *Historia General y Natural de*

las Indias, Islas, y Tierra-Firme del Mar Océano, 4 vols. (1851–1855; Chapel Hill: University of North Carolina Press, 1959), 4: 325–30.

8. Quattlebaum, *Land of Chicora*, 15; The various plans of Thomas Nairn, Thomas Coram, Sir Robert Mountgomery, Jean-Pierre Purry, Joshua Gee, and, ultimately, James Oglethorpe and the Trustees for Establishing the Colony of Georgia in America will be discussed in the following chapter. However, it would appear that many, if not all, of these planners were aware of Ayllón's claims of silk production—most likely through Peter Martyr's work, which was familiar throughout Europe, although none mention their source of information.

9. Quattlebaum, *Land of Chicora*, appendix F, 139.

10. These accounts come mainly from text of litigation proceedings against Ayllón filed by Juan Ortiz de Matienzo in an effort to recover his costs in the failed slave expedition of 1521 and to claim part of Ayllón's spoils from the new land. Additional information comes from the ship's log of the voyage found in Alonso de Chaves's manuscript "Espejo de Navigantes" of circa 1530. This is the same report that was used for Juan Vespucci's map of 1526. These are reproduced in Peter Martyr's *De Orbo Novo*, 2: 258.

11. David Hurst Thomas, "The Spanish Mission Experience in La Florida," in *Columbus and the Land of Ayllón: The Exploration and Settlement of the Southeast,* Jeannine Cook, ed. (Darien, Ga.: Darien News, 1992), 53.

12. Jane Landers, "Africans in the Land of Ayllón: The Exploration and Settlement of the Southeast," in *Columbus and the Land of Ayllón: The Exploration and Settlement of the Southeast,* Jeannine Cook, ed. (Darien, Ga.: Darien News, 1992), 110.

13. Hoffman, "Lucas Vásquez de Ayllón," 34–35; Joseph Judge, "Exploring Our Lost Century," *National Geographic* 173 (1988): 337; Quinn, *Earliest Discovery,* 145.

14. There has been much debate about the precise location of Ayllón's colony, the first European settlement within the present boundaries of the United States. Traditionally, the site has been situated in Santa Elena on the Port Royal Sound on the coast of South Carolina. Some historians have placed it near Cape Fear, North Carolina (Lowery, *Spanish Settlements,* and Quattlebaum, *Land of Chicora*), while others have it located on the Savannah River in Georgia (J. R. Swanton, *Indians of the Southeastern United States* [New York: Greenwood Press, 1969]). However, a recent examination of the testimony given during the Matienzo lawsuit against Ayllón provides an insight to the real location of the colony known as San Miguel de Gualdape. Hoffman places the settlement "on or close to the shores of Sapelo Sound," in the region later known as Guale (*New Andalucia,* 328). This is the location of the present county of McIntosh in Georgia and also the location of the Highland Scots' colony in British North America. Although De Vorsey in "Early Maps" disagrees with some of Hoffman's reasoning and explanation as to how he arrived at the location of McIntosh County, he nevertheless agrees with Hoffman's findings. He suggests that archeological evidence of San Miguel de Gualdape may have been observed and recorded

more than two centuries ago. In his report personally presented to King George III, De Brahm included a description of a site he located in Sapelo Sound, which De Vorsey included in his work *Report of the General Survey in the Southern District of North America* (Louis De Vorsey, Jr., ed. [Columbia: University of South Carolina Press, 1971], 147):

> Between the Mouth of Midway or North Newport [river], and the Mouth of South Newport [river], as also between the Ocean and the Eastermost Creek communing with the two Newports, is situated Saint Catherine's Island. Out of South Newport makes a creek into the next salt water Stream (called Sapelo), which Creek is bordered to the west by an open Marsh country, in which lays Demetrius Island; on this Island the Author [De Brahm] found in 1753 the Vestiga of an Intrenchment of a mile and a quarter in Length; as also many ruins of ancient houses, by all appearance proving a settlement made there before, or in the Beginning of the 17th Century. For no Carolinian, much less Georgian can give any account of it, so that by the Author's [De Brahm's] Opinion, it has been a Settlement, which was neither favored by the Spanish nor left quiet by the Indians, and was at last extirpated or its inhabitants forced to leave the Place. The length of the intrenchment indicates that it had many Hands for its Constructors and Defenders: By its Situation it does not appear to have been a Spanish Out-Post, stationed there to be guarded by a Detachment from Saint Augustine, in order to discover and intercept surprises and Hostilities from the English settled in Virginia; as the high Land on the East side of the mouth of Black Beard's Creek on Blackbeard's Island, would have suited much better for a good Battery 1¼ mile due west of the Intrenchment on a Point of Sapelo Island (a) Passage, and from the Intrenchment, to discover whatever passes along the shore: (a) Commanding Sapelo Creek, from the latter to Dispute the Inland passage.

Demetrius Island is the area now known as Harris Neck in McIntosh County, Georgia. De Vorsey asserts that De Brahm apparently could not find any reasonable explanation as to why the settlement would have been located where it was if it had been a recent defense post. It was situated away from the intercoastal waterway that was then in use by both the British and Spanish. The extensive earthworks and the many ruins of ancient houses meet the criteria that Hoffman has set for the site of San Miguel de Gualdape. It is situated close to Sapelo Sound; it has an extensive area of cultivable land; and archeological surveys have shown the area to have sustained large Indian populations during the Contact Period. It is interesting to note that this section of Georgia coastline should have been the site of the first and last appearances of Spanish conquest in the debatable land.

15. The name of the settlement itself may be an indication as to its location. Named in honor of Michael the Archangel (San Miguel) and of the land or people where it was founded—Guale (Gualdape).

16. Hoffman, *New Andalucia*, 67–77.

17. Hoffman, "Lucas Vásquez de Ayllón," 36–37; Quinn, *Earliest Discovery*, 146.

18. Landers, "Africans in the Land of Ayllón," 111. She cites Peter Wood's *Black Majority: Negroes in Colonial South Carolina from 1670 through the Stono Rebellion* (New York: Knopf, 1974) and William Loren Katz, "A Tradition of Freedom, Black/ Indian Community," *Southern Exposure* (Sept.–Oct. 1984): 16–19, as her sources for this information; however, there seems to be little or no historical or archeological evidence for such an assertion in relation to Ayllón's settlement at San Miguel de Gualdape.

19. Quinn, *Earliest Discovery*, 146; Oviedo, *Historia General*, 4: 537.

20. Quinn, *Earliest Discovery*, 148–51; Charles M. Hudson, "The Genesis of Georgia's Indians," in *Forty Years of Diversity: Essays on Colonial Georgia*, Harvey H. Jackson and Phinizy Spalding, eds. (Athens: University of Georgia Press, 1984), 26; Jerald T. Milanich, ed., *The Hernando de Soto Expedition* (New York: Garland Publishing, 1991); Jean Ribault, *The Whole and True Discovery of Terra Florida: A Facsimile Reprint of the London Edition of 1563, Together with a Transcript of an English Version in the British Museum, with Notes by H. M. Biggar and a Biography by Jeannette Thurber Connor* (Deland, Fla.: The Florida State Historical Society, 1927), 90; Hoffman, "Lucas Vásquez de Ayllón," 38–39; Hoffman, *New Andalucia*, 216–17; Antonio de Arrendondo, *Demostracion Historiographica* (1742), reprinted as "Arrendondo's Historical Proof of Spain's Title to Georgia" in *The Debatable Land: A Sketch of the Anglo-Spanish Contest for the Georgia Country*, Herbert Eugene Bolton and Mary Ross (Berkeley: University of California Press, 1925), 226–325, with relevant section for Ribault at capitulo 2: 234–42; J. Randolph Anderson, "The Spanish Era in Georgia History," *GHQ* 20 (1936): 216–17.

21. Spalding, "Spain and the Coming of the English," 10–11.

22. William Roy Smith, *South Carolina as a Royal Province, 1719–1776* (Freeport, N.Y.: Books for Library Press, 1970), 3; Verner Crane, *The Southern Frontier, 1670–1732* (1977; New York: W. W. Norton, 1981), 3; see Bolton and Ross, *Debatable Land*, 28.

23. Bolton and Ross, *Debatable Land*, 28; Bailes, "Scottish Colonization of Georgia," 7; Smith, *South Carolina*, 3.

24. Joseph Dalton to Lord Ashley, 9 Sept. 1670, "Shaftesbury Papers," *Collections* (Charleston: South Carolina Historical Society, 1897), 5: 183; see Kenneth Coleman, "The Southern Frontier: Georgia's Founding and the Expansion of South Carolina," *GHQ* 56 (1972): 163–64. Coleman, a noted Georgia historian, has claimed that the founding of Charleston in 1670 began the real struggle for the "debatable land" between the English, based at Charleston, and the Spanish at Saint Augustine. This is an anglocentric view, given the fact that there was already a history of 150 years of warfare over this land among the Spanish, Indians, and French—which was to continue with the recent arrival of the English in South Carolina.

25. Crane, *Southern Frontier*, 9.

26. Bolton and Ross, *Debatable Land*, 36–37.

27. J. Randolph Anderson, "Spanish Era in Georgia History," 223; Crane, *Southern Frontier*, 17–18; "Shaftesbury Papers," 5: 197.

28. William R. Brock, *Scotus Americanus: A Survey of the Sources for Links between Scotland and America in the Eighteenth Century* (Edinburgh: Edinburgh University Press, 1982), 5.

29. George Pratt Insh, *Scottish Colonial Schemes, 1620–1686* (Glasgow: Maclehose, Jackson and Company, 1992), chap. 6, 186–211, is the best narrative concerning the Scottish settlement; however, it ignores the intensity of conflict between the Scots Indian traders and the traders from Charlestown; Crane, *Southern Frontier*, 28.

30. Insh, *Scottish Colonial Schemes*, 189; Dobson, *Scottish Emigration*, 63.

31. Dobson, *Scottish Emigration*, 63.

32. Brock, *Scotus Americanus*, 5.

33. Insh, *Scottish Colonial Schemes*, 192–201.

34. *CSP, A&WI, 1681–85*, nos. 808–9, p. 339.

35. 25 June 1684, Lords Proprietors of Carolina to [the Governor of Carolina] *CSP, A&WI, 1681–85*, no. 1774, p. 661: "The Scotts that are now just going have desired that the town they pitch on may be the seat of justice for that county: we have no objection."

36. Crane, *Southern Frontier*, 28–29.

37. Crane, *Southern Frontier*, 29; *CSP, A&WI, 1685–88*, no. 173, p. 40.

38. *CSP, A&WI, 1685–88*, no. 173, p. 40.

39. 21 May 1685, *CSP, A&WI, 1685–88*, no. 194, p. 46.

40. *CSP, A&WI, 1685–88*, no. 206, p. 46; 17 July 1685, Cardross to Robert Quarry (Secretary to Carolina Colony), no. 286, p. 67; 22 April 1686, no. 639, p. 178.

41. 21 Feb. 1685, Caleb Westbrooke to (Deputy-Governor Colonel John Godfrey?), *CSP, A&WI, 1685–88*, no. 28, p. 5; 21 March 1685, Dr. Henry Woodward to Deputy-Governor John Godfrey, *CSP, A&WI, 1685–88*, no. 83, p. 19.

42. 6 May 1685, *CSP, A&WI, 1685–88*, no. 174, p. 40; Insh, *Scottish Colonial Schemes*, 210; Crane, *Southern Frontier*, 30; Bolton and Ross, *Debatable Land*, 40.

43. *CSP, A&WI, 1685–88*, no. 1029, p. 295, no. 1161, p. 336; Insh, *Scottish Colonial Schemes*, 210–11.

44. Dobson, *Scottish Emigration*, 65.

45. Bolton and Ross, *Debatable Land*, 42; Insh, *Scottish Colonial Schemes*, 211.

46. *St. Augustine Report*, 4.

47. 10 Oct. 1687, Lords Proprietors to Governor James Colleton, *CSP, A&WI, 1685–88*, no. 1457, pp. 451–52.

48. 10 Oct. 1687, Lords Proprietors to Governor James Colleton, *CSP, A&WI, 1685–88*, no. 1457, p. 452.

49. Spalding, "Spain and the Coming of the English," 13.

50. An interesting account of Pierre LeMoyne d'Iberville's activities in the Mississippi Gulf are recorded in his journals translated and edited by Richebourg Gaillard

McWilliams in *Iberville's Gulf Journals* (Tuscaloosa: University of Alabama Press, 1981).

51. Crane, *Southern Frontier*, chaps. 3–5.

52. Coleman, "The Southern Frontier," 164.

53. McWilliams, *Iberville's Gulf Journals*, 14.

54. Crane, *Southern Frontier*, 68–69.

55. Bolton and Ross, *Debatable Land*, 59–63.

56. For a historiographical overview see Christopher A. Whatley's *Bought and Sold for English Gold: Explaining the Union of 1707* (Dundee: Economic and Social History Society of Scotland, 1994).

57. John Archdale, "A New Description of That Fertile and Pleasant Province of Carolina with a Brief Account of Its Discovery, Settling, and the Government Thereof to This Time," in *Narratives of Early Carolina 1650–1708*, A. S. Salley, ed. (New York: Charles Scribner's Sons, 1911), 124. Switzers refer to mercenary Swiss soldiers.

58. Crane, *Southern Frontier*, 168–69.

59. Coleman, "The Southern Frontier," 165.

60. See appendix A.

61. See chapter 4 for a discussion on the impact of these Highlanders in Carolina and Georgia.

62. 4 Dec. 1717, Richard Beresford to Council of Trade and Plantations, *CSP, A&WI, 1717–18*, no. 238, p. 119.

63. 12 Dec. 1717, Council of Trade and Plantations to Mr. Secretary Addison, *CSP, A&WI, 1717–18*, no. 256, p. 123.

64. 12 Jan. 1720, Governor Johnson to Council of Trade and Plantations, *CSP, A&WI, 1719–20*, no. 516, pp. 300–8.

65. 29 Jan. 1720, Council and Assembly in South Carolina to the Council of Trade and Plantations, *CSP, A&WI, 1719–20*, no. 531, pp. 318–23.

66. *Journals of the Commissioners for Trade and Plantations*, 14 vols. (London: His Majesty's Stationery Office, 1920–1938), 16 and 23 Aug. 1720; Crane, *Southern Frontier*, 234.

67. 23 Sept. 1720, Council of Trade and Plantations to Lords Justices, *CSP, A&WI, 1720–21*, no. 237, pp. 145–47.

68. Coleman, "The Southern Frontier," 168.

69. 10 March 1722, Don Francisco Menendez Marques to the Governor and Council of South Carolina, *CSP, A&WI, 1722–23*, no. 427, p. 202.

70. Spalding, "Spain and the Coming of the English," 15.

71. 10 July 1709, *CSP, A&WI, 1708–9*, no. 632, pp. 421–24.

72. Crane, *Southern Frontier*, 168–69.

73. Coleman, "The Southern Frontier," 165.

74. Paul S. Taylor, *Georgia Plan: 1732–1752* (Berkeley: Institute of Business and Economic Research, 1972), 10.

75. Taylor, *Georgia Plan*, 10–11.

76. Taylor, *Georgia Plan*, 10–12.

77. Robert Mountgomery, "A Discourse Concerning the Design'd Establishment of a New Colony to the South of Carolina, in the Most Delightful Country of the Universe" (1717), facsimile reprinted in *The Most Delightful Golden Islands, Being a Proposal for the Establishment of a Colony in the Country to the South of Carolina by Sir Robert Mountgomery, Baronet and Colonel John Barnwell*, with introduction by Kenneth Coleman (Atlanta: Cherokee Publishing Company, 1969).

78. Mountgomery, "The Most Delightful Country," 1.

79. Mountgomery, "The Most Delightful Country," 1.

80. *Journals of the Commissioners for Trade and Plantations*, 20 February 1717/18.

81. Mountgomery, "The Most Delightful Country," 16.

82. The Azilia plans are documented in *CSP, A&WI, 1717–18*, no. 360, p. 178, no. 389, pp. 187–88, no. 424, p. 207, no. 459, p. 223, no. 493, pp. 232–33, no. 671, p. 341.

83. Mountgomery, "The Most Delightful Country," 7.

84. Kenneth Coleman, "The Founding of Georgia," in *Forty Years of Diversity: Essays on Colonial Georgia*, Harvey H. Jackson and Phinizy Spalding, eds. (Athens: University of Georgia Press, 1984), 4–5.

85. Mountgomery, "The Most Delightful Country," 6; Trevor R. Reese, ed., *The Most Delightful Country of the Universe: Promotional Literature of the Colony of Georgia, 1717–1734* (Savannah: Beehive Press, 1972), x.

86. Coleman, "The Southern Frontier," 164–65.

87. Jean-Pierre Purry, "Memorial Presented to His Grace My Lord the Duke of Newcastle, Chamberlain of his Majesty King George, &c., and Secretary of State: Upon the Present Condition of Carolina, and the Means of Its Amelioration" (1724), reprinted in *The Most Delightful Country of the Universe: Promotional Literature of the Colony of Georgia, 1717–1734*, Trevor R. Reese, ed. (Savannah: Beehive Press, 1972), 63.

88. Purry, "Memorial," 60.

89. Joshua Gee, *The Trade and Navigation of Great Britain Considered: Shewing the Surest Way for a Nation to Increase Its Riches, Is to Prevent the Importation of Such Foreign Commodities as May Be Rais'd at Home* (London: Printed by Sam Buckley, 1729).

90. Gee, *Trade and Navigation*, "Conclusion," 13.

91. Gee, *Trade and Navigation*, 61.

92. Crane, *Southern Frontier*, 314–15.

93. Milton L. Ready, "Philanthropy and the Origins of Georgia," in *Forty Years of Diversity: Essays on Colonial Georgia*, Harvey H. Jackson and Phinizy Spalding, eds. (Athens: University of Georgia Press, 1984), 49.

94. Bailes, "Scottish Colonization of Georgia," 37.

95. Amos Aschbach Ettinger, *Oglethorpe: A Brief Biography*, edited by Phinizy Spalding (Macon: Mercer University Press, 1984), 17.

96. 13 Feb. 1730, *Egmont Diary*, 1: 45.

97. For the procedures and activities in council for the Georgia Plan see *CSP, A&WI, 1730*, no. 546, pp. 357–58, no. 586, pp. 383–84, no. 619, pp. 394–97; *CSP, A&WI, 1731*, no. 7, pp. 3–4, no. 15, pp. 12–13, no. 547, p. 369; *Journals of the Commissioners for Trade and Plantations*, January 1728/9 to December 1734, 165–69, 175, 259; see also *Egmont Diary*, 1: 127–29, 154, 157, 165, 193, 204, 209.

98. The charter is published in *CRG*, 1: 11–26.

99. *CRG*, 1: 11–26.

100. *Caledonian Mercury*, no. 1963, 6 Nov. 1732, 9965; *Gentleman's Quarterly* 2 (Oct.–Nov. 1732): 1029, 1079–80.

101. *Gentleman's Quarterly* 2 (Oct.–Nov. 1732): 1079–80.

102. *Caledonian Mercury*, 9965.

103. Phinizy Spalding, "Oglethorpe and the Founding of Georgia," in *A History of Georgia*, 2nd edition, Kenneth Coleman, et al., eds. (Athens: University of Georgia Press, 1991), 18.

104. 14 Aug. 1734, *Egmont Diary*, 2: 120; reprinted in *CRG*, 3: 413–19.

105. 12 March 1735, *Egmont Diary*, 2: 158, 160.

106. *CRG*, 3: 386.

107. *Egmont Diary*, 2: 160.

108. Benjamin Martyn, "An Account Showing the Progress of the Colony of Georgia in America from Its First Establishment," *CRG*, 3: 387.

109. *Egmont Diary*, 2: 183.

110. Edith Duncan Johnston, *The Houstouns of Georgia* (Athens: University of Georgia Press, 1950), 44–45.

111. *Egmont Diary*, 2: 185.

112. *CRG*, 2: 10–11; *CRG*, 32: 141.

113. *CRG*, 3: 373.

114. *CRG*, 3: 387.

115. T. C. Smout, *A History of the Scottish People, 1560–1830* (London: Fontana Press, 1969), 311–21. A deeper discussion of land relations and leases will develop in the next chapter.

116. Daniel McLachlan to [?], 9 May 1735, *CRG*, 20: 338–40.

117. Private Instructions to Lieutenant Hugh Mackay and Mr. George Dunbar, *CRG*, 32: 144.

Chapter 2. Changing Conditions in the Highlands of Scotland

1. G. Simpson, ed., *The Scottish Soldier Abroad, 1247–1967* (Edinburgh: John Donald, 1991).

2. M. Percival-Maxwell, *Scottish Migration to Ulster in the Reign of James I* (London: Routledge and Kegan Paul, 1973), 278.

3. T. C. Smout, Ned Landsman, and T. M. Devine, "Scottish Emigration in the Seventeenth and Eighteenth Centuries," *Europeans on the Move*, ed. Nicolas Canny (Oxford: Clarendon Press, 1994), 4.

4. A. J. Youngson, *Beyond the Highland Line: Three Journals of Travel in Eighteenth Century Scotland—Burt, Pennant, Thorton* (London: William Collins Sons and Company, 1974), 13–16.

5. J. M. Bumsted, *The People's Clearances: Highland Emigration to British North America, 1770–1815* (Edinburgh: Edinburgh University Press, 1982), 29–30.

6. William Ramsey Kermack, *The Scottish Highlands: A Short History (c. 300–1746)* (Edinburgh: W. and A. K. Johnston, 1957), 7.

7. See *Steuart's Letter-Book*.

8. William Mackenzie to William B. Hodgson, 28 Sept. 1844, GHS, Manuscript Collection no. 532, William Mackenzie Papers, folder 1; Youngson, *Beyond the Highland Line*, 16; Cashin, *Lachlan McGillivray*, 6–14.

9. Smout, *Scottish People*, 41. For an excellent discussion on clanship see T. M. Devine, *Clanship to Crofters' War: The Social Transformation of the Scottish Highlands* (Manchester: Manchester University Press, 1994), chap. 1; see also Robert A. Dodgshon, *Land and Society in Early Scotland* (Oxford: Clarendon Press, 1981), 277–320, and Allan I. Macinnes, "Scottish Gaeldom: The First Phase of Clearance," *People and Society in Scotland, 1760–1830, Volume 1*, T. M. Devine and Rosalind Mitchison, eds. (Edinburgh: John Donald Publishers, 1988), 70–88.

10. There has been much controversy on the identity of Captain Burt. Many publishers and historians in the past have erroneously named him "Edward"; however, I have located several letters and orders signed "Edmund Burt" in Scottish Records Office GD/176, Mackintosh of Mackintosh Muniments, Number 1708 in particular notifying Mackintosh of General Wade's road construction in 1728. Also, for the definitive argument on Burt's identity see David Stevenson, "Who Was Edmund Burt?" in *Essays for Professor R. E. H. Mellor*, W. Ritchie, J. C. Stone, and A. S. Mather, eds. (Aberdeen: University of Aberdeen, 1986), 250–59.

11. Bailie John Steuart to his son, 8 March 1729, *Steuart's Letter-Book*, 312; Stevenson, "Who Was Edmund Burt?" 254.

12. Edmund Burt, *Letters from a Gentleman in the North of Scotland to His Friend in London; Containing the Description of a Capital Town in That Northern Country; with an Account of some Uncommon Customs of the Inhabitants: Likewise an Account of the Highlands, with the Customs and Manners of the Highlanders. To Which Is Added, a Letter Relating to the Military Ways among the Mountains, Began in the Year 1726. The Whole Interspersed with Facts and Circumstances Intirely New to the Generality of People in England, and Little Known in the Southern Parts of Scotland*, 2 vols. (1754; Edinburgh: William Paterson, 1876), 2: 41.

13. Devine, *Clanship to Crofters' War*, 7.

14. The Macphails, a sept of Clan Chattan, were found in Sutherland and were burgesses of Dornoch; Charles Fraser-Mackintosh, *An Account of the Confederation of Clan Chattan: Its Kith and Kin* (Glasgow: John Mackay, 1898), 58.

15. Fraser-Mackintosh, *Confederation of Clan Chattan*, 8.

16. See appendix B.

17. Smout, *Scottish People*, 41.

18. Burt, *Letters from a Gentleman*, 2: 246–47.

19. Devine, *Clanship to Crofters' War*, 14–16.

20. Devine, *Clanship to Crofters' War*, 15; Macinnes, "Scottish Gaeldom," 71.

21. Throughout his letters, Bailie John Steuart cites several orders from Highland chiefs for hundreds of bolls of meal to feed their clansmen during difficult times; *Steuart's Letter-Book*, xi–xii.

22. E. R. Cregeen, "The Tacksmen and Their Successors: A Study of Tenurial Reorganization in Mull, Morvern and Tiree in the Early Eighteenth Century," *Scottish Studies* 13 (1969): 102; A. Richardson Love Jr. "North Carolina's Highland Scots: Cultural Continuity and Change in Eighteenth-Century Scotland and Colonial America" (M.A. thesis, University of North Carolina at Chapel Hill, 1981), 2.

23. Burt, *Letters from a Gentleman*, 1: 160.

24. William Mackenzie to William Hodgson, 28 Sept. 1844, GHS, Mackenzie Papers.

25. Samuel Johnson, "Journey to the Western Isles of Scotland," in *Johnson's Journey to the Western Isles of Scotland and Boswell's Journal of a Tour to the Hebrides with Samuel Johnson, LL.D.*, R. W. Chapman, ed. (1930; London: Oxford University Press, 1951), 79.

26. SRO GD128/21.1, Fraser-Mackintosh Collection, 1728.

27. Charles Fraser-Mackintosh, *Antiquarian Notes Regarding Families and Places in the Highlands* (Stirling: Æneas Mackay, 1913), 40.

28. SRO GD176/1400, Mackintosh of Mackintosh Muniments.

29. See chapter 4.

30. Smout, *Scottish People*, 316–17.

31. R. J. Brien, *The Shaping of Scotland: Eighteenth Century Patterns of Land Use and Settlement* (Aberdeen: Aberdeen University Press, 1989), chap. 1: 1–3.

32. Dodgshon, *Land and Society in Early Scotland*, 301.

33. Daniel McLachlan to [?], 9 May 1735, C.O. 5/636, 327–28: McLachlan complained that rents were raised and that Highland people were in a starving condition; Cashin, *Lachlan McGillivray*, 10.

34. Smout, *Scottish People*, 317.

35. R. A. Dodgshon, "The Nature of Scottish Clans," in *Scottish Society, 1500–1800*, R. A. Houston and I. D. Whyte, eds. (Cambridge: Cambridge University Press, 1989), 189; Youngson, *Beyond the Highland Line*, 20.

36. Kermack, *The Scottish Highlands*, 107. For an example of an Inverness merchant see *Steuart's Letter-Book*.

37. Bruce Lenman, *The Jacobite Risings in Britain, 1689–1746* (1980; Aberdeen: Scottish Cultural Press, 1995), chap. 6; see also T. C. Smout, "Where Had the Scottish Economy Got to by the Third Quarter of the Eighteenth Century?" in *Wealth and Virtue: The Shaping of Political Economy in the Scottish Enlightenment,* Istvan Hont and Michael Ignatieff, eds. (Cambridge: Cambridge University Press, 1983), 48.

38. Henry Grey Graham, *The Social Life of Scotland in the Eighteenth Century* (London: Adam and Charles Black, 1901), 35.

39. John Macky, *A Journey through Scotland in Familiar Letters from a Gentleman Here, to His Friend Abroad,* 2nd edition (London: Printed for J. Pemberton and J. Hooke, 1729), 190.

40. Disarming acts seldom had the desired effect; however, the orders were posted on the parish church doors. An example of the summons to disarm is found in the manuscripts of the Fraser-Mackintosh Collection, SRO 128/38.4, sent by General Wade to the Mackintosh Clan. See appendix E.

41. Burt, *Letters from a Gentleman,* 2: 226–29; Martin Martin, *A Description of the Western Islands of Scotland,* 2nd edition (1716; Edinburgh: James Thin, Bookseller, 1970), 101.

42. Burt, *Letters from a Gentleman,* 2: 226.

43. Burt, *Letters from a Gentleman,* 2: 227; this account coincides with George Wade's "Report, &c, Relating to the Highlands, 1724," in *Historical Papers Relating to the Jacobite Period, 1699–1750,* James Allardyce, ed. (Aberdeen: Printed for the New Spalding Club, 1895), 134–35.

44. Burt, *Letters from a Gentleman,* 2: 227.

45. Burt, *Letters from a Gentleman,* 2: 230–31.

46. Martin, *Description of the Western Islands,* 101.

47. Ian Charles Cargill Graham, *Colonists from Scotland: Emigration to North America, 1707–1783* (Ithaca: Cornell University Press, 1956), 1, 3–4.

48. For a complete discussion of the changes made by the Duke of Argyll see Cregeen, "The Tacksmen and Their Successors"; see also Dodgshon, *Land and Society in Early Scotland,* 306–8; Macinnes, "Scottish Gaeldom," 71; William Ferguson, *Scotland: 1689 to the Present,* Edinburgh History of Scotland, vol. 4 (1968; Edinburgh: Oliver and Boyd, 1978), 4: 176.

49. William Mackintosh of Borlum, *An Essay on Ways and Means for Inclosing, Fallowing, Planting, &c. Scotland; and That in Sixteen Years at Farthest* (Edinburgh: Mr. Freebairn's Shop, 1729).

50. Devine, *Clanship to Crofters' War,* 17.

51. T. C. Smout, ed., "Sir John Clerk's Observations on the Present Circumstances of Scotland, 1730," in *Miscellany of the Scottish History Society,* vol. 10. (Edinburgh: Printed for the Scottish History Society by T. and A. Constable, 1965), 195.

52. Smout, "Where Had the Scottish Economy Got To?" 47.

53. Mackintosh, *Ways and Means,* 232.

54. Burt, *Letters from a Gentleman,* 1: 83.

55. A. J. S. Gibson and T. C. Smout, "Scottish Food and Scottish History, 1500–1800," in *Scottish Society, 1500–1800*, R. A. Houston and I. D. Whyte, eds. (Cambridge: Cambridge University Press, 1989), 77.

56. Devine, *Clanship to Crofters' War*, 15.

57. Burt, *Letters from a Gentleman*, 2: 125.

58. As evidenced by Bailie John Steuart (*Steuart's Letter-Book*), John Hossack (SRO T82/312), Alexander Mackintosh of Termit, brother of Mackintosh of Borlum (SRO GD23/6.48–53), Bailie Gilbert Gordon (SRO 23/6.112), and Bailie John Mackintosh (SRO GD128/24.1–5), among others.

59. Both Bailie John Steuart (*Steuart's Letter-Book*) and Alexander Mackintosh (SRO GD23/6.48–53, Bught Papers) had extensive trade dealings with England and the European continent.

60. Burt, *Letters from a Gentleman*, 2: 250–51.

61. SRO GD128/11.2, correspondence of Mackintosh of Mackintosh in the Fraser-Mackintosh Collection.

62. David Murray, *The York Buildings Company: A Chapter in Scotch History* (Edinburgh: T. and A. Constable, 1883), 57.

63. Murray, *York Buildings Company*, 59, note 2; Stephens became the secretary for the Trustees for Establishing the Colony of Georgia in America in 1737. He later became the first president of the colony, 1741–1751.

64. Jean Munro, ed., *The Inventory of Chisolm Writs, 1456–1810* (Edinburgh: Scottish Record Society, 1992), no. 871, 125–26.

65. Burt, *Letters from a Gentleman*, 2: 10–11.

66. Kermack, *The Scottish Highlands*, 117.

67. Smout, "Sir John Clerk's Observations," 198. Clerk was overly optimistic about York Buildings Company and its endeavors in the Highlands; however, his attitude reflects the sentiment of many people in Scotland in 1730.

68. *Caledonian Mercury*, 27 Aug. 1728.

69. *Caledonian Mercury*, 7 Aug. 1729.

70. SRO GD176/2094, Mackintosh of Mackintosh Muniments, 3 July 1730, John Smith to Lachlan Mackintosh of Mackintosh.

71. M. G. Jones, *The Charity School Movement* (Cambridge: Cambridge University Press, 1964), 176.

72. Smout, *Scottish People*, 433–34.

73. Cashin, *Lachlan McGillivray*, 11.

74. Sir Robert Gordon, quote in Ian Grimble, *Chief of Mackay* (London: Routledge and Kegan Paul, 1965), 183.

75. Bruce Lenman, *The Jacobite Clans of the Great Glen, 1650–1784* (1984; Aberdeen: Scottish Cultural Press, 1995), 77–87.

76. See appendix A.

77. Cashin, *Lachlan McGillivray*, 7.

78. Their contributions and activities will be addressed in chapter 6.

79. [Duncan Forbes of Culloden], "Memoriall Anent the True State of the Highlands as to Their Chieftenries, Followings and Dependances Before the Late Rebellion," in *Historical Papers Relating to the Jacobite Period, 1699–1750*, James Allardyce, ed. (Aberdeen: Printed for the New Spalding Club, 1895), 173.

80. *Steuart's Letter-Book*, xli.

81. "Duncan Forbes of Culloden to John, Duke of Argyll and Greenwich, 24 September 1737," *Report of Her Majesty's Commissioners of Inquiry into the Condition of the Crofters and Cottars in the Highlands and Islands of Scotland, with Appendices* (Edinburgh: Neill and Company, 1884), appendix 85: 387–94.

82. "Duncan Forbes of Culloden to John, Duke of Argyll and Greenwich, 24 September 1737," appendix 85: 391.

83. Cregeen, "The Tacksmen and Their Successors," 107.

84. Dodgshon, *Land and Society in Early Scotland*, 289–92; Dodgshon estimates that the general average of arable acreage per person on all estates in the Highlands by the mid–eighteenth century was two acres or less.

85. Kermack, *The Scottish Highlands*, 111.

86. Daniel McLachlan to the Trustees for Establishing the Colony of Georgia, 9 May 1735, *CRG*, 20: 339.

87. *CRG*, 20: 339.

88. A. J. S. Gibson and T. C. Smout, *Prices, Food and Wages in Scotland, 1550–1780* (Cambridge: Cambridge University Press, 1995), table 6.13, 214; exceptionally good records of cattle prices were kept throughout this period by Archibald Campbell, SRO GD14/10, 3 vols., Letter Books of James and Archibald Campbell of Stonefield.

89. McLachlan to Trustees, 9 May 1735, *CRG*, 20: 339.

90. James Cromb, *The Highlands and Highlanders of Scotland: Papers Historical, Descriptive, Biographical, Legendary, and Anecdotal* (Dundee: J. Leng, 1883), 32.

91. See appendix E.

92. Wade, "Report, &c," 139.

93. Wade, "Report, &c," 158–59.

94. Edmund Burt to Mackintosh of Mackintosh, 22 April 1728, SRO GD76/1708, Mackintosh of Mackintosh Muniments.

95. Smout, "Where Had the Scottish Economy Got To?" 48.

Chapter 3. Highland Recruitment: Fertile Fields for Georgia Settlers

1. *Caledonian Mercury*, 11 Feb.; 15 June; 20, 25, 29, 31 July; 3, 8, 10, 14 Aug.; 7 Sept.; 3, 18, 24 Oct.; 23 Nov.; 28 Dec. 1732; 6, 15 March; 23 April; 3, 7 May; 17, 25, July 1733; etc. to 18 Aug. 1735. *Edinburgh Eccho*, 25 July, 12 Dec. 1733; 10 April 1734.

2. *Caledonian Mercury*, 27 June 1734.

3. Harman Verelst to Lieutenant Hugh Mackay at Inverness, 12 July 1735, *CRG*, 29: 73–74.

4. Common Council Instructions to Lieutenant Hugh Mackay as to Scots Highlanders he is to secure to go to Georgia, 16 July 1735, *CRG*, 32: 141.

5. *CRG*, 32: 141–42.

6. *CRG*, 32: 142.

7. *CRG*, 32: 142.

8. *CRG*, 32: 142.

9. *CRG*, 2: 381; Harman Verelst to James Oglethorpe, 18 Sept. 1741, *CRG*, 30: 210.

10. Common Council Instructions to Lieutenant Hugh Mackay, 16 July 1735, *CRG*, 32: 143.

11. Harman Verelst to Lieutenant Hugh Mackay, 19 July 1735, *CRG*, 29: 77.

12. Hugh Mackay to the Trustees, 24 July 1735, *CRG*, 21: 11.

13. See appendix B.

14. Most of the Monroes were farmers who paid their own passage to Georgia. In Egmont's list, he describes them as "labourers" but that term is incorrect.

15. Hugh Mackay to the Trustees, 24 July 1735, *CRG*, 21: 11.

16. Meyer, *Highland Scots of North Carolina*, 42.

17. Hugh Mackay to the Trustees, 24 July 1735, *CRG*, 21: 12.

18. Mackay to Trustees, *CRG*, 21: 12.

19. Harman Verelst to Lieutenant Hugh Mackay, 23 Aug. 1735, *CRG*, 29: 85.

20. Common Council Grant of 500 acres of land to Lieutenant Hugh Mackay, 24 July 1735, *CRG*, 32: 144.

21. Harman Verelst to Lieutenant Hugh Mackay at Dorneck, 26 July 1735, granting him land in Georgia, *CRG*, 29: 78.

22. Compiled from the list found in E. Merton Coulter and Albert B. Saye, eds., *A List of the Early Settlers of Georgia* (Athens: University of Georgia Press, 1949). The list is taken from the manuscripts of John Percival, First Earl of Egmont and president of the Georgia Trustees.

23. Hugh Mackay to James Oglethorpe, 1 Sept. 1735, from Kirktomie, *CRG*, 21: 13–14.

24. *CRG*, 21: 13–14.

25. *CRG*, 21: 13–14.

26. *CRG*, 21: 13–14.

27. Lieutenant Hugh Mackay to "Sir" [Oglethorpe?], from Tain, 24 Sept. 1735, PRO, CO 5/638: 43–44.

28. In the Earl of Egmont's list of early settlers, printed in Coulter and Saye, *List of Early Settlers of Georgia*, no fewer than ten of the Mackays and two MacDonalds are listed as coming from Tar, and most came on the expense of the Georgia Trustees.

29. Private instructions to Lieutenant Hugh Mackay and Mr. George Dunbar [16 July 1735], *CRG*, 32: 143–44.

30. This "Mackey" is in all probability one of three Mackay brothers, Patrick, William, or John, who had emigrated from Sutherland on 1 Feb. 1733 (Coulter and Saye, *List of the Early Settlers of Georgia,* 84: nos. 706, 712, 714.) These brothers were the sons of Hugh Mackay of Scourie and are dealt with in greater detail later in this chapter.

31. Mackay to [Oglethorpe], 24 Sept. 1735, PRO, CO 5/638: 44.

32. Mackay to Oglethorpe, 1 Sept. 1735, *CRG,* 21: 13–14.

33. Trustee Petition to the Queen for cannon for use in Georgia, 30 July 1735, *CRG,* 32: 150–51.

34. A small bronze mortar mounted on a wooden block, used for throwing high shells. Granadoes were probably shells for the cohorns.

35. Trustee Petition to the Queen, 30 July 1735, *CRG,* 32: 151.

36. Harman Verelst to Thomas Causton, 22 Aug. 1735, advising him of Oglethorpe's and the Highlanders' arrival in Georgia. By the *Prince of Wales,* Captain Dunbar, *CRG,* 29: 85.

37. *CRG,* 29: 85.

38. Harman Verelst to John Hossack at Inverness, 22 Aug. 1735, asking him to check passengers on ship to Georgia, *CRG,* 29: 82–83.

39. Fraser-Mackintosh, *Antiquarian Notes,* 312.

40. Harman Verelst to Nicholas Spencer, secretary to the Society for Promoting Christian Knowledge in the Highlands of Scotland, 23 Aug. 1735, asking him to recommend a minister to go to Georgia, *CRG,* 29: 83.

41. Nick Spence[r] to Trustee Adam Anderson in London, 11 Aug. 1735, from Edinburgh concerning support for a Scots minister in Georgia, *CRG,* 20: 456–57.

42. Verelst to Spencer, 23 Aug. 1735, *CRG,* 29: 83–84.

43. *CRG,* 29: 83–84.

44. *CRG,* 29: 83–84.

45. Mackay to Oglethorpe, 1 Sept. 1735, *CRG,* 21: 13–14.

46. *CRG,* 21: 13–14.

47. George Dunbar to the Trustees for Establishing the Colony of Georgia in America, 21 Oct. 1735, *CRG,* 21: 26.

48. Lenman, *Jacobite Clans of the Great Glen,* 199.

49. From the Minutes of Directors of the Committee of the Society in Scotland for Propagating Christian Knowledge, 2 Oct. 1735, Edinburgh, extracts found in the Mackenzie Papers, Georgia Historical Society, Savannah.

50. Directors' Minutes, 2 Oct. 1735, GHS, Mackenzie Papers.

51. Directors' Minutes, 2 Oct. 1735, GHS, Mackenzie Papers.

52. Minutes of the Meeting of the Society in Scotland for Propagating Christian Knowledge, 15 Oct. 1735, Jo: Walker, Praeses, Edinburgh, Mackenzie Papers, Georgia Historical Society, Savannah.

53. 29 Oct. 1735, *Egmont Diary,* 2: 201.

54. Harman Verelst to Lieutenant Hugh Mackay, 23 Aug. 1735, concerning Scottish servants for Georgia. To be left at the Post House at Inverness, *CRG*, 29: 85.

55. *CRG*, 29: 85.

56. *CRG*, 29: 85.

57. Trustee Instructions to Captain George Dunbar for his voyage to Scotland and Georgia, 23 Aug. 1735, *CRG*, 32: 152–54.

58. Tilbury is on the Thames, twenty-two miles east of London, on the north shore opposite Gravesend.

59. Trustee Instructions to Dunbar, *CRG*, 32: 152.

60. *CRG*, 32: 152.

61. *CRG*, 32: 152.

62. Referring to Dunbar's private instructions of 16 July 1735, *CRG*, 32: 143–44.

63. Trustee Instructions to Dunbar, *CRG*, 32: 152.

64. *CRG*, 32: 152–53; this list, although evidenced by the Egmont list in Coulter and Saye, is not in the records of the Trustees for Georgia in the Public Record Office, the extensive collection of Egmont papers in the Keith Read Collection at the University of Georgia, the Georgia State Archives, which house several volumes of Georgia Colonial Records in manuscript form, or the collections of the Georgia Historical Society.

65. *CRG*, 32: 153.

66. "Theracle" or "treacle" is defined as a remedy for poison, any effective remedy, or molasses.

67. Trustee Instructions to Dunbar, *CRG*, 32: 153.

68. *CRG*, 32: 153.

69. *CRG*, 32: 153.

70. "Pettiauguas" or "periaguas" were small vessels, generally propelled by rowing or poling and sometimes equipped with one or two small sails, mostly used for river and coasting traffic, *CRG*, 29: 84.

71. Trustee Instructions to Dunbar, *CRG*, 32: 153–54.

72. *CRG*, 32: 153–54.

73. *CRG*, 32: 153–54.

74. George Dunbar to James Oglethorpe, 20 Sept. 1735, Inverness, *CRG*, 21: 20–21.

75. *CRG*, 21: 20–21.

76. "That day the said Magistrates and Council having a particular regard for the Honourable James Oglethorpe Esq., one of the Trustees for the Colony of Georgia on account of his public spirit in promoting the settlement of that colony to the great advantage of the trade of the nation did create to receive and admit the said James Oglethorpe burgess and guild brother of the said burgh. Captain George Dunbar commander of one of the ships pertaining to be employed for the advancement of the said colonists as his proxie ordaining a Burgess Act to be given the said

Honourable James Oglethorpe in token of their particular esteem for him" (Extract from the Inverness Town Council Records, Nov. 1720 to Oct. 1749 [manuscript volume in Inverness Town Hall, Inverness], 321); copies of which are also found in the James Edward Oglethorpe Papers, 1733–1742, William Hartridge Collection, Eighteenth Century Manuscript Collection, Georgia Historical Society, Savannah.

77. Oglethorpe to the Trustees, 13 Feb. 1736, *CGHS*, 3: 10–13; also *CRG*, 21: 450.

78. George Dunbar to James Oglethorpe, 20 Sept. 1735, *CRG*, 21: 20–21.

79. Mackay to Oglethorpe, 1 Sept. 1735, *CRG*, 21: 13–14.

80. Dunbar to Oglethorpe, 20 Sept. 1735, *CRG*, 21: 20–21.

81. Dunbar to Trustees, 22 Oct. 1735, *CRG*, 21: 27.

82. *CRG*, 21: 27.

83. *CRG*, 21: 27.

84. Mackay to Oglethorpe, 1 Sept. 1735, *CRG*, 21: 14.

85. *Caledonian Mercury*, 18 Aug. 1735.

86. Harman Verelst to Captain George Dunbar, 30 Aug. 1735, *CRG*, 29: 86–87.

87. Common Council Grant of 500 Acres of land to Patrick Mackay, 3 Sept. 1735, *CRG*, 32: 160.

88. Lee Ann Caldwell, "Women Landholders of Colonial Georgia," in *Forty Years of Diversity: Essays on Colonial Georgia*, Harvey H. Jackson and Phinizy Spalding, eds. (Athens: University of Georgia Press, 1984), 185–86.

89. Common Council Grant of 500 Acres of land to George Dunbar, 3 Sept. 1735, *CRG*, 32: 160; Common Council Grant of 500 Acres of land to Lieutenant Hugh Mackay, 24 July 1735, *CRG*, 32: 144.

90. As discussed in chapter 2.

91. Common Council Instructions to Lieutenant Hugh Mackay as to Scots Highlanders he is to secure to go to Georgia, 16 July 1735, *CRG*, 32: 141; it is safe to assume the same criteria existed for Dunbar.

92. Cashin, *Lachlan McGillivray*, 13.

93. Charles Fraser-Mackintosh, *Letters of Two Centuries: Chiefly Connected with Inverness and the Highlands, from 1616 to 1815* (Inverness: A. and W. Mackenzie, 1890), 386–87.

94. There are no fewer than nine John Mackintoshes listed in Egmont's list (Coulter and Saye, *List of Early Settlers of Georgia*).

95. These men are listed in the section of Egmont's list entitled "Persons Who Went from Europe to Georgia on Their Own Account" (Coulter and Saye, *List of Early Settlers of Georgia*).

96. Fraser-Mackintosh, *Letters of Two Centuries*, 203–4.

97. Fraser-Mackintosh, *Letters of Two Centuries*, 204.

98. See appendix B.

99. Mackay to Trustees, 21 Oct. 1735, Inverness, PRO, CO 5/638: 46.

100. George Dunbar to the Trustees, 21 Oct. 1735, *CRG*, 21: 26.

101. *Egmont Journal*, 114.

102. James Oglethorpe to the Trustees, 13 Feb. 1736, *CRG*, 21: 449.

Chapter 4. The Founding of Darien

1. See appendix B.

2. Benjamin Martyn to James Oglethorpe, 1 April 1736, *CRG*, 29: 126; 10 Jan. 1736, *Egmont Journal*, 123.

3. Harman Verelst to Thomas Causton, 22 Aug. 1735, *CRG*, 29: 84.

4. See chap. 3, note 70.

5. 10 Jan. 1736, *Egmont Journal*, 124; Francis Moore, "A Voyage to Georgia: Begun in the Year 1735," *Our First Visit in America: Early Reports from the Colony of Georgia, 1732–1740*, Trevor R. Reese, ed. (Savannah: Beehive Press, 1974), 93.

6. Jackson, *Lachlan McIntosh and the Politics of Revolutionary Georgia*, 1; MacLean, *Settlements of Scotch Highlanders in America*, 152.

7. Martyn, "An Account Showing the Progress of the Colony of Georgia," 3: 387; 10 Jan. 1736, *Egmont Journal*, 124. For a short time the settlement was known as New Inverness and the district known as Darien; however, as time went on, use of New Inverness was dropped and the town continued to be called Darien. A detailed discussion on the naming and confusion over the names is found in Bessie Mary Lewis, "Darien, a Symbol of Defiance and Achievement," *GHQ* 20 (1936): 186–98. For this study the name Darien is used.

8. Patrick Tailfer, Hugh Anderson, and David Douglas, "A True and Historical Narrative of the Colony of Georgia in America from the First Settlement Thereof until This Present Period: Containing the Most Authentick Facts, Matters, and Transactions Therein; Together with His Majesty's Charter, Representations of the People, Letters, &c. and a Dedication to His Excellency General Oglethorpe" (1741), reprinted in *The Clamorous Malcontents: Criticisms and Defenses of the Colony of Georgia, 1741–1743*, Trevor R. Reese, ed. (Savannah: Beehive Press, 1973), 111–12.

9. Harvey H. Jackson, "General Lachlan McIntosh, 1727–1806: A Biography" (Ph.D. dissertation, University of Georgia, 1973), 1.

10. James Oglethorpe to the Trustees, 27 Feb. 1736, *Oglethorpe Letters*, 1: 239.

11. *Oglethorpe Letters*, 1: 239; also James Oglethorpe to the Trustees, 27 Feb. 1736, *CRG*, 21: 76.

12. *CRG*, 21: 76.

13. Moore, "Voyage to Georgia," 110–11; although Moore called them oranges in his diary, the fruit must have been persimmons.

14. Moore, "Voyage to Georgia," 112; Oglethorpe to Trustees, 27 Feb. 1736, *Oglethorpe Letters*, 1: 239.

15. "An Act for More Effectual Disarming of the Highlands in That Part of Great Britain called Scotland of 1726," reported in Wade, "Report, &c.," 150, and a summons found in manuscripts of the Fraser-Mackintosh Collection, SRO 128/38.4.

16. 5 May 1736, *Egmont Diary,* 2: 268. Moore, "Voyage to Georgia," 112.

17. Samuel Eveleigh to Harman Verelst, 24 March 1736, *Oglethorpe Letters,* 1: 254.

18. *Oglethorpe Letters,* 1: 254; see also Buddy Sullivan, *Early Days on the Georgia Tidewater: The Story of McIntosh County and Sapelo* (Darien: McIntosh County Board of Commissioners, 1990), chap. 2, 16–23.

19. Moore, "Voyage to Georgia," 112.

20. Burt, *Letters from a Gentleman,* 2: 119.

21. Oglethorpe to the Trustees, 28 March 1736, *Oglethorpe Letters,* 1: 257.

22. PRO, CO 5/434: 11.

23. Moore, "Voyage to Georgia," 112.

24. Moore, "Voyage to Georgia," 104–5, 112.

25. Moore, "Voyage to Georgia," 105.

26. Oglethorpe to Egmont, 1 Feb. 1736, *Oglethorpe Letters,* 1: 237.

27. *Oglethorpe Letters,* 1: 105; Larry E. Ivers, *British Drums on the Southern Frontier: The Military Colonization of Georgia, 1733–1749* (Chapel Hill: University of North Carolina Press, 1974), 51.

28. Moore, "Voyage to Georgia," 118.

29. 11 Dec. 1736, *Egmont Journal,* 217.

30. McWhiney, *Cracker Culture.*

31. John Brownfield to the Trustees, 6 March 1736, *Oglethorpe Letters,* 1: 250.

32. Moore, "Voyage to Georgia," 113.

33. Moore, "Voyage to Georgia," 113.

34. For the purpose of identification and to avoid confusion with other John Mackintoshes in the colony, I maintain the use of "John Mohr Mackintosh" or "Mohr Mackintosh" as leader of the Darien community. I also retain the spelling of Mackintosh instead of the changed and current spelling McIntosh.

35. 11 Dec. 1736, *Egmont Journal,* 217; Elisha Dobree to the Trustees, 17 Dec. 1736, *CRG,* 21: 285.

36. An anonymous letter, 12 April 1736, *Oglethorpe Letters,* 1: 260.

37. Benjamin Martyn, "An Impartial Enquiry into the State and Utility of the Province of Georgia" (1741), reprinted in *The Clamorous Malcontents: Criticisms and Defenses of the Colony of Georgia, 1741–1743,* Trevor R. Reese, ed. (Savannah: Beehive Press, 1973), 155.

38. "Egmont Journal," 2 July 1740, *CRG,* 5: 381.

39. James Oglethorpe to the Trustees, 20 Oct. 1739, *Oglethorpe Letters,* 2: 418–19.

40. *Oglethorpe Letters,* 2: 418–19.

41. *Oglethorpe Letters,* 2: 419.

42. James Oglethorpe to the Duke of Newcastle, 17 April 1736, *Oglethorpe Letters,* 2: 263–64; Moore, "Voyage to Georgia," 126–27.

43. 26 March 1736, *Egmont Journal,* 143; James Oglethorpe to Thomas Broughton, 28 March 1736, *Oglethorpe Letters,* 1: 258–59. Although a few local people with romantic notions of the past still call it "The Highlands," the island in Georgia is now known only as Cumberland Island.

44. Moore, "Voyage to Georgia," 126.

45. Moore, "Voyage to Georgia," 129.

46. Moore, "Voyage to Georgia," 129.

47. Moore, "Voyage to Georgia," 129; Anonymous Letter, 12 April 1736, *Oglethorpe Letters,* 1: 261–62.

48. Moore, "Voyage to Georgia," 143.

49. James Oglethorpe to the Trustees, June 1736, *Oglethorpe Letters,* 1: 269.

50. *Oglethorpe Letters,* 1: 269–70.

51. Moore, "Voyage to Georgia," 145.

52. Moore, "Voyage to Georgia," 145.

53. Moore, "Voyage to Georgia," 131; James Oglethorpe to the Trustees, 18 May 1736, *Oglethorpe Letters,* 1: 265–67; Duke of Newcastle to the Council of Trade and Plantations, *CSP, A&WI, 1735–36,* no. 348i, pp. 234–36.

54. James Oglethorpe to the Trustees, June 1736, *Oglethorpe Letters,* 1: 269.

55. *Oglethorpe Letters,* 1: 269.

56. 8 Dec. 1736, *Egmont Diary,* 2: 313.

57. George Dunbar to the Trustees, 22 Oct. 1735, *CRG,* 21: 27.

58. James Oglethorpe to the Duke of Newcastle, 17 April 1736, *Oglethorpe Letters,* 1: 264.

59. James Oglethorpe to the Trustees, 18 May 1736, *Oglethorpe Letters,* 1: 266.

60. James Oglethorpe to the Trustees, June 1736, *Oglethorpe Letters,* 1: 271.

61. Moore, "Voyage to Georgia," 153.

62. Moore, "Voyage to Georgia," 153; James Oglethorpe to the Trustees, June 1736, *Oglethorpe Letters,* 1: 272.

63. *Oglethorpe Letters,* 1: 272.

64. *Oglethorpe Letters,* 1: 273–74. Details of the debates between Spain and Great Britain are found in *CSP, A&WI, 1735–36,* no. 348, pp. 234–43, and in *CRG,* 29: 151, 160–65, 172–74, 188–89, and *CRG,* 32: 213–14.

65. *CSP, A&WI, 1737,* no. 68i, p. 33.

66. *CSP, A&WI, 1737,* no. 68i, p. 33.

67. *CSP, A&WI, 1737,* no. 68i, p. 33.

68. *CSP, A&WI, 1737,* no. 68i, p. 33.

69. Thomas Causton to the Trustees, 8 March 1737, *Oglethorpe Letters,* 1: 304–5; in this letter Causton mentions a letter he received from William Horton dated 28 February 1737, which makes note of the situation at Darien.

70. James Oglethorpe to the Trustees, June 1736, *Oglethorpe Letters,* 1: 275, in

which he states that 400 more servants [i.e., soldiers] are needed: 100 from the north and 100 from the west of Scotland, 100 from Ireland or Wales, and 100 from Germany; 11 Dec. 1736, *Egmont Journal*, 217; Harman Verelst to John Hossack & Co. at Inverness, 23 April 1737, *CRG*, 29: 189.

71. 11 Dec. 1736, *Egmont Diary*, 2: 316–17; 11 Dec. 1736, *Egmont Journal*, 217. It is not stated in any of the documentary evidence whether the bear was dead or alive.

72. Archibald MacBean to James Oglethorpe, 8 Jan. 1737, *CSP, A&WI, 1737*, no. 6, pp. 4–5.

73. Letter from Daniel M'Lachlan [to Trustees?], 26 Feb. 1737, *CSP, A&WI, 1737*, no. 112, p. 57.

74. McLachlan's claim that it was a bad time for the people in the Highlands is supported by the average price of cattle dropping from £16.15.7 at Knockbury, Argyll, in 1731 to £12.6.8 in 1737 and back to £16.15.0 in 1742. The 1737 average price was the lowest in the twenty-year period between 1729 and 1749; see Gibson and Smout, *Prices, Food and Wages*, table 6.13, 214.

75. Daniel M'Lachlan [to Trustees?], 26 Feb. 1737, *CSP, A&WI, 1737*, no. 112, p. 57–58.

76. Lenman, *Jacobite Clans of the Great Glen*, 21.

77. Daniel McLachlan to the Trustees, 9 May 1735, *CRG*, 20: 338–40.

78. 30 March 1737, *Egmont Diary*, 2: 380.

79. *Egmont Diary*, 2: 380.

80. 6 April 1737, *Egmont Journal*, 255; also 6 April 1737, *Egmont Diary*, 2: 384.

81. Daniel McLachlan to James Oglethorpe, 6 April 1737, *CSP, A&WI, 1737*, no. 204, p. 103.

82. 6 April 1737, *Egmont Diary*, 2: 384; 6 April 1737, *Egmont Journal*, 255.

83. 6 April 1737, *Egmont Journal*, 255.

84. 6 April 1737, *Egmont Diary*, 2: 385.

85. Lachlan McLachlan and Donald Cameron to Trustees for Georgia, 30 March 1737, *CSP, A&WI, 1737*, no. 189, pp. 97–98.

86. *CSP, A&WI, 1737*, no. 189, pp. 97–98.

87. Minutes of the Common Council of Georgia, 29 April 1737, *CSP, A&WI, 1737*, no. 256, p. 127.

88. 11 May 1737, *Egmont Diary*, 2: 405; Minutes of the Common Council of Georgia, 11 May 1737, *CSP, A&WI, 1737*, no. 281, p. 144.

89. 11 May 1737, *Egmont Diary*, 2: 405.

90. [Archibald MacBean] to Harman Verelst, 26 March 1737, *CSP, A&WI, 1737*, no. 178, p. 93.

91. MacBean wrote to Oglethorpe: "I meet with all imaginable encouragement from Provost Hossack in levying servants" (25 March 1737, *CSP, A&WI, 1737*, no. 179, p. 93).

92. John Hossack to Harman Verelst, 25 March 1737, *CSP, A&WI, 1737*, no. 177, p. 93.

93. Minutes of the Common Council of Georgia, 18 April 1737, *CSP, A&WI, 1737*, no. 220, pp. 112–13.

94. *CSP, A&WI, 1737*, no. 220, pp. 112–13.

95. *CSP, A&WI, 1737*, no. 220, p. 113.

96. *CSP, A&WI, 1737*, no. 220, p. 113.

97. Harman Verelst to John Hossack, 23 April 1737, *CRG*, 29: 189.

98. *CRG*, 29: 189.

99. *CRG*, 29: 190.

100. This list is not in the colonial records.

101. Harman Verelst to Thomas Causton, 27 May 1737, *CRG*, 29: 194–96.

102. Archibald MacBean to Harman Verelst, 21 May 1737, *CSP, A&WI, 1737*, no. 308, p. 163.

103. 16 Nov. 1737, Stephens, *Proceedings in Georgia*, 1: 25.

104. Harman Verelst to Messrs. John Hossack & Co. at Inverness, 28 May 1737, *CRG*, 29: 197.

105. *CRG*, 29: 197.

106. Archibald MacBean to Harman Verelst, 28 May 1737, *CSP, A&WI, 1737*, no. 323, p. 173.

107. John Hossack to Harman Verelst, 10 June 1737, *CSP, A&WI, 1737*, no. 336, p. 177.

108. *CSP, A&WI, 1737*, no. 336, p. 177.

109. That Mackay felt he was not valued as much in the colony as he thought he should have been is reflected in Egmont's list of settlers. He reports that Hugh Mackay "quitted the Colony and Regiment upon not being promoted to Major of the Regiment 1740" (see appendix B).

110. Captain William Thomson to Harman Verelst, 25 June 1737, *CSP, A&WI, 1737*, no. 368, p. 188.

111. *CSP, A&WI, 1737*, no. 368, p. 188.

112. *CSP, A&WI, 1737*, no. 368, p. 188.

113. Archibald MacBean to Harman Verelst, 9 July 1737, *CSP, A&WI, 1737*, no. 390, p. 195.

114. John Hossack to Harman Verelst, 15 July 1737, *CSP, A&WI, 1737*, no. 405, p. 204.

115. Harman Verelst to Lieutenant Moore Mackintosh at Darien, 12 Aug. 1737, *CRG*, 29: 225.

116. 15 Nov. 1737, Stephens, *Proceedings in Georgia*, 22.

117. No large number of any clan was listed among the Trust servants. The most prominent names were Frazer, Grant, and McDonald (see appendix B).

Chapter 5. War Comes to Darien: The Battle at Fort Mosa

1. Lieutenant-Governor Thomas Broughton to Duke of Newcastle, 6 Feb. 1737, *CSP, A&WI, 1737*, no. 57, p. 25; Martyn, "An Account Showing the Progress of the Colony of Georgia"; Thomas Causton to the Trustees, 24 Feb. 1737, *Oglethorpe Letters*, 1: 298; Lieutenant-Governor Thomas Broughton to the Trustees for Georgia, 7 Feb. 1737, *CRG*, 21: 335.

2. Governor Richard Fitzwilliam to the Duke of Newcastle, 18 Feb. 1737, *CSP, A&WI, 1737*, no. 92, pp. 43–46.

3. Martyn, "Progress of the Colony," 207.

4. See Affidavits of Henry Welden, Thomas Lynch, John Darkins, Jacob Phenix, James Wilson, and John Salter in *CSP, A&WI, 1737*, nos. 92iii–92viii, pp. 44–46.

5. *CSP, A&WI, 1737*, nos. 92iii–92viii, pp. 44–46.

6. Harman Verelst to Thomas Causton, 23 March 1737, *CSP, A&WI, 1737*, no. 164, p. 86.

7. Martyn, "Progress of the Colony," 207.

8. Martyn, "Progress of the Colony," 207.

9. John Mackintosh Moore to James Oglethorpe, 15 Nov. 1737, *CSP, A&WI, 1737*, no. 573, p. 278.

10. John Mackintosh Moore to Harman Verelst, 15 Nov. 1737, *CSP, A&WI, 1737*, no. 574, p. 279.

11. 20 July 1737, *Egmont Journal*, 293; 20 July 1737, *Egmont Diary*, 2: 423.

12. *Egmont Diary*, 2: 423.

13. William Horton to Thomas Causton, 7 May 1737, *Oglethorpe Letters*, 1: 311–12; this letter is also printed in *CSP, A&WI, 1737*, no. 273, p. 138.

14. *CSP, A&WI, 1737*, no. 273, p. 138.

15. 18 April 1737, *Egmont Journal*, 260.

16. Captain James Gascoigne to [Benjamin Martyn], 10 Aug. 1737, *CSP, A&WI, 1737*, no. 442, p. 216.

17. John Mackintosh Moore to James Oglethorpe, 15 Nov. 1737, *CSP, A&WI, 1737*, no. 573, p. 279.

18. Deposition of Alexander Monroe, Darien, 29 Nov. 1741, in Trevor R. Reese, ed., *The Clamorous Malcontents: Criticisms and Defenses of the Colony of Georgia, 1741–1743* (Savannah: Beehive Press, 1973), 301–4.

19. John Mackintosh Moore to James Oglethorpe, 15 Nov. 1737, *CSP, A&WI, 1737*, no. 573, p. 279.

20. 4 Feb. 173[8], Stephens, *Proceedings in Georgia*, 1: 99.

21. John Mackintosh Moore to Harman Verelst, 21 Dec. 1738, *CSP, A&WI, 1738*, no. 553, p. 272.

22. William Stephens to the Trustees for Georgia, 20 Dec. 1737, *CSP, A&WI, 1737*, no. 642, p. 307.

23. *CSP, A&WI, 1737*, no. 642, p. 307.

24. Thomas Causton to the Trustees for Georgia, 20 April 1738, *CSP, A&WI, 1738,* no. 157, p. 68.

25. William Stephens to the Trustees for Georgia, 27 May 1738, *CSP, A&WI, 1738,* no. 255, p. 119; 27 May 1738, *Egmont Journal,* 366.

26. 29 June 1738, Stephens, *Proceedings in Georgia,* 1: 233; Lewis is identified by Lilla Mills Hawes in *Lachlan McIntosh Papers in the University of Georgia Libraries* (Athens: University of Georgia Press, 1968), 2.

27. William Stephens to Trustees for Georgia, 25 July 1738, *CSP, A&WI, 1738,* no. 368, p. 169.

28. *CSP, A&WI, 1738,* no. 368, p. 169.

29. William Horton to the Trustees for Georgia, 28 Aug. 1738, *CSP, A&WI, 1738,* no. 431, p. 205.

30. Monroe Deposition, in Reese, *The Clamorous Malcontents,* 301–4.

31. Monroe Deposition, in Reese, *The Clamorous Malcontents,* 301–4.

32. Reese, *The Clamorous Malcontents,* 302, and Deposition of the Reverend John McLeod, Darien, 12 Nov. 1741, 299–300.

33. 4 Dec. 1738, Stephens, *Proceedings in Georgia,* 1: 344.

34. 4 Dec. 1738, Stephens, *Proceedings in Georgia,* 1: 344.

35. Monroe Deposition, in Reese, *The Clamorous Malcontents,* 302.

36. Reese, *The Clamorous Malcontents,* 302–3.

37. 4 Dec. 1738, Stephens, *Proceedings in Georgia,* 1: 344; 17 March 1739, *Egmont Diary,* 3: 38.

38. *Egmont Diary,* 3: 38.

39. 4 Dec. 1738, Stephens, *Proceedings in Georgia,* 1: 345.

40. 5 Dec. 1738, Stephens, *Proceedings in Georgia,* 1: 345–46.

41. This petition, signed by 121 inhabitants of Georgia, including both English and Scots, is reprinted in Reese, *The Clamorous Malcontents,* 75–80; also found in 21 April 1739, *Egmont Diary,* 3: 52.

42. See depositions of McLeod, Monroe, and George Philp in Reese, *The Clamorous Malcontents,* 299–300, 301–4, 304–6; see also Harvey H. Jackson, "The Darien Antislavery Petition of 1739 and the Georgia Plan," *William and Mary Quarterly,* 3rd series, 34 (Oct. 1977): 618–31; Clarence L. Ver Steeg, ed., *A True and Historical Narrative of the Colony of Georgia, by Pat. Tailfer and Others, with Comments by the Earl of Egmont* (Athens: University of Georgia Press, 1960), note 178, 98–99.

43. Monroe Deposition, in Reese, *The Clamorous Malcontents,* 303.

44. McLeod Deposition, in Reese, *The Clamorous Malcontents,* 299–300.

45. "The Petition of the Inhabitants of New Inverness," 3 Jan. 1739, reprinted in Reese, *The Clamorous Malcontents,* 249–50; see appendix C.

46. Letter from the Saltzburgers at Ebenezer to His Excellency General Oglethorpe, signed by John Martin Bolzius, 13 March 1739, extract reprinted in Reese, *The Clamorous Malcontents,* 164–65.

47. 5 Nov. 1739, *Egmont Diary*, 3: 88. For a detailed and complete survey on the slavery issue in Georgia, see Betty Wood, *Slavery in Colonial Georgia, 1730–1775* (Athens: University of Georgia Press, 1984).

48. 5 Nov. 1739, *Egmont Diary*, 3: 88–89.

49. Monroe Deposition, in Reese, *The Clamorous Malcontents*, 301.

50. Philp Deposition, 16 Feb. 1740, in Reese, *The Clamorous Malcontents*, 304–6.

51. Report of Robert Williams to the Earl of Egmont, 14 Nov. 1739, *Egmont Diary*, 3: 90.

52. James Oglethorpe to Egmont, 13 June 1739, *Oglethorpe Letters*, 2: 405.

53. *Oglethorpe Letters*, 2: 405.

54. *Oglethorpe Letters*, 2: 405.

55. James Oglethorpe to Harman Verelst, 15 June 1739, *Oglethorpe Letters*, 2: 406–7.

56. "A Ranger's Report of Travels with General Oglethorpe 1739–1742," reprinted in *Travels in the American Colonies*, Newton D. Mereness, ed. (New York: Antiquarian Press, 1961), 219; this document is also found in the James Oglethorpe Papers in the Georgia Historical Society, Savannah.

57. "Ranger's Report," 219.

58. "Ranger's Report," 219.

59. "Ranger's Report," 220.

60. "Ranger's Report," 222; the full agreement is found in *GHQ* 4 (1920): 5–8; see also *CRG*, 26: 485–90.

61. Oglethorpe to Trustees, 5 Oct. 1739, *CRG*, 22: part 2, 218.

62. "Ranger's Report," 223.

63. Cashin, *Lachlan McGillivray*, 28–29; Phinizy Spalding, *Oglethorpe in America* (Athens: University of Georgia Press, 1984), 103. For a more detailed discussion of the War of Jenkins' Ear, see Ivers, *British Drums*, chaps. 6–13; see also John Tate Lanning, *The Diplomatic History of Georgia: A Study of the Epoch of Jenkins' Ear* (Chapel Hill: University of North Carolina Press, 1936).

64. James Oglethorpe to the Trustees, 16 Nov. 1739, *Oglethorpe Letters*, 2: 420; MacLean, *Settlements of Scotch Highlanders in America*, 162; Ivers, *British Drums*, 90.

65. John Mackintosh Moore to Alexander Mackintosh, 20 June 1741, CRG Ms, 35: 340–43; John Mackintosh Moore to Harman Verelst, 24 June 1741, CRG Ms, 35: 344–46.

66. James Oglethorpe to the Trustees, 16 Nov. 1739, *Oglethorpe Letters*, 2: 421.

67. *Oglethorpe Letters*, 2: 421; 9 March 1740, *Egmont Diary*, 3: 120.

68. Spalding, *Oglethorpe in America*, 101; "Captain James Howell's Affidavit of the Spaniards Design to Attack Georgea," 21 April 1738, South Carolina Council Chamber, Egmont Papers, University of Georgia Library, Athens, vol. 14203: 115.

69. Governor Don Manuel de Montiano to Don Juan Francisco de Güemes y Hor-

casitas, postscript to letter of 3 Jan. 1739 (N. S.), translated by C. de Witt Willcox, *CGHS*, 7, part 1 (1909): 29.

70. 20 Nov. 1739, Stephens, *Proceedings in Georgia*, 2: 196.

71. Stephens, *Proceedings in Georgia*, 2: 196.

72. Thomas Eyre to His Brother, 23 Dec. 1739, *Oglethorpe Letters*, 2: 422–23.

73. Oglethorpe to the Trustees, 5 Oct. 1739, "Letters from General Oglethorpe," *CGHS*, 3 (1873): 82.

74. James Oglethorpe to William Stephens, 2 Feb. 1740, *Oglethorpe Letters*, 2: 451–52.

75. *Oglethorpe Letters*, 2: 451–52.

76. James Oglethorpe to the Duke of Newcastle, 22 Jan. 1740, *Oglethorpe Letters*, 2: 442–44; Mark Carr to James Campbell, 28 Jan. 1740, *Oglethorpe Letters*, 2: 444–50.

77. It is recorded in the "Farr Manuscripts," MS9854: 94–95, National Library of Scotland, Edinburgh, that this command was the first Highland Company of the king stationed in America.

78. Ivers, *British Drums*, 101.

79. George Whitefield to the Trustees, 7 April 1740, *Oglethorpe Letters*, 2: 440.

80. 24 June 1740, *Egmont Diary*, 3: 149.

81. *Egmont Diary*, 3: 149; George Whitefield to the Trustees, 7 April 1740, *Oglethorpe Letters*, 2: 440.

82. 13 Feb. 1740, Stephens, *Proceedings in Georgia*, 2: 279–80.

83. Stephens, *Proceedings in Georgia*, 2: 279–280.

84. 27 Feb. 1740, Stephens, *Proceedings in Georgia*, 296.

85. Ivers, *British Drums*, 140. This John Mackintosh could only be the one identified by Egmont in his list as no. 738: "Mackintosh, Jo.—age 15; farmer; embark'd 20 Oct. 1735; arrived 10 Jan. 1735–6. Of the Highland Company of Rangers, and as such return'd by Col. Oglethorpe 6 May 1741" (Coulter and Saye, *List of the Early Settlers of Georgia*, 85). The designation "farmer" in relationship to the Scottish immigrants in Egmont's list usually denotes a gentleman or cadet of a clan.

86. *St. Augustine Report*, 18.

87. *St. Augustine Report*, 23.

88. Ivers, *British Drums*, 114; Spalding, *Oglethorpe in America*, 110–13.

89. Hugh Mackay, *A Letter from Lieut. Hugh Mackay of Genl. Oglethorpe's Regiment, to John Mackay, Esq; in the Shire of Sutherland in Scotland* (London, 1741), 26.

90. Mackay, *A Letter*, 28; *St. Augustine Report*, 33; see also Depositions of Thomas Jones, 9 April 1741, 120; William Palmer, 19 Feb. 174[1], 123; and William Steads, 13 March 174[1], 126, in *St. Augustine Report;* Deposition of Capt. John Mackintosh, Quartermaster James McQueen, and Private Ronald Mackdonald, 1743, CRG Ms, 35: 431.

91. CRG Ms, 35: 431.

92. Mackay, *A Letter,* 27–28; Deposition of Mackintosh, McQueen, and Mackdonald, CRG Ms, 35: 431.

93. *St. Augustine Report,* 38.

94. *St. Augustine Report,* 38.

95. *St. Augustine Report,* 38.

96. Steads Deposition, *St. Augustine Report,* 126.

97. Governor Don Manuel de Montiano to Don Juan Francisco de Güemes y Horcasitas, 24 June 1740, *CGHS,* 7, part 1 (1909), 56; Ivers, *British Drums,* 119.

98. Mackay, *A Letter,* 31; Steads Deposition, *St. Augustine Report,* 127.

99. *St. Augustine Report,* 127.

100. *St. Augustine Report,* 39.

101. *St. Augustine Report,* 39; Steads Deposition, *St. Augustine Report,* 127.

102. Mackay, *A Letter,* 31.

103. *St. Augustine Report,* 39.

104. *St. Augustine Report,* 39.

105. Mackay, *A Letter,* 31.

106. Deposition of Captain William Palmer, 19 Feb. 174[1], *St. Augustine Report,* 124; Mackay, *A Letter,* 31.

107. *St. Augustine Report,* 39.

108. Mackay, *A Letter,* 32.

109. Mackay, *A Letter,* 32.

110. Mackay, *A Letter,* 33; *St. Augustine Report,* 39–40.

111. Mackay, *A Letter,* 33.

112. John Mackintosh Moore, San Sebastian, to Alexander Mackintosh of Lothbury, 20 June 1741, CRG Ms, 35: 341; Steads Deposition, *St. Augustine Report,* 127.

113. John Mackintosh Moore to Andrew Stone, 20 June 1741, CRG Ms, 35: 340; same to Harman Verelst, 24 June 1741, CRG Ms, 35: 344.

114. 24 Nov. 1740, *Egmont Diary,* 3: 166.

115. Ivers, *British Drums,* 129; Spalding, *Oglethorpe in America,* 112; Orders of James Oglethorpe, 4 July 1740, *St. Augustine Report,* 61.

Chapter 6. Darien and the Aftermath of Fort Mosa, 1740–1748

1. John Mackintosh Moore, San Sebastian, to Alexander Mackintosh of Lothbury, 20 June 1741, CRG Ms, 35: 340–43.

2. CRG Ms, 35: 342.

3. Mackay, *A Letter,* 33; Jackson, *Lachlan McIntosh,* 4.

4. *Stephens Journal,* 6 Aug. 1742, 1: 117.

5. *Stephens Journal,* 6 Aug. 1742, 1: 117; Jackson, *Lachlan McIntosh,* 4.

6. Tailfer, Anderson, and Douglas, "A True and Historical Narrative of the Colony of Georgia in America," 104.

7. The Malcontents were a group of disgruntled settlers under the leadership of some discontented Lowland Scots in Savannah. Many of these men left the colony in the late fall of 1740 and went to South Carolina. There were some of the Darien people among them. See note 42 of chapter 5 for the naming of the Malcontents.

8. Tailfer, Anderson, and Douglas, "A True and Historical Narrative of the Colony of Georgia in America," 111–12.

9. Thomas Hawkins to Benjamin Martyn, 9 Aug. 1740, in Lane, *Oglethorpe Letters*, 2: 467.

10. Thomas Causton to the Trustees, 19 Feb. 1741, *Oglethorpe Letters*, 2: 568.

11. James Oglethorpe to Harman Verelst, 21 Dec. 1738, *CSP, A&WI, 1738*, no. 554, p. 272.

12. *CSP, A&WI, 1738*, no. 554, p. 272.

13. 20 April 1741, *Egmont Diary*, 3: 213, 217.

14. Deposition of John M'Leod, 12 Nov. 1741, in Reese, *The Clamorous Malcontents*, 300.

15. In addition to McGillivray having kinsmen, i.e., Archibald and John McGillivray, in Charleston, he had gained passage to Georgia as a servant to John Mackintosh of Holmes, who also went to Charleston (see appendix B and also Coulter and Saye, *List of Early Settlers of Georgia*, no. 683, 83–84).

16. Cashin, *Lachlan McGillivray*, 34–35.

17. 13 April 1741, *Egmont Diary*, 3: 211.

18. *Egmont Diary*, 3: 211; Harman Verelst to William Stephens, 17 Sept. 1741, *CRG*, 30: 195; "Egmont Journal," 13 April 1741, *CRG*, 5: 492.

19. 24 April 1741, *Egmont Diary*, 3: 218.

20. *Egmont Diary*, 3: 218.

21. 25 April 1741, *Egmont Diary*, 3: 218.

22. Harman Verelst to Messrs. John Hossack & Co. at Inverness, 29 April 1741, *CRG*, 30: 181.

23. "Egmont Journal," 23 July 1741, *CRG*, 5: 539; according to the ship's list there were forty-three persons on board, *CRG*, 30: 197–99.

24. "Egmont Journal," 15 Sept. 1741, *CRG*, 5: 549.

25. Harman Verelst to William Stephens, 17 Sept. 1741, *CRG*, 30: 195.

26. *CRG*, 30: 207.

27. See chapters 4 and 5 for the details of the previous two recruitments in Scotland.

28. "Egmont Journal," 24 April 1741, *CRG*, 5: 505.

29. Harman Verelst to James Oglethorpe, 18 Sept. 1741, *CRG*, 30: 210.

30. Harman Verelst to James Oglethorpe, 6 Nov. 1741, *CRG*, 30: 221.

31. Harman Verelst to William Stephens, 17 Sept. 141, *CRG*, 30: 197; see chapter 5 for details of the controversy over provisions in Darien.

32. Harman Verelst to James Oglethorpe, 18 Sept. 1741, *CRG*, 30: 210.

33. See appendix D, "List of Highlanders on the *Loyal Judith*, 17 September 1741."

34. 2 Dec. 1741, *Stephens Journal*, 1: 14.

35. 10 Dec. 1741, *Stephens Journal*, 1: 16.

36. 15 Dec. 1741, *Stephens Journal*, 1: 18.

37. "Egmont Journal," 5 Oct. 1741, *CRG*, 5: 556.

38. "Egmont Journal," 5 Oct. 1741, *CRG*, 5: 557.

39. James Oglethorpe to the Trustees, 28 May 1742, *Oglethorpe Letters*, 2: 612.

40. James Oglethorpe to the Duke of Newcastle, 28 April 1741, CRG Ms, 32: 327; "Stephens' Journal," 30 March 1741, *CRG*, 4 Supplement: 117; Ivers, *British Drums*, 144–45.

41. James Oglethorpe to the Duke of Newcastle, 12 May 1741, *Oglethorpe Letters*, 2: 579.

42. The St. John's River was the dividing line between the British-held territory and land held by the Spanish.

43. 18 Dec. 1741, *Stephens Journal*, 1: 21.

44. 8 Jan. 1742, *Stephens Journal*, 1: 28.

45. Spalding, *Oglethorpe in America*, 129.

46. José de Campillo, King's Minister, to Don Juan Francisco de Güemes, 31 Oct. 1741, translated by C. de Witt Willcox, *CGHS*, 7, part 3 (1913): 22. For a detailed account of the Spanish invasion of 1742 and the resulting actions see Ivers, *British Drums*, chap. 12: "The Spanish Invasion of Georgia, May-July 1742," 151–61, and chapter 13: "Oglethorpe's Revenge, July-September 1742," 162–72; also see Spalding, *Oglethorpe in America*, chap. 9: "The Spanish Invasion of Georgia," 127–50, and Bailes, "Scottish Colonization of Georgia," 218–35.

47. Campillo to Güemes, 31 Oct. 1741, *CGHS*, 7, 23; Don Juan Francisco de Güemes y Horcasitas to Don Manuel de Montiano, 14 May 1742, *CGHS*, 7, 30; Güemes to Montiano, 2 June 1742, *CGHS*, 7, 33.

48. Güemes to Montiano, 2 June 1742, *CGHS*, 7, 33–34; 7 June 1742, *Stephens Journal*, 1: 91; James Oglethorpe had been aware of Spanish intrigues with the slaves in Carolina and warned the authorities in London of such in the summer of 1741, James Oglethorpe to the Trustees, 29 June 1741, *Oglethorpe Letters*, 2: 585; Ivers, *British Drums*, 151.

49. Betty Wood, *Slavery in Colonial Georgia*, 8–9.

50. Don Juan Francisco de Güemes y Horcasitas to Don Manuel de Montiano, 14 May 1742, *CGHS*, 7, part 3: 27; James Oglethorpe to the Duke of Newcastle, 30 June 1742, *Oglethorpe Letters*, 2: 616.

51. See Bolton and Ross, *Debatable Land;* included in this volume is Arrendondo's "Spanish Claim to Georgia."

52. Güemes to Montiano, 2 June 1742, *CGHS*, 7, part 3: 32–35; Ivers, *British Drums*, 151.

53. Don Antonio de Arrendondo, "Journal Kept by Don Antonio de Arrendondo, Chief Engineer of the Present Expedition," *CGHS*, 7, part 3: 56.

54. 7 June 1742, *Stephens Journal*, 1: 91; James Oglethorpe to the Duke of Newcastle, 30 July 1742, *Oglethorpe Letters*, 2: 618; 15 June 1742, Arrendondo, "Journal Kept by Don Antonio de Arrendondo," 57; Lieutenant Patrick Sutherland, "An Account of the Late Invasion of Georgia Drawn Out by Lieutenant Patrick Sutherland, December 1742," CRG Ms, 35: 530; Ivers, *British Drums*, 152; Bailes, "Scottish Colonization of Georgia," 220.

55. 15 June 1742, Arrendondo, "Journal Kept by Don Antonio de Arrendondo," 57.

56. 21 June 1742, Arrendondo, "Journal Kept by Don Antonio de Arrendondo," 61; Marquess of Casinas, 20 June 1742, "Details of What Occurred in the Present Expedition, Entrusted to the Care of Brigadier Don Manuel de Montiano, from the [4th day of] June on Which the Convoy Arrived from Havana at St. Augustine, the Whole Being Contained in a Journal Kept by the Marquess of Casinas," *CGHS*, 7, part 3: 65.

57. Casinas, "Details of What Occurred," 65–66; Ivers, *British Drums*, 152–53; James Oglethorpe numbered the fleet at fifty-one sail (James Oglethorpe to the Duke of Newcastle, 30 July 1742, *Oglethorpe Letters*, 2: 618).

58. Oglethorpe to Newcastle, *Oglethorpe Letters*, 2: 618–19; Francis Moore to the Trustees, 9 July 1742, *Oglethorpe Letters*, 2: 627.

59. Moore to Trustees, 9 July 1742, *Oglethorpe Letters*, 2: 627.

60. 20 July 1742, Casinas, "Details of What Occurred," 75–76.

61. Moore to Trustees, 9 July 1742, *Oglethorpe Letters*, 2: 627.

62. Moore to Trustees, 9 July 1742, *Oglethorpe Letters*, 2: 627; James Oglethorpe to the Duke of Newcastle, 30 July 1742, *Oglethorpe Letters*, 2: 619.

63. Ivers, *British Drums*, 154; 27 June 1742, *Stephens Journal*, 1: 100; Sutherland, "An Account of the Late Invasion of Georgia," 35: 530; Oglethorpe to Newcastle, 30 July 1742, *Oglethorpe Letters*, 2: 619.

64. Oglethorpe to Newcastle, 30 July 1742, *Oglethorpe Letters*, 2: 619.

65. Oglethorpe to Newcastle, 30 July 1742, *Oglethorpe Letters*, 2: 619; Ivers, in his account of the engagement, justified Tolson's actions by saying that "his evasion may have saved a scout boat and a large detachment of regulars." He fails to realize that without Tolson's support, Oglethorpe and his men were left to face the attack alone and were placed in a more vulnerable condition (*British Drums*, 155).

66. Francis Moore to the Trustees, 9 July 1742, *Oglethorpe Letters*, 2: 628.

67. Oglethorpe to Newcastle, 30 July 1742, *Oglethorpe Letters*, 2: 619.

68. Oglethorpe to Newcastle, 30 July 1742, *Oglethorpe Letters*, 2: 619; a brief sketch of this encounter is discussed in J. Randolph Anderson, "The Spanish Era in Georgia History," *GHQ* 20 (1936): 235; Bessie Lewis, *They Called Their Town Darien* (Darien, Ga.: Darien News, 1975), 21; MacLean, *Settlements of Scotch Highlanders in America*, 167.

69. Moore to Trustees, 9 July 1742, *Oglethorpe Letters*, 2: 628.

70. 18 July 1742, *Stephens Journal*, 1: 110.

71. Oglethorpe to Newcastle, 30 July 1742, *Oglethorpe Letters*, 2: 619; 4 July 1742, Casinas, "Details of What Occurred," 66; Ivers, *British Drums*, 156–57; Bailes, "Scottish Colonization of Georgia," 224; Spalding, *Oglethorpe in America*, 134–35.

72. Oglethorpe to Newcastle, 30 July 1742, *Oglethorpe Letters*, 2: 619; Moore to Trustees, 9 July 1742, *Oglethorpe Letters*, 2: 631; 17 July 1742, Casinas, "Details of What Occurred," 69.

73. 17 July 1742, Casinas, "Details of What Occurred," 69; Ivers, *British Drums*, 159; Oglethorpe to Newcastle, 30 July 1742, *Oglethorpe Letters*, 2: 619.

74. Moore to trustees, 9 July 1742, *Oglethorpe Letters*, 2: 631; 16 July 1742, Casinas, "Details of What Occurred," 69–70.

75. Spalding, *Oglethorpe in America*, 135; Oglethorpe to Newcastle, 30 July 1742, *Oglethorpe Letters*, 2: 620; Ivers, *British Drums*, 161.

76. Ivers, *British Drums*, 163; 18 July 1742, Casinas, "Details of What Occurred," 72–73.

77. Sutherland, "An Account of the Late Invasion of Georgia," 35: 534; "Ranger's Report," 234–36; Spalding, *Oglethorpe in America*, 136.

78. Oglethorpe to Newcastle, 30 July 1742, *Oglethorpe Letters*, 2: 620.

79. Moore to Trustees, 9 July 1742, *Oglethorpe Letters*, 2: 632.

80. Ivers, *British Drums*, 164.

81. Ivers, *British Drums*, 164; Sutherland, "An Account of the Late Invasion of Georgia," 35: 534.

82. Oglethorpe to Newcastle, 30 July 1742, *Oglethorpe Letters*, 2: 620.

83. Ivers, *British Drums*, 165.

84. Oglethorpe to Newcastle, 30 July 1742, *Oglethorpe Letters*, 2: 621; Moore to Trustees, 9 July 1742, *Oglethorpe Letters*, 2: 633; Sutherland, "An Account of the Late Invasion of Georgia," 35: 535; Ivers, *British Drums*, 165; Spalding, *Oglethorpe in America*, 136. Spalding rightly expresses the confusion over what happened next by writing, "[the] surviving accounts are either too brief and conflicting or hopelessly romantic in the light of modern scholarship." He was referring to the differing accounts given not only by those on the scene—i.e., Sutherland and Oglethorpe for the British and Barba, Casinas, and Montiano for the Spanish—but also in the histories written by Thomas Spalding, "A Sketch in the Life of James Oglethorpe," *CGHS*, 1 (1840), 281–84; Bessie Lewis, *They Called Their Town Darien*, 22; Margaret D. Cate, "Fort Frederica—Battle of Bloody Marsh," *GHQ* 27 (1943): 148–50; Bailes, "Scottish Colonization of Georgia," 229–30; and Ivers, *British Drums*, 165–67, who perhaps gives the most balanced and accurate assessment of the action, an opinion based on this author's examination of the existing evidence. The most romantic versions, which placed the Highlanders of Darien as the sole British participants in the battle known as Bloody Marsh, were penned by MacLean, *Settlements of Scotch*

Highlanders in America, 167–69, and Alexander R. MacDonell, "The Settlement of the Scotch Highlanders at Darien," *GHQ* 20 (1936): 257–58.

85. 3 Aug. 1742, "Montiano's Report of the Expedition to the King, St. Augustine, in Florida, August 3 1742," *CGHS,* 7, part 3: 91.

86. Casinas, "Details of What Occurred," 73.

87. Casinas, "Details of What Occurred," 73.

88. Sutherland, "An Account of the Late Invasion of Georgia," 35: 536–37; Moore to Trustees, 9 July 1742, *Oglethorpe Letters,* 2: 633; Casinas, "Details of What Occurred," 73.

89. Oglethorpe to Newcastle, 30 July 1742, *Oglethorpe Letters,* 2: 621.

90. Oglethorpe to Newcastle, 30 July 1742, *Oglethorpe Letters,* 2: 621.

91. Oglethorpe to Newcastle, 30 July 1742, *Oglethorpe Letters,* 2: 621; Moore to Trustees, 9 July 1742, *Oglethorpe Letters,* 2: 635.

92. James Oglethorpe to Mary Mathews, 20 July 1742, *CRG,* 27: 4.

93. Spalding, *Oglethorpe in America,* 140; Casinas, "Details of What Occurred," 79.

94. MacLean, *Settlements of Scotch Highlanders in America,* 170; Ivers, *British Drums,* 178–83; Spalding, *Oglethorpe in America,* 145.

95. Spalding, *Oglethorpe in America,* 146.

96. This story was recounted by Thomas Spalding, grandson of William Mackintosh, and printed in Hawes, *Lachlan McIntosh Papers,* 5.

97. 6 August 1742, *Stephens Journal,* 1: 117; Marjory was the daughter of John Fraser of Garthmore, "Farr Manuscript," MS9854: 93, National Library of Scotland, Edinburgh.

98. Ivers, *British Drums,* 186.

99. Ivers, *British Drums,* 187; 1 June 1743, *Stephens Journal,* 1: 211.

100. 4 Dec. 1743, 30 Aug. 1744, 2 Aug. 1745, *Stephens Journal,* 2: 47, 140, 234.

101. Ivers, *British Drums,* 194; see also John Prebble, *Mutiny: Highland Regiments in Revolt 1743–1804* (London: Penguin Books, 1975), 85–86.

102. Prebble, *Mutiny,* 62.

103. Prebble, *Mutiny,* 75, 80–87.

104. Not much is known about the history of Darien between 1 January 1746 and 2 January 1749, when Oglethorpe's regiment was disbanded, the obvious reason being that the two most copious keepers of Georgia's journals, William Stephens and the Earl of Egmont, no longer provide a commentary. While it is known that Stephens continued keeping his journal for the Trustees as late as 11 September 1749 (*CRG,* 1: 495, 541; 2: 485), the only surviving journals go through 31 December 1745. The Earl of Egmont, due to ill health and dissatisfaction over the government's handling of Georgia during the War of Jenkins' Ear, resigned from the Georgia Trustees Council on the very day of the Battle of Bloody Marsh, 7 July 1742 (*Egmont Diary,* 3: 265). Additionally, there seem to be no surviving letters of a personal nature from any of the Darien settlers, except those already noted in the study.

Conclusion

1. Martyn, "An Impartial Enquiry," 132.

2. *Georgia Gazette*, 11 Feb. 1796, p. 2, col. 2, quoted in Hawes, *Lachlan McIntosh Papers*, 2.

3. Johnson, "Journey to the Western Isles of Scotland," 87.

4. Cashin, *Lachlan McGillivray*, 42, 292.

5. Kenneth Coleman, "Georgia in the American Revolution, 1775–1782," in *A History of Georgia*, 2nd edition, Kenneth Coleman, et al., eds. (Athens: University of Georgia Press, 1991), 73.

6. Benjamin Martyn to the President and his Assistants in Georgia, 2 Jan. 1749, *CRG*, 31: 117. With the disbanding of Oglethorpe's regiment, the Highland regiment known as the Black Watch became the Forty-Second Regiment.

7. Hawes, *Lachlan McIntosh Papers*, 82.

8. The State of Georgia Survey Office has published the Crown grants in Georgia from 1755 to 1775 in three volumes. These records indicate that Lachlan Mackintosh owned 9,712 acres in and around Darien while George, his brother, was granted 7,938 acres (Pat Bryant, *English Crown Grants in St. Andrew Parish in Georgia, 1755–1775; English Crown Grants for Islands in Georgia, 1755–1775; English Crown Grants for Parishes of St. David, St. Patrick, St. Thomas and St. Mary in Georgia, 1755–1775* [Atlanta: State of Georgia Surveyor General Department, 1972–73]). William Brock incorrectly attributes to Lachlan Mackintosh 8,512 acres in St. Andrews, when in fact it was only 5,812 acres (*Scotus Americanus*, 79).

9. Benjamin Martyn to the Vice President and Assistants in Georgia, 15 Aug. 1750, *CRG*, 31: 207–8.

10. Bessie Lewis, *They Called Their Town Darien*, 27.

11. Cashin, *Lachlan McGillivray*, 42.

12. For an outstanding view of Lachlan Mackintosh's political and military career see Jackson, *Lachlan McIntosh and the Politics of Revolutionary Georgia*.

13. Dobson, *Scottish Emigration*, 167.

14. Lillian B. Schaitberger, *Scots of McIntosh* (Darien, Ga.: Printed for the Lower Altamaha Historical Society by the Darien News, 1992), 13. Population figure for Darien comes from the 1990 census, Town Clerk, Darien Town Hall.

SELECTED BIBLIOGRAPHY

Manuscript Collections

Georgia Department of Archives and History, Atlanta, Georgia
  The Colonial Records of the State of Georgia, 14 vols., typescript
Georgia Historical Society, Savannah, Georgia
  William Hartridge Collection
  William Mackenzie Papers
  James Edward Oglethorpe Papers
National Library of Scotland, Edinburgh
  Index to Manuscripts
  Farr Manuscripts
Public Record Office, Kew Gardens, London
  Colonial Office
Scottish Record Office, Edinburgh
  Bught Papers
  Fraser-Mackintosh Collection
  Mackintosh of Mackintosh Muniments
  Letter-Books of James and Archibald Campbell of Stonefield
University of Georgia Library, Athens, Georgia
  Keith Read Collection
  Phillipps Collection of Egmont Manuscripts
University of St. Andrews Library, St. Andrews, Scotland
  Lady Edith Haden Guest Papers
  Roy's Maps of Scotland

Published Sources

Abbot, W. W. *The Royal Governors of Georgia, 1754–1775.* Chapel Hill: University of North Carolina Press, 1959.

Allardyce, Colonel James, ed. *Historical Papers Relating to the Jacobite Period, 1699–1750.* Aberdeen: Printed for the New Spalding Club, 1895.

Anderson, J. Randolph. "The Spanish Era in Georgia History." *Georgia Historical Quarterly* 20 (1936).

Archdale, John. "A New Description of That Fertile and Pleasant Province of Carolina with a Brief Account of Its Discovery, Settling, and the Government Thereof to This Time." *Narratives of Early Carolina, 1650–1708.* Edited by A. S. Salley. New York: Charles Scribner's Sons, 1911.

Arnade, Charles W. *The Siege of St. Augustine in 1702.* Gainesville: University of Florida Press, 1959.

Arrendondo, Antonio de. *Demostracion Historiographica* (1742). Reprinted as "Arrendondo's Historical Proof of Spain's Title to Georgia" in *The Debatable Land: A Sketch of the Anglo-Spanish Contest for the Georgia Country.* Herbert Eugene Bolton and Mary Ross. Berkeley: University of California Press, 1925.

———. "Journal Kept by Don Antonio de Arrendondo, Chief Engineer of the Present Expedition." *Collections of Georgia Historical Society.* Savannah: Published by the Society, 1840– .

Avilés, Pedro Menéndez de. "Laudonnière and Fort Caroline, History and Documents." *Voices of the Old South: Eyewitness Accounts, 1528–1861.* Edited by Alan Gallay. Athens: University of Georgia Press, 1994.

Bailes, Edna Sue. "The Scottish Colonization of Georgia in America, 1732–1742." Ph.D. dissertation, University of Edinburgh, 1977.

Bailyn, Bernard. *Voyagers to the West: A Passage in Peopling of America on the Eve of the Revolution.* New York: Vintage Books, 1986.

Baldwin, John R., ed. *Firthlands of Ross and Sutherland.* Edinburgh: Scottish Society for Northern Studies, 1988.

Bolton, Herbert Eugene, and Mary Ross. *The Debatable Land: A Sketch of the Anglo-Spanish Contest for the Georgia Country.* Berkeley: University of California Press, 1925.

Boyer, Paul S., Clifford E. Clark Jr., Joseph F. Kett, Neal Salisbury, Harvard Sitkoff, and Nancy Woloch, eds. *The Enduring Vision: A History of the American People.* 2nd edition. Lexington, Mass.: D. C. Heath and Company, 1993.

Brien, R. J. *The Shaping of Scotland: Eighteenth Century Patterns of Land Use and Settlement.* Aberdeen: Aberdeen University Press, 1989.

Britt, Albert Sidney, Jr., and Lilla Mills Hawes, eds. *The MacKenzie Papers.* Savannah: Society of Colonial Wars in the State of Georgia, 1973.

Brock, William R. *Scotus Americanus: A Survey of the Sources for Links between Scotland and America in the Eighteenth Century.* Edinburgh: Edinburgh University Press, 1982.

Brown, P. Hume. *A Short History of Scotland.* Revised edition. Edited by Henry W. Meikle. Edinburgh: Oliver and Boyd, 1955.

Bruce, Henry. *Life of General Oglethorpe.* New York: Dodd, Mead, and Company, 1890.

Bryant, Pat. *English Crown Grants for Islands in Georgia, 1755–1775.* Atlanta: State of Georgia Surveyor General Department, 1972.

———. *English Crown Grants for Parishes of St. David, St. Patrick, St. Thomas, St. Mary in Georgia, 1755–1775.* Atlanta: State of Georgia Surveyor General Department, 1973.

———. *English Crown Grants in St. Andrew Parish in Georgia, 1755–1775.* Atlanta: State of Georgia Surveyor General Department, 1972.

Bumsted, J. M. *The People's Clearance: Highland Emigration to British North America, 1770–1815.* Edinburgh: Edinburgh University Press, 1982.

Burt, Edmund. *Letters from a Gentleman in the North of Scotland to His Friend in London; Containing the Description of a Capital Town in That Northern Country; with an Account of Some Uncommon Customs of the Inhabitants: Likewise an Account of the Highlands, with the Customs and Manners of the Highlanders. To Which Is Added, a Letter Relating to the Military Ways among the Mountains, Began in the Year 1726. The Whole Interspersed with Facts and Circumstances Intirely New to the Generality of People in England, and Little Known in the Southern Parts of Scotland.* 2 vols. 1754. Reprint, Edinburgh: William Paterson, 1876.

Cabeza de Vaca, Álvar Núñez. "The Narrative of Álvar Núñez Cabeza de Vaca, in Spanish Explorers in the Southern United States, 1528–1543." *Voices of the Old South: Eyewitness Accounts, 1528–1861.* Edited by Alan Gallay. Athens: University of Georgia Press, 1994.

———. *Relación.* Edited by Frederick Hodge and translated by Buckingham Smith in *Spanish Explorers in the Southern United States, 1528–1543.* New York: Charles Scribner's Sons, 1907.

Caldwell, Lee Ann. "Women Landholders of Colonial Georgia." *Forty Years of Diversity: Essays on Colonial Georgia.* Edited by Harvey H. Jackson and Phinizy Spalding. Athens: University of Georgia Press, 1984.

Calender of State Papers, Colonial Series, America and the West Indies. London: His Majesty's Stationery Office, 1899.

Candler, Allen D., Lucian Lamar Knight, Kenneth Coleman, and Milton Ready, eds. *The Colonial Records of the State of Georgia.* 32 vols. to date. Atlanta and Athens: various printers, 1904–1916, 1976– .

Cashin, Edward. *Lachlan McGillivray, Indian Trader: The Shaping of the Southern Colonial Frontier.* Athens: University of Georgia Press, 1992.

Casinas, Marquess of. "Details of What Occurred in the Present Expedition, Entrusted to the Care of Brigadier Don Manuel de Montiano, from the [4th day of] June on Which the Convoy Arrived from Havana at St. Augustine, the Whole Being Contained in a Journal Kept by the Marquess of Casinas." *Collections of Georgia Historical Society,* 7, part 3: 65.

Cate, Margaret D. "Fort Frederica—Battle of Bloody Marsh." *Georgia Historical Quarterly* 27 (1943).

Challeux, Nicolas le. "A True and Perfect Description, of the Last Voyage or Navigation, Attempted by Capitaine Jean Rybaut" (1566). *Voices of the Old South: Eyewitness Accounts, 1528–1861.* Edited by Alan Gallay. Athens: University of Georgia Press, 1994.

Coleman, Kenneth. "The Founding of Georgia." *Forty Years of Diversity: Essays on
Colonial Georgia.* Edited by Harvey H. Jackson and Phinizy Spalding. Athens: University of Georgia Press, 1984. 4–20.

———. "Georgia in the American Revolution, 1775–1782." *A History of Georgia.*
2nd edition. Edited by Kenneth Coleman, et al. Athens: University of Georgia
Press, 1991.

———. "The Southern Frontier: Georgia's Founding and the Expansion of South
Carolina." *Georgia Historical Quarterly* 56 (1972).

Coleman, Kenneth, et al., eds. *A History of Georgia.* 2nd edition. Athens: University
of Georgia Press, 1991.

Collections of the Georgia Historical Society. 20 vols. to date. Savannah: Georgia Historical Society, 1840–.

Coulter, E. Merton, ed. *The Journal of William Stephens, 1741–1743, 1743–1745.*
2 vols. Athens: University of Georgia Press, 1958.

———. *Wormsloe: Two Centuries of a Georgia Family.* Athens: University of Georgia Press, 1955.

Coulter, E. Merton, and Albert B. Saye, eds. *A List of the Early Settlers of Georgia.*
Athens: University of Georgia Press, 1949.

Crane, Verner W. *The Southern Frontier, 1607–1732.* 1977. Reprint, New York:
W. W. Norton, 1981.

Cregeen, E. R. "The Tacksmen and Their Successors: A Study of Tenurial Reorgani-
sation in Mull, Morvern, and Tiree in the Early Eighteenth Century." *Scottish
Studies* 13 (1969).

Cromb, James. *The Highlands and Highlanders of Scotland: Papers Historical, Descriptive, Biographical, Legendary, and Anecdotal.* Dundee: J. Leng, 1883.

Davis, Harold E. *The Fledgling Province: Social and Cultural Life in Colonial Georgia, 1733–1776.* Chapel Hill: University of North Carolina Press, 1976.

Davis, T. Frederick. "History of Juan Ponce de León's Voyages to Florida." *Florida
Historical Quarterly* 14, 1 (July 1935).

Devine, T. M. *Clanship to Crofters' War: The Social Transformation of the Scottish
Highlands.* Manchester: Manchester University Press, 1994.

Devine, T. M., and Rosalind Mitchison, eds. *People and Society in Scotland.* Vol. 1,
1760–1830. Edinburgh: John Donald Publishers, 1988.

De Vorsey, Louis, Jr. "Early Maps and the Land of Ayllón." *Columbus and the Land
of Ayllón: The Exploration and Settlement of the Southeast.* Edited by Jeannine
Cook. Darien, Ga.: Darien News, 1992.

———. *Report of the General Survey in the Southern District of North America.*
Columbia: University of South Carolina Press, 1971.

Dobson, David. *Scottish Emigration to Colonial America, 1607–1785.* Athens: University of Georgia Press, 1994.

Dodgshon, R. A. *Land and Society in Early Scotland.* Oxford: Clarendon Press, 1981.

———. "The Nature of Scottish Clans." *Scottish Society, 1500–1800.* Edited by R. A. Houston and I. D. Whyte. Cambridge: Cambridge University Press, 1989.

"Duncan Forbes of Culloden to John, Duke of Argyll and Greenwich, 24 September 1737." *Report of Her Majesty's Commissioners of Inquiry into the Condition of the Crofters and Cottars in the Highlands and Islands of Scotland, with Appendices.* Edinburgh: Neill and Company, 1884.

Egmont, John Percival, First Earl of. *Manuscripts of the Earl of Egmont: Diary of the First Earl of Egmont (Viscount Percival).* 3 vols. London: His Majesty's Stationery Office, 1923.

Ettinger, Amos Aschbach. *James Edward Oglethorpe, Imperial Idealist.* Oxford: Clarendon Press, 1936.

———. *Oglethorpe: A Brief Biography.* Edited by Phinizy Spalding. Macon: Mercer University Press, 1984.

Ferguson, William. *Scotland: 1689 to the Present.* Edinburgh History of Scotland, vol. 4. 1968. Reprint, Edinburgh: Oliver and Boyd, 1978.

Fischer, David Hackett. *Albion's Seed: Four British Folkways in America.* Oxford: Oxford University Press, 1989.

Floyd, Marmaduke. "The Spanish Missions." *Georgia's Disputed Ruins.* Edited by E. Merton Coulter. Chapel Hill: University of North Carolina Press, 1937.

[Forbes, Duncan]. "Memoriall Anent the True State of the Highlands as to Their Chieftenries, Followings and Dependances Before the Late Rebellion." *Historical Papers Relating to the Jacobite Period, 1699–1750.* Edited by Colonel James Allardyce. Aberdeen: Printed for the New Spalding Club, 1895.

Fraser-Mackintosh, Charles. *An Account of the Confederation of Clan Chattan: Its Kith and Kin.* Glasgow: John Mackay, 1898.

———. *Antiquarian Notes Regarding Families and Places in the Highlands.* Stirling: Æneas Mackay, 1913.

———. *Letters of Two Centuries: Chiefly Connected with Inverness and the Highlands, from 1616 to 1815.* Inverness: A. and W. Mackenzie, 1890.

Friedman, Arthur, ed. *The Collected Works of Oliver Goldsmith.* 4 vols. Oxford: Oxford University Press, 1966.

Gailey, R. A. "Agrarian Improvement and the Development of Enclosure in the South-West Highlands of Scotland." *Scottish Historical Review* 17 (1963).

Gee, Joshua. *The Trade and Navigation of Great Britain Considered: Shewing That the Surest Way for a Nation to Increase Its Riches, Is to Prevent the Importation of Such Foreign Commodities as May Be Rais'd at Home.* London: Printed by Sam Buckley, 1729.

Geiger, Maynard. *The Franciscan Conquest of Florida.* Studies in Hispanic-American History 1. Washington: Catholic University of America, 1937.

Gibson, A. J. S., and T. C. Smout. *Prices, Food and Wages in Scotland 1550–1780.* Cambridge: Cambridge University Press, 1995.

——. "Scottish Food and Scottish History, 1500–1800." *Scottish Society, 1500–1800.* Edited by R. A. Houston and I. D. Whyte. Cambridge: Cambridge University Press, 1989.

Graham, Ian Charles Cargill. *Colonists from Scotland: Emigration to North America, 1707–1783.* Ithaca: Cornell University Press, 1956.

Graham, Henry Grey. *The Social Life of Scotland in the Eighteenth Century.* London: Adam and Charles Black, 1901.

Grimble, Ian. *Chief of Mackay.* London: Routledge and Kegan Paul, 1965.

Hamilton, Henry, ed. *Selections from the Monymusk Papers, 1713–1755.* Edinburgh: University Press by T. and A. Constable for the Scottish History Society, 1945.

Hawes, Lilla Mills, ed. *Lachlan McIntosh Papers in the University of Georgia Libraries.* Athens: University of Georgia Press, 1968.

Hoffman, Paul E. "Lucas Vásquez de Ayllón." *Columbus and the Land of Ayllón: The Exploration and Settlement of the Southeast.* Edited by Jeannine Cook. Darien, Ga.: Darien News, 1992.

——. *A New Andalucia and a Way to the Orient: The American Southeast during the Sixteenth Century.* Baton Rouge: Louisiana State University Press, 1990.

Hudson, Charles M. "The Genesis of Georgia's Indians." *Forty Years of Diversity: Essays on Colonial Georgia.* Edited by Harvey H. Jackson and Phinizy Spalding. Athens: University of Georgia Press, 1984.

Insh, George Pratt. *Scottish Colonial Schemes, 1620–1686.* Glasgow: Maclehose, Jackson and Company, 1922.

Ivers, Larry E. *British Drums on the Southern Frontier: The Military Colonization of Georgia, 1733–1749.* Chapel Hill: University of North Carolina Press, 1974.

Jackson, Harvey H. "The Darien Antislavery Petition of 1739 and the Georgia Plan." *William and Mary Quarterly,* 3rd series, 34 (Oct. 1977).

——. "General Lachlan McIntosh, 1727–1806: A Biography." Ph.D. dissertation, University of Georgia, 1973.

——. *Lachlan McIntosh and the Politics of Revolutionary Georgia.* Athens: University of Georgia Press, 1979.

Johnston, Edith Duncan. *The Houstouns of Georgia.* Athens: University of Georgia Press, 1950.

Johnson, Samuel. "Journey to the Western Isles of Scotland." *Johnson's Journey to the Western Isles of Scotland and Boswell's Journal of a Tour to the Hebrides with Samuel Johnson LL.D.* Edited by R. W. Chapman. 1930. Reprint, London: Oxford University Press, 1951.

Jones, Grant. "The Ethnohistory of the Guale Coast through 1684." *Anthropological Papers of the American Museum of Natural History* 55, 2 (1978).

Jones, M. G. *The Charity School Movement.* Cambridge: Cambridge University Press, 1964.

Journals of the Commissioners for Trade and Plantations, 1704–1782. 14 vols. London: His Majesty's Stationery Office, 1920–1938.

Judge, Joseph. "Exploring Our Lost Century." *National Geographic* 173 (1988).

Katz, William Loren. "A Tradition of Freedom, Black/Indian Community." *Southern Exposure* (Sept.–Oct. 1984).

Kermack, William Ramsey. *The Scottish Highlands: A Short History (c. 300–1746).* Edinburgh: W. and A. K. Johnston, 1957.

King, Horace Maybray. *James Edward Oglethorpe's Parliamentary Career.* Milledgeville, Ga.: Committee on Faculty Research, Georgia College, 1968.

Landers, Jane. "Africans in the Land of Ayllón: The Exploration and Settlement of the Southeast." *Columbus and the Land of Ayllón: The Exploration and Settlement of the Southeast.* Edited by Jeannine Cook. Darien, Ga.: Darien News, 1992.

Lane, Mills, ed. *General Oglethorpe's Georgia: Colonial Letters 1733–1743.* 2 vols. Savannah: Beehive Press, 1975.

Lanning, John Tate. *The Diplomatic History of Georgia: A Study of the Epoch of Jenkins' Ear.* Chapel Hill: University of North Carolina Press, 1936.

———, ed. *The St. Augustine Expedition of 1740: A Report to the South Carolina General Assembly.* Columbia: South Carolina Archives Department, 1954.

———. *The Spanish Missions of Georgia.* Chapel Hill: University of North Carolina Press, 1935.

Lenman, Bruce. *The Jacobite Clans of the Great Glen, 1650–1784.* 1984. Reprint, Aberdeen: Scottish Cultural Press, 1995.

———. *The Jacobite Risings in Britain, 1689–1746.* 1980. Reprint, Aberdeen: Scottish Cultural Press, 1995.

Lewis, Bessie Mary. "Darien, a Symbol of Defiance and Achievement." *Georgia Historical Quarterly* 20 (1936).

———. *They Called Their Town Darien.* Darien, Ga.: Darien News, 1975.

Lewis, Theodore H., ed. "The Narratives of the Expedition of Hernando de Soto by the Gentleman of Elvas." *South Carolina: A Documentary Profile of the Palmetto State.* Edited by Elmer D. Johnson and Kathleen Lewis Sloan. Columbia: University of South Carolina Press, 1971.

Love, A. Richardson, Jr. "North Carolina's Highland Scots: Cultural Continuity and Change in Eighteenth-Century Scotland and Colonial America." M.A. thesis, University of North Carolina at Chapel Hill, 1981.

Lowery, Woodbury. *Spanish Settlements within the Present Limits of the United States 1513–1561.* New York and London: G. P. Putnam's Sons, 1901.

Lynch, John. *Spain under the Habsburgs.* 2 volumes. Vol. 2, *Spain and America, 1598–1700.* New York: Macmillan, 1969.

Lyon, Eugene. *The Enterprise of Florida: Pedro Menéndez de Avilés and the Spanish Conquest of 1565–1568.* Gainesville: University Presses of Florida, 1976.

———. "Pedro Menéndez's Strategic Plan for the Florida Peninsula." *Florida Historical Quarterly* 67 (1988).

MacDonell, Alexander R. "The Settlement of the Scotch Highlanders at Darien." *Georgia Historical Quarterly* 20 (1936).

Macinnes, Allan I. "Scottish Gaeldom: The First Phase of Clearance." *People and Society in Scotland, 1760–1830, Volume 1.* Edited by T. M. Devine and Rosalind Mitchison. Edinburgh: John Donald Publishers, 1988.

Mackay, Hugh. *A Letter from Lieut. Hugh Mackay of Genl. Oglethorpe's Regiment, to John Mackay, Esq; in the Shire of Sutherland in Scotland.* London, 1741.

Mackay, William, ed. *The Letter-Book of Bailie John Steuart of Inverness, 1715–1752.* Edinburgh: University Press by T. and A. Constable for the Scottish History Society, 1915.

MacKenzie, William. *The MacKenzie Papers.* Edited by Albert Sidney Britt Jr. and Lilla M. Hawes. Savannah: The Society of Colonial Wars in the State of Georgia, 1973.

Mackintosh of Borlum, William. *An Essay on Ways and Means for Inclosing, Fallowing, Planting, &c. Scotland; and That in Sixteen Years at Farthest.* Edinburgh: Mr. Freebairn's Shop, 1729.

Macky, John. *A Journey through Scotland in Familiar Letters from a Gentleman Here, to His Friend Abroad.* 2nd edition. London: Printed for J. Pemberton and J. Hooke, 1729.

MacLean, J. P. *An Historical Account of the Settlements of Scotch Highlanders in America Prior to the Peace of 1783 Together with Notices of Highland Regiments and Biographical Sketches.* Cleveland: Helman-Taylor Company, 1900.

Martin, Martin. *A Description of the Western Islands of Scotland.* 2nd edition. 1716. Reprint, Edinburgh: James Thin, Bookseller, 1970.

Martyn, Benjamin. "An Account Showing the Progress of the Colony of Georgia in America from Its First Establishment." *The Colonial Records of the State of Georgia.* Edited by Allen D. Candler, Lucian Lamar Knight, Kenneth Coleman, and Milton Ready. 32 vols. to date. Atlanta and Athens: various printers, 1904–1916, 1976– .

———. "An Impartial Enquiry into the State and Utility of the Province of Georgia." *The Clamorous Malcontents: Criticisms and Defenses of the Colony of Georgia, 1741–1743.* Edited by Trevor R. Reese. Savannah: Beehive Press, 1973.

Martyr, Peter. *De Orbo Novo: The Eight Decades of Peter Martyr d'Anghera.* 2 vols. Translated by Francis MacNutt. New York: G. P. Putnam's Sons, 1912.

McPherson, Robert, ed. *The Journal of the Earl of Egmont: Abstracts of the Trustees' Proceedings for Establishing the Colony of Georgia, 1732–1738.* Athens: University of Georgia Press, 1962.

McWhiney, Grady. *Cracker Culture: Celtic Ways in the Old South.* Tuscaloosa: University of Alabama Press, 1988.

McWilliams, Richebourg Gaillard, ed. and trans. *Iberville's Gulf Journals.* University: University of Alabama Press, 1981.

Meyer, Duane. *The Highland Scots of North Carolina, 1732–1776.* Chapel Hill: University of North Carolina Press, 1957.

Milanich, Jerald T., ed. *The Hernando de Soto Expedition.* New York: Garland Publishing, 1991.

Millar, A. H., ed. *A Selection of Scottish Forfeited Estates Papers, 1715; 1745.* Edinburgh: University Press by T. and A. Constable for the Scottish History Society, 1909.

Mountgomery, Sir Robert, Baronet. "A Discourse Concerning the Design'd Establishment of a New Colony to the South of Carolina, in the Most Delightful Country of the Universe" (1717). *The Most Delightful Golden Islands, Being a Proposal for the Establishment of a Colony in the Country to the South of Carolina by Sir Robert Mountgomery, Baronet and Colonel John Barnwell,* with introduction by Kenneth Coleman. Atlanta: Cherokee Publishing Company, 1969.

Moore, Francis. "A Voyage to Georgia: Begun in the Year 1735." *Our First Visit in America: Early Reports from the Colony of Georgia, 1732–1740.* Edited by Trevor R. Reese. Savannah: Beehive Press, 1974.

Munro, Jean, ed. *The Inventory of Chisolm Writs, 1456–1810.* Edinburgh: Scottish Record Society, 1992.

Murray, David. *The York Buildings Company: A Chapter in Scotch History.* Edinburgh: T. and A. Constable, 1883.

Oviedo y Valdés, Gonzalo Fernández de. *Historia General y Natural de las Indias, Islas, y Tierra-Firme del Mar Océano.* 4 vols. 1851–1855. Reprint, Chapel Hill: University of North Carolina Press, 1959.

Peck, Douglas T. *Reconstruction and Analysis of the 1513 Discovery Voyage of Juan Ponce de León.* Bradenton, Fla.: Privately printed, 1990.

Percival-Maxwell, M. *Scottish Migration to Ulster in the Reign of James I.* London: Routledge and Kegan Paul, 1973.

Prebble, John. *Mutiny: Highland Regiments in Revolt 1743–1804.* London: Penguin Books, 1975.

Purry, Jean-Pierre. "Memorial Presented to His Grace My Lord the Duke of Newcastle, Chamberlain of His Majesty King George, &c., and Secretary of State: Upon the Present Condition of Carolina, and the Means of its Amelioration" (1724). *The Most Delightful Country in the Universe: Promotional Literature of the Colony of Georgia, 1717–1734.* Edited by Trevor R. Reese. Savannah: Beehive Press, 1972.

Quattlebaum, Paul. *The Land of Chicora: The Carolinas under Spanish Rule with French Intrusions 1520–1670.* Gainesville: University of Florida Press, 1956.

Quinn, David B., ed. *New American World: A Documentary History of North America to 1612.* New York: Arno Press and Hector Bye, 1979.

———. *North America from Earliest Discovery to First Settlements: The Norse Voyages to 1612.* New York: Harper and Row, 1975.

"A Ranger's Report of Travels with General Oglethorpe 1739–1742." *Travels in the American Colonies.* Edited by Newton D. Mereness. New York: Antiquarian Press, 1961.

Ranjel, Rodrigo. "A Narrative of de Soto's Expedition." *Narratives of the Career of Hernando de Soto.* 4 vols. Edited by Edward G. Bourne. New York: AMS Press, 1904.

Ready, Milton L. "Philanthrophy and the Origins of Georgia." *Forty Years of Diversity: Essays on Colonial Georgia.* Edited by Harvey H. Jackson and Phinizy Spalding. Athens: University of Georgia Press, 1984.

Reese, Trevor R., ed. *The Clamorous Malcontents: Criticisms and Defenses of the Colony of Georgia, 1741–1743.* Savannah: Beehive Press, 1973.

————. *The Most Delightful Country of the Universe: Promotional Literature of the Colony of Georgia, 1717–1734.* Savannah: Beehive Press, 1972.

Ribault, Jean. *The Whole and True Discovery of Terra Florida: A Facsimile Reprint of the London Edition of 1563, Together with a Transcript of an English Version in the British Museum, with Notes by H. M. Biggar and a Biography by Jeannette Thurber Conner.* Deland, Fla.: The Florida State Historical Society, 1927.

Ross, Mary. "The Restoration of the Spanish Missions in Georgia, 1598–1606." *Georgia Historical Quarterly* 10 (1926).

Schaitberger, Lillian B. *Scots of McIntosh.* Darien, Ga.: Printed for the Lower Altamaha Historical Society by the Darien News, 1992.

Scisco, L. D. "The Track of Ponce de León in 1513." *Bulletin of the American Geographical Society* 45, 10 (1913).

"Shaftesbury Papers." *Collections.* Charleston: South Carolina Historical Society, 1897.

Simpson, G., ed. *The Scottish Soldier Abroad, 1247–1967.* Edinburgh: John Donald, 1991.

Smith, William Roy. *South Carolina as a Royal Province, 1719–1776.* Freeport, N.Y.: Books for Library Press, 1970.

Smout, T. C. *A History of the Scottish People, 1560–1830.* London: Fontana Press, 1969.

————, ed. "Sir John Clerk's Observations on the Present Circumstances of Scotland, 1730." *Miscellany of the Scottish History Society,* vol. 10. Edinburgh: Printed for the Scottish History Society by T. and A. Constable Ltd., 1965.

————. "Where Had the Scottish Economy Got to by the Third Quarter of the Eighteenth Century?" *Wealth and Virtue: The Shaping of Political Economy in the Scottish Enlightenment.* Edited by Istvan Hont and Michael Ignatieff. Cambridge: Cambridge University Press, 1983.

Smout, T. C., Ned Landsman, and T. M. Devine. "Scottish Emigration in the Seventeenth and Eighteenth Centuries." *Europeans on the Move.* Edited by Nicolas Canny. Oxford: Clarendon Press, 1994.

Spalding, Phinizy. "Oglethorpe and the Founding of Georgia." *A History of Georgia.* 2nd edition. Edited by Kenneth Coleman, et al. Athens: University of Georgia Press, 1991.

————. *Oglethorpe in America.* Athens: University of Georgia Press, 1984.

————. "Spain and the Coming of the English." *A History of Georgia.* 2nd edition. Edited by Kenneth Coleman, et al. Athens: University of Georgia Press, 1991.

Stephens, William. *A Journal of the Proceedings in Georgia Beginning October 20, 1737: To Which Is Added, a State of That Province, as Attested upon Oath in the Court of Savannah, November 10, 1740.* 2 vols. London: Printed for W. Meadows, 1742. New York: Readex Microprint, 1966.

Stevenson, David. "Who Was Edmund Burt?" *Essays for Professor R. E. H. Mellor.* Edited by W. Ritchie, J. C. Stone, and A. S. Mather. Aberdeen: University of Aberdeen, 1986.

Sullivan, Buddy. *Early Days on the Georgia Tidewater: The Story of McIntosh County and Sapelo.* Darien, Ga.: McIntosh County Board of Commissioners, 1990.

Sutherland, Patrick. "An Account of the Late Invasion of Georgia Drawn Out by Lieutenant Patrick Sutherland, December 1742." Typescript Colonial Records of Georgia, Georgia Department of Archives and History, Atlanta.

Swanton, J. R. *Indians of the Southeastern United States.* New York: Greenwood Press, 1969.

Tailfer, Patrick, Hugh Anderson, and David Douglas. "A True and Historical Narrative of the Colony of Georgia in America from the First Settlement Thereof until This Present Period: Containing the Most Authentick Facts, Matters, and Transactions Therein; Together with His Majesty's Charter, Representations of the People, Letters, &c. and a Dedication to His Excellency General Oglethorpe" (1741). *The Clamorous Malcontents: Criticisms and Defenses of the Colony of Georgia, 1741–1743.* Edited by Trevor R. Reese. Savannah: Beehive Press, 1973.

Taylor, Paul S. *Georgia Plan: 1732–1752.* Berkeley: Institute of Business and Economic Research, 1972.

Temple, Sarah B. Gober, and Kenneth Coleman. *Georgia Journeys: Being an Account of the Lives of Georgia's Original Settlers and Many Other Early Settlers from the Founding of the Colony in 1732 until the Institution of Royal Government in 1754.* Athens: University of Georgia Press, 1961.

Thomas, David Hurst. "The Spanish Mission Experience in La Florida." *Columbus and the Land of Ayllón: The Exploration and Settlement of the Southeast.* Edited by Jeannine Cook. Darien, Ga.: Darien News, 1992.

Ver Steeg, Clarence L. *Origins of a Southern Mosaic: Studies of Early Carolina and Georgia.* Athens: University of Georgia Press, 1975.

————. *A True and Historical Narrative of the Colony of Georgia, by Pat. Tailfer and Others, with Comments by the Earl of Egmont.* Athens: University of Georgia Press, 1960.

Wade, General George. "Report, &c, Relating to the Highlands, 1724." *Historical Papers Relating to the Jacobite Period, 1699–1750.* Edited by Colonel James Allardyce. Aberdeen: Printed for the New Spalding Club, 1895.

Whatley, Christopher A. *Bought and Sold for English Gold: Explaining the Union of 1707.* Dundee: Economic and Social History Society of Scotland, 1994.

Wood, Betty. *Slavery in Colonial Georgia, 1730–1775*. Athens: University of Georgia Press, 1984.

Wood, Peter. *Black Majority: Negroes in Colonial South Carolina from 1670 through the Stono Rebellion*. New York: Knopf, 1974.

Wroth, Lawrence C. *Voyages of Giovanni de Verrazzano, 1524–1528*. New Haven: Yale University Press, 1970.

Youngson, A. J. *Beyond the Highland Line: Three Journals of Travel in Eighteenth Century Scotland — Burt, Pennant, Thorton*. London: William Collins Sons and Company, 1974.

INDEX